WAR

ADAPTED FOR YOUNG READERS

by Charles Flato

from *The American Heritage Picture History of the Civil War*
by the Editors of AMERICAN HERITAGE
with narrative by Bruce Catton

INTRODUCTION BY Bruce Catton

 GOLDEN PRESS NEW YORK

WESTERN PUBLISHING COMPANY, INC.
RACINE, WISCONSIN

CONTENTS

Third limp bound printing, 1976

Library of Congress Catalog Card Number: 61-66512

Maps on pages 34-35, 44-45, 56-57, 59, 61, 77, 78, 82-83, 94-95, 98-99, 104-105, 108-109, 116-117, 136-137, 142-143, 150-151, 185, and 187 copyrighted separately, © 1960, by American Heritage Publishing Co., Inc.

GOLDEN, A GOLDEN BOOK® and GOLDEN PRESS® are trademarks of Western Publishing Company, Inc.

The City of Atlanta

Collection of Mrs. John Nicholas Brown

INTRODUCTION

THE CIVIL WAR ended a long time ago, and everybody who ever had anything to do with it is dead and gone by now, and yet somehow people still want to know all about it. The interest in the war does not come primarily from people who had an immediate, direct connection with it; it just seems to be something that grows out of the American soil, and more people seem to want to hear about it in the 1960's than ever before. Why?

One reason, of course, is that the Civil War makes one of the most fascinating stories ever told. Some of the men who took part in it became very famous, so that today there are statues in their memory, with books written about them and towns and colleges named for them; most of the rest were completely unknown people, ordinary men from farms and villages and cities all across the United States, utterly undistinguished except that at one time in their lives they were a part of something ever so much larger and more important than themselves. But in either case, the men who enacted the terrible, tragic drama of the Civil War were men who have to be remembered. They have not been flattened out by the age of big cities, machinery, mass transportation, and unending television shows. They stand out: whether the Civil War veteran was a private soldier unknown outside of his own company, or a General Grant, a General Lee, a Stuart or a Sherman or a Jackson, he is somebody you feel like taking a second look at.

And these men, in what they were and what they did, illustrate all of the virtues, and unhappily sometimes all of the vices, which are part of the common lot of humanity. Civil War soldiers were very brave, very gallant, very determined and fearless—some of them. Others were a little more ordinary, brave part of the time and very badly scared at other times, average human beings who could be heroic if the men around them were heroic, or if some unusual leader inspired them, but pretty anxious to save their own skins the rest of the time. And of course there were some who were just plain scamps, men who faded out of the firing lines when the guns began to fire, disappearing in the hazy area behind the lines and quietly joining up again a day or so later when the dangerous time was over.

They were typical human beings, in other words—some of them very good, some of them pretty poor, most of them just average. But for four dreadful years they somehow carried on their shoulders the heaviest burden that has ever been laid on the people of the United States, and by and large they carried it so well that we still marvel at their endurance and their manliness. Perhaps what they really prove is that the ordinary man can be pretty good when the heat is on him—good enough to inspire other ordinary folk who come along a century later.

Beyond that, the Civil War was the great turning point in American history.

More than anywhere else, here is where our greatness comes from; this is where it really is rooted. We got a great deal out of the pioneer period and we got more out of the Revolution, but the Civil War put it all to the test. Here, once and for all, we decided what sort of country we were going to be.

Until the Civil War Americans did not know, actually, what they were citizens of—a state, a region, a nation, a loose association of states, or what. In the North, for the most part, people looked on themselves as citizens of the nation; in the South, most people considered that to begin with they came from a state, from a special part of the country with its own customs and its own traditions. When the big showdown came in 1861, people chose their sides without stopping too long to think about it, and the big fight began.

The fighting lasted for four years, from 1861 to 1865, and it killed more than 600,000 young Americans. It may be worth remembering that more young men lost their lives in our Civil War than in all other American wars put together, beginning with the Revolution and ending with Korea. It was a tremendous fight, and if it did nothing else it would at least prove that the Americans have a good deal of stamina and determination.

But of course it did a great deal more.

To begin with, it made one nation out of us. It showed that there is a unity in human affairs, that men of the same language and the same traditions do better working together than working separately, that this American continent was somehow meant to have one great nation, rather than several, between Canada and Mexico. The nation that was hammered together then was destined for greatness. It had the people, the resources and the room to go on and assume world leadership, to show the rest of the world how much a united democracy can do for the welfare of the people who live in it, to prove that men of different races and different origins can live together in peace and harmony and can do much to promote their own and one another's happiness.

Beyond that, the Civil War broadened the base of American freedom. It ended human slavery, and left us forever dedicated to the ideal of the equality of all men and women; in a very real way, it committed America to the attempt to establish here on earth a good working model of the brotherhood of man. That we have not yet perfected this working model makes no difference; the point is that it is what we have to work toward, and the magnificent ideal that we try to follow is something that those 600,000 young Americans died for in our Civil War.

Its story is something to be enjoyed as a story, to be studied as a piece of history, and to be brooded on as the biggest, most colorful and exciting and meaningful chapter in American life. It may be that another century will pass before we entirely understand what it was and what it meant. Meanwhile, it is fascinating—sometimes sad, sometimes terrifying, very often inspiring, and always full of meaning.

The story is told, as briefly as such a complicated story can be told, in this book. May it at the very least help to bring about a better understanding of what this country is all about and what Americans are really like.

BRUCE CATTON

The War Begins

IT WAS April 12, 1861. At four o'clock in the morning, night still lingered in Charleston, South Carolina. Darkness lay over the harbor, hiding the squat outline of Fort Sumter. At dawn, the flag of the United States was raised over it. Shortly after, there was a quick flash, like heat lightning. Then there was a red glow and the roar of a bursting bomb. The Civil War had begun.

The fort, still uncompleted, was a five-sided brick structure on an island near the mouth of the harbor. It had been built there to protect the city from an attack by sea. But, on this April morning, the attack came from the land. Even more strange, the guns trained on the fort belonged to no foreign enemy. They were fired by Americans—Americans who, less than five months before, had left the Union to set up an independent nation, the Confederate States of America.

The men in the fort also were Americans. Under the command of Major Robert Anderson, a regular officer of the United States Army, were nine commissioned officers and sixty-eight noncommissioned officers and privates. Unlike the citizens of Charleston, they were loyal to the Union. Besides the soldiers, eight musicians and forty-three workmen were in the fort when the attack came.

Major Anderson and his men had been told to leave by the Confederate authorities in Charleston. But they had orders to stay from the new President of the United States, Abraham Lincoln. In his inaugural address, Lincoln had said that the new administration in

General "Stonewall" Jackson's statue stands at Bull Run, where two battles were fought in the Civil War.

Washington would do everything it could to "hold, occupy, and possess" all Federal property in Confederate territory. No one could doubt that he had Fort Sumter in mind. Its seizure by the Confederacy would mean that the South was prepared to fight for independence. Its defense would mean that the North was determined to preserve the Union. The result would be war.

Until several days before the attack on Fort Sumter, it was not clear whether the government in Washington really meant what it said. It had not been clear for months. While politicians talked, the tiny garrison at Fort Sumter was running out of food and supplies.

On November 15, 1860, when Major Anderson had taken command of the Federal forts in Charleston harbor, the Confederacy was not yet formed. But secession talk was common in Charleston, and the forts were weak and undermanned. Fort Moultrie was the only one with a garrison on it. Built during the Revolution, it was in bad repair. There were gaps in the landward walls through which enemy forces could pass without too much trouble. Major Anderson saw that Fort Moultrie could not be defended, and moved his men to Fort Sumter.

That winter was a time of anxious waiting for the men on Sumter. Anderson had asked Washington for reinforcements and supplies, but they never came. Food was running low, and the authorities in Charleston refused to send any to the fort. Only by the hardest kind of work were the men able to get forty-eight pieces of artillery ready for use.

On March 4, Abraham Lincoln became President. For more than a month nothing

happened, and there was little food in the fort besides some flour and salt pork. On April 8, word came that Lincoln had decided to send a naval relief expedition. Its instructions were to land provisions only. It was to make no attempt to put men or munitions ashore unless attacked.

To avoid the charge that the Federal government was taking warlike steps against the South, Lincoln notified the Governor of South Carolina of the plan. On April 9, the relief ships sailed from New York—but things did not work out as Lincoln had calculated. Instead, the Confederacy immediately went into action. Jefferson Davis, president of the Confederacy, ordered General P. G. T. Beauregard, provisional commander of the Southern forces, to take possession of the fort.

On April 11, Beauregard sent a polite but firm message to Major Anderson. He demand-

ed immediate evacuation of the fort, offering the garrison safe conduct out of Confederate territory. Anderson replied at once, refusing to surrender. Beauregard repeated his order to surrender, and again Anderson refused. At 3:20 A.M. on April 12, Beauregard issued an ultimatum. If the fort was not evacuated within an hour, he would open fire.

Anderson continued to stand firm, although he knew that the odds were heavily against him. The Rebels had thousands of troops in gun pits and encampments all around the harbor. And if the fort was not battered to pieces by artillery fire, the Federals would be starved out in a few days. Anderson's only hope was that the relief ships would arrive in time and could get safely past the Rebel batteries.

The ships did arrive—at least, some of them did—but none succeeded in entering the har-

On April 12, 1861, at 4:30 A.M., the Civil War began with the Confederate bombardment of Fort Sumter in Charleston Harbor. This painting shows the fort as it looked during an unsuccessful Federal attack in 1863.

bor before the bombardment began. The little fleet had to stand by helplessly while the big guns pounded Sumter. The Confederate fire was deadly, and Anderson's was weak. For thirty-four hours the defenders of Fort Sumter fought on, but on April 13, at 2:30 P.M., they were forced to surrender. General Beauregard kept his promise to allow Anderson a final salute to the colors. At noon on Sunday, April 14, the small company on Sumter fell into formation, and the flag was lowered. It would not be raised over the fort again until April 14, 1865, after four years of war.

During the firing of the last salute to the flag, a charge of powder exploded and killed a gunner. He was the only man on either side to lose his life. The actual fighting for Sumter was bloodless. But to the people of both

the North and the South, news of the battle came like an electric shock. In Boston, church bells rang. In New York, cheering crowds poured into the streets. And in Columbus, Ohio, when the news was announced in the state legislature, a lady abolitionist in the gallery rose and screamed, "Glory to God!" War brought a feeling of relief; the tension was over.

It was the same in the South. Reports from Montgomery, Alabama, said that the people were "delighted." In New Orleans, everyone was "highly pleased." In Charleston, the harbor was gay with streamers flying the Stars

(Next page) Enthusiastic crowds lined the streets to cheer New York's Seventh Regiment, a crack parade unit, as it marched down Broadway on April 19, 1861.

Seventh Regiment Armory, New York

Georgians of the Sumter Light Guard rally around the new Confederate flag in April of 1861.

and Bars. Even the Confederate Cabinet was in a festive mood. It listened to a proclamation from President Lincoln "amid bursts of laughter."

There was little gaiety in Washington. Abraham Lincoln knew what war meant. He moved quickly to raise troops for the army.

His proclamation, which the Confederate Cabinet found so amusing, called for the states to place 75,000 of the militia at the service of the Federal government for ninety days. He hoped that he could restore order and put down the rebellion in that short time. The North hailed the proclamation with

NOT FOR THE SUNNY SOUTH.

RENSSELAER COUNTY REGIMENT
OF VOLUNTEERS.

REGIMENTAL
HEADQUARTERS,

69 FIRST STREET,
TROY, N.Y.

COL. W. T. WILLARD,

Having entered upon the duties and command of this Regiment, calls upon all Patriots and Lovers of their country to step forward at this most important crisis, in aid of their beloved country, in her efforts to

Preserve the UNION. Protect the CONSTITUTION.

With united effort we shall soon be in the m........ender aid to crush Rebellion, and restore the Laws to their protecting influence, enabling the Citizens of this great Republic once more to meet on terms of harmony and friendship, banishing the demon Rebellion, and ambitious Traitors who have brought this evil day upon us.

Company Officers for Six Companies, are active in obtaining Volunteers at this moment, with flattering success. The other Companies will be organized immediately. YOUNG MEN of Character, Energy, and Capacity, are invited to come forward to fill up the unoccupied positions, and complete the organization. It is intended and desirable to pass the winter in a milder climate than our latitude affords. An early organization will do this, and enable the Regiment to participate in the operations now going on in the field of War.

Nov. 18, 1861.

W. T. WILLARD, Col. Com'g.

West Point Museum

The recruiting poster at left called for volunteers to "crush rebellion" and fight "ambitious Traitors."

Collection of Mrs. Katharine McCook Knox

GOD, OUR COUNTRY AND LIBERTY.!!

THE SPIRIT OF '61.

Up with the Standard and bear it on. | Remember the deeds of Washington,
Let its folds to the wind expand. | And the flag of our native land.

The patriotic feeling that stirred the North in the early days of the war is shown in the poster above.

Colonel Elmer Ephraim Ellsworth (arms folded) modelled his company of Zouaves after the famous French fighting forces. The uniforms made a handsome sight, but proved to be unsuitable for battle.

Collection of Mrs. John Nicholas Brown

15

enthusiasm and a rush of volunteers. In the South, four more states—Virginia, North Carolina, Tennessee, and Arkansas—seceded within a month.

Neither the North nor the South was prepared for war. Few persons had any idea of the number of men and the amount of material that would be necessary. The North had the regular army, but it consisted of scarcely 16,000 men. It was up to the ninety-day volunteers to do the job, and the weapons they would fire and the uniforms they would wear did not yet exist. It did not seem to matter to the young men of the North. Everywhere, from quiet New England towns to the rough frontier of Wisconsin, they hurried to the recruiting offices.

The men of the Confederacy were on the march, too. Lean backwoodsmen with a taste for fighting and the elegant sons of the slave-holding aristocrats answered Jefferson Davis' call for 100,000 volunteers. As Davis was getting ready to move his capital from Montgomery to Richmond, he announced that he had 19,000 men under arms. Thousands more were on their way to Virginia, and the governors of the Southern states were busy raising still more troops to fill their quotas.

As for weapons, the South had even less than the North. Some had been taken from government arsenals which fell into Southern hands when the war broke out. But few of them were modern rifles. Many were similar to the flintlock, the Brown Bess of Revolutionary War days. In the weeks after Sumter, the Southern army was small in size, poorly outfitted, and almost completely untrained.

If the troops on both sides were green, so were most of their officers. As often as not, the company commanders had little or no military experience. It was the custom for volunteer companies to elect their own officers. They were chosen for various reasons. Some were prominent citizens; others had paid for the outfitting of their companies; still others were merely good vote-getters. The rival armies were amateurs led by amateurs.

There were, of course, officers of the regular army in both the Northern and the Southern forces. Most had served in the Mexican War and in the Indian fighting, and from their ranks would come the generals whose names would go down in history. The majority were graduates of West Point, and often classmates would oppose each other on the battlefields of the Civil War.

The commanding general of the United States Army was Winfield Scott. A hero of the War of 1812, he had led the United States forces in the war against Mexico. But when the Civil War began, General Scott was an old man of seventy-five, failing in his health. Actual command of the army defending Washington—later to be known as the Army of the Potomac—was given to a younger man, General Irvin McDowell. Opposing him was General Beauregard, who had been his classmate at West Point.

One of General Scott's staff officers was a Virginian named Robert E. Lee. He resigned his commission when his native state left the Union and offered his services to Jefferson Davis. Ulysses S. Grant, a veteran of the Mexican War, quit his father's leather business in Illinois and joined the Northern forces. An army being raised in Ohio was led by a brilliant West Pointer named George B. McClellan—"Little Mac." In time his path would cross that of an old classmate, Thomas J. Jackson, who would become famous as "Stonewall" Jackson. Still another West Point graduate who joined the South was General A. P. Hill. He and McClellan had been rivals for the hand of Ellen Marcy, until Ellen decided to marry "Little Mac."

Altogether, about one-third of the West Pointers in the regular army resigned to serve with the South. Among them were some of the ablest officers in the country. Lincoln was forced to appoint politicians to replace them. Some of the politicians in uniform became good soldiers; others were embarrassingly bad. Good or bad, Lincoln was almost always under pressure to make military appointments for political reasons.

These political generals added to Lincoln's worries—and he had much to worry about. During the early days of the war, the safety of Washington, the capital of the Union, was constantly on his mind. The city was in the midst of hostile slave territory. It was surrounded by Virginia, which had seceded, and by Maryland, whose sympathies were divided. To defend his capital, Lincoln had only six companies of regulars, fifteen of volunteers, and a handful of marines at the Navy Yard. There was real danger that Washington would be cut off from the rest of the North, and something that happened in Baltimore increased Lincoln's fears.

On the morning of April 19, 1861, a troop train entered Baltimore. It was carrying the Sixth Massachusetts Regiment, on the way to Washington. Forced to cross the city to change trains at another station, the soldiers were attacked by mobs of Southern sympathizers, first with rocks, then with bullets. Loading their guns, the soldiers returned the fire. Men fell on both sides. After fighting their way through the town, the soldiers arrived in Washington that evening.

At the start of the war, the Union's capital was open to attack by the Confederates. By 1862, however, the city was defended by fortifications. Each red dot on the map represents a Union fort.

TOPOGRAPHICAL MAP
OF THE ORIGINAL
District of Columbia
AND ENVIRONS
Showing the Fortifications around the
CITY OF WASHINGTON.
By E. G. Arnold C.E.
1862.

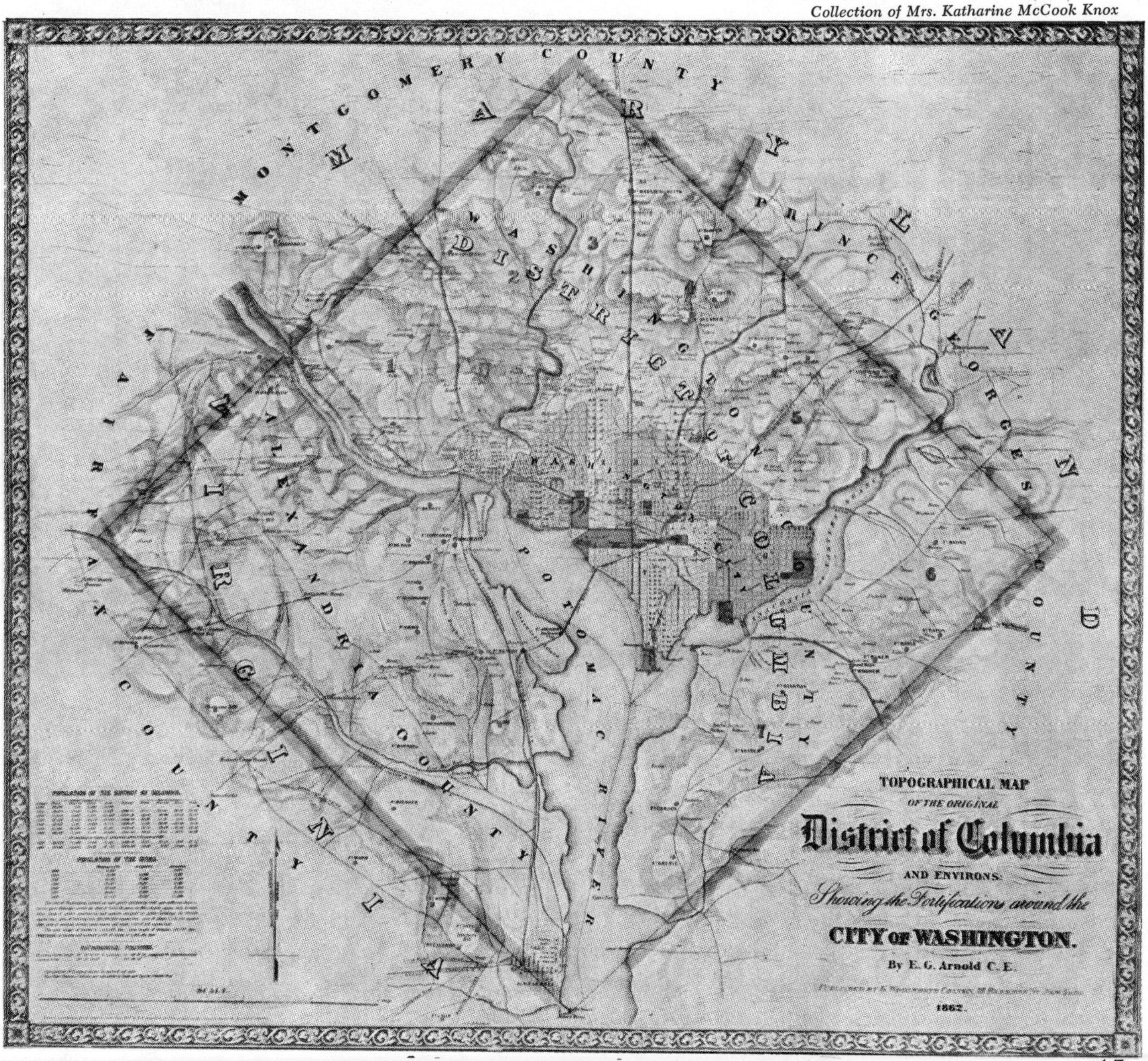

A Rebel bullet knocked Nathaniel Lyon dead from his horse during fighting at Wilson's Creek, Missouri.

As the days passed, Lincoln grimly paced the floor of his office. He peered out the window, impatient for the arrival of more troops. Where were the Seventh Regiment of New York, the First of Rhode Island, the Eighth of Massachusetts? Once he was heard to say, "Why don't they come? Why don't they come?" By April 24, Washington was like a city under siege—its offices and stores closed, its streets empty. Speaking to the wounded men of the Sixth Massachusetts, Lincoln said, "I don't believe there is any North! The Seventh Regiment is a myth. Rhode Island is not known in our geography any longer. You are the only real things!"

But the Seventh New York proved to be real, too, when it marched into Washington two days later. The regiment had been forced to come by water from Philadelphia to Annapolis, then overland to the capital. Soon other regiments came pouring into the city from the Northern states. Among them were the colorful Fire Zouaves of New York, commanded by Colonel Elmer Ellsworth. He led his troops through spectacular drills before cheering crowds.

With Washington less open to attack, Lincoln took action against the secessionists in Maryland. The mayor of Baltimore and nineteen members of the state legislature were jailed, along with a number of other Southern sympathizers. Federal troops took up positions on a hill overlooking downtown Baltimore. A number of places in eastern Maryland, where the secessionists were particularly strong, were also occupied by Union contingents. Once again Washington had a direct link with the North. By early May, Washington was defended by 10,000 troops and Maryland was under control. For the time being, at least, the capital was safe.

But trouble between Northern and Southern forces was coming to a head in another border state. Governor Jackson of Missouri and his armed militia were pro-slavery. The Federal troops, mainly pro-Union German immi-

An actual sketch, made on the spot by one of the Special Artists of Frank Leslie's Illustrated Newspaper.
Mr. Leslie holds the copyright and reserves the exclusive right of publication.

grants, were led by a fiery young regular, Captain Nathaniel S. Lyon. Fearing an attack on the Union arsenal at St. Louis, Lyon raided the militia camp. He disarmed the men and marched them through the streets of the city. A hostile crowd jeered, shoved, and threw bricks. At last someone opened fire, and the troops returned it. Before the shooting was over, twenty-eight men were dead or dying.

The Governor and his legislature at once took war measures, but the Federal commander of the area, General W. A. Harney, arranged a temporary truce. Then Lyon replaced Harney in command. He refused to abide by the truce and drove the Governor out of the capital. Marching his little army into southwest Missouri, he tried to rid the state of all armed Confederates. At a little place called Wilson's Creek, he got into a sharp fight with a larger force and was killed.

The Confederates kept their hold on southwestern Missouri, and there was fighting throughout the war. But Missouri did not leave the Union, which was all Washington cared about at the time.

One way or another, the Federal government was making the border secure.

19

Cotton was King in the South, and slaves worked in the fields of the large plantations.

A House Divided

THE FIRING on Fort Sumter was a mighty explosion at the end of a long quarrel between the North and the South. Many things were involved in the quarrel, but the most important was slavery. Without slavery, the problems between the two sections could probably have been worked out in one way or another. With slavery, they could not be solved.

And yet, early in the nation's history, slavery itself was no problem. There were slaves in all parts of Colonial America. Nor did there seem to be much difference between the North and the South. Most people in both sections made their living by farming.

After the Revolution, the big change began. In the North, commerce and industry grew rapidly. Hundreds of immigrants arrived. Great cities came into being almost overnight. New York City, for example, nearly doubled in size in less than twenty years. The South remained agricultural, with few immigrants and few large cities. It manufactured little.

Trade between the North and the South was brisk, but it was the cause of much bad feeling. A good part of the South's crops went north to be processed. Cotton, for example, was made into cloth in Northern mills. As the largest buyer, the North set the price, which the Southern planters always thought too low. At the same time, the South bought most of the manufactured goods it needed from the North. Again the North set the price, and to the planters it seemed too high.

Not all of the South's trade was with the North. Tobacco, rice, and cotton were exported to foreign lands, chiefly England. Once again the South was at a disadvantage. Northern banks and brokers controlled the overseas trade and collected fees for their services. Northerners owned the vessels on which Southern goods were shipped and collected the shipping charges.

Other things divided the two sections. Their ways of living and thinking were different, and each side often misunderstood the other. But the big thing that set them apart was slavery.

Slavery gradually died out in the North, simply because it did not pay. At the beginning of the nineteenth century, most Americans, Southerners and Northerners alike, thought that in time slavery would go out of existence everywhere. And then a Connecticut Yankee, Eli Whitney, invented the cotton gin.

Whitney's invention was a simple device, which made it possible for textile mills to use the short-staple cotton the Southern states could grow so easily. Within a few years, cotton was being planted on every acre where it could grow. The world had a great appetite for cotton, and the textile mills gobbled up every bale that was produced. More and more slaves were needed to work in the fields, and on the plantations there was no more talk of slavery going out of existence.

In the South, cotton was King, and the kingdom was growing. Planters looked westward for new land, to the black soil of Alabama and the yellow-gray loam of Mississippi. After that, King Cotton's rule extended into Mexican Texas and Missouri. And in Missouri came the first head-on clash between the North and the South. It happened in 1818, when Southern settlers in the territory applied for admission to the Union as a slave state.

To Thomas Jefferson, this was a danger signal. The "momentous question," he wrote, "like a firebell in the night, awakened and filled me with terror." He feared that the republic he had helped to establish would split apart over the slavery issue.

The split was prevented, at least for a time, by the Missouri Compromise of 1820. Missouri was admitted as a slave state, Maine as a free state. Congress also said that it would admit no more slave states north of the parallel that marked Missouri's southern boundary. Americans everywhere hoped that the argument over slavery was ended once and for all. But John Quincy Adams knew better. He

The North had many factories and shops, such as this chisel and steel-square works in Vermont.

A slave auction in 1852, when slaves were forty per cent of the South's population.

called the compromise merely "a title-page to a great, tragic volume," and what happened after the Mexican War proved that he was right.

As a result of the war, the United States gained an immense new territory. It included areas that would later be the states of Texas, California, Arizona, and New Mexico. A Congressman from Pennsylvania, David Wilmot, was determined to keep slavery out of the new lands. He introduced a bill, known as the Wilmot Proviso, forbidding slavery in any part of the territory.

A Congressman from Georgia answered him angrily: "In the presence of the living God, if by your legislation you seek to drive us from the territories...I am for disunion."

Disunion...the ugly word had been used at last. But, after much wrangling and argument, another compromise was reached. Called the Compromise of 1850, it was the work of three giants in the Senate—Daniel Webster from the North, John C. Calhoun from the South, and Henry Clay from the border state of Kentucky. California was to be admitted as a free state. New Mexico and Utah would come into the Union as either free or slave states, depending on the wishes of the settlers there. The slave trade in the District of Columbia was abolished. The Fugitive Slave Act, providing for the capture and return of runaway slaves to their masters, was made much stronger.

Once again, people hoped that the slavery issue had been settled for good. This hope soon exploded, mostly because of the Fugitive Slave Act. As manhunts for runaway slaves became common in the streets of cities and towns, Northerners grew more and more opposed to slavery. Some broke open jails to release captured slaves. Others worked for the Underground Railroad, a system by which

After making a speech against slavery in the U.S. Senate, Charles Sumner was beaten with a walking stick by Preston Brooks.

slaves were helped to escape to Canada. In 1852, with the excitement at a high pitch, Harriet Beecher Stowe brought out her novel, *Uncle Tom's Cabin*. She had tried to write "something which would make the whole nation feel what an accursed thing slavery is," and she succeeded—at least, in the North.

The book sold 300,000 copies in its first year and won over many of its readers to the cause of anti-slavery.

Two years later, Senator Stephen A. Douglas of Illinois introduced the Kansas-Nebraska Act. The bill created the territories of Kansas and Nebraska, but it did much more than

Border Ruffians from Missouri crossed the line into Kansas, determined to make Kansas a new slave state.

Hoping to start an uprising among the slaves, John Brown raided Harpers Ferry. At his trial for treason, he said, "I did no wrong, but right."

that. It did away with the Missouri Compromise, and stated that the people of each territory would decide for themselves, when time for statehood came, whether or not to allow slavery.

The Kansas-Nebraska Act was passed, and the feeling between the North and the South became even more bitter. Many Northerners who had been friendly to the South now felt that the "slave power" was trying to extend slavery across the nation. Abolitionists angrily called for an end to slavery. In the South, the "fire-eaters" spoke just as angrily. They quoted the Bible to prove that slavery was good. "Give us slavery, or give us death!" they cried. There were moderates in both the North and the South, but their voices could not be heard in the uproar. Worse yet, Kansas was thrown open for settlement under conditions that made bloodshed practically certain.

Into Kansas, from the North, came settlers determined to make Kansas free soil; from the South came settlers just as determined to win Kansas for slavery. From Missouri came the Border Ruffians. They were hardfisted men who crossed the line to cast illegal votes for slavery, threaten free-soil settlers, and sometimes raid abolitionist towns. From New England came boxes of rifles, known as Beecher's

Bibles. They were named for Henry Ward Beecher, a Brooklyn minister and abolitionist, who said that there might be spots where a gun was more useful than a Bible.

Confusion and hatred hung over Kansas like a blinding fog. Patrols of free-soil men clashed with patrols of pro-slavery men. There were barn-burnings, horse-stealings, occasional shootings. On May 21, 1856, a mob of pro-slavery settlers rode into the free-soil town of Lawrence. In a few hours the town was destroyed and two of its inhabitants killed. The sack of Lawrence was soon avenged by John Brown, a fanatical abolitionist. With six followers, he killed five Southern settlers at Pottawatomie Creek.

On the same day that Lawrence was sacked, Charles Sumner, an abolitionist senator from Massachusetts, ended a two-day speech in Washington. Speaking on "the crime against Kansas," he harshly attacked Senator Andrew Butler of South Carolina.

The next day, Sumner was alone in the Senate chamber, writing at his desk. Looking up, he saw that someone had come in and was standing beside him. It was Congressman Preston Brooks, Butler's nephew.

"I have read your speech twice over, carefully," Brooks said. "It is a libel on South

Carolina and on Senator Butler, who is a relative of mine."

Brooks raised his walking stick and brought it down as hard as he could on Sumner's head. He struck again and again. When the stick broke, he went on clubbing Sumner with the splintered butt.

Some other Senators, who had been talking in the nearby cloakroom, came running in. They found Sumner lying on the floor, blood on his head and clothing. They helped him to a sofa in the cloakroom, where he was examined by a doctor. Made an invalid by the beating, he would not return to the Senate for more than three years.

With the country torn by mistrust and hatred, the Supreme Court added to the bitterness. It announced its decision in the case of Dred Scott, a Negro slave. Scott's master had taken him to Illinois, and later to Wisconsin, both states where there was no slavery. Scott sued for freedom, stating that he lived in free territory and could not be held in bondage. The court ruled against him, which was no surprise. But the reasons given by the court stunned the North. A Negro born of a

Abraham Lincoln (to right of doorway) at an election rally in the front yard of his home at Springfield.

slave could not be a citizen of any state, had no rights, and could not sue anyone. Even more alarming, the Constitution gave slavery ironclad protection. Congress had no right to forbid slavery in the Northern territories. In fact, there was no legal way to keep slavery out of any territory.

Truly, the United States seemed a house divided against itself. And, as a lawyer in Illinois said, "A house divided against itself cannot stand. I believe this government cannot endure half slave and half free."

That lawyer from Illinois was Abraham Lincoln, and in 1858 he ran for the Senate against Stephen A. Douglas. The two toured the state, holding a series of debates that stirred the nation. Lincoln lost the election, but the debates made him known far beyond the boundaries of his home state.

Although Lincoln was clearly opposed to slavery, he was no abolitionist. He was against bringing more slave states into the Union. At the same time, he was against interfering with slavery where it existed.

His moderate words failed to satisfy John Brown, who had already shed the blood of pro-slavery men in Kansas. "These men all talk," Brown said. "What is needed is action —action!"

On October 16, 1859, John Brown showed what he meant. With eighteen followers, he captured the Federal arsenal at Harpers Ferry, Virginia. He had a wild scheme to arm the slaves and start a revolt in the South. He took possession of an enginehouse and managed to hold out until the morning of the eighteenth. Then a detachment of U. S. Marines, under the command of Colonel Robert E. Lee of the U. S. Army, stormed the building. Brown was quickly put on trial for treason, and early in December he was hanged.

To some abolitionists, Brown was a martyr who had died for their great cause. To the people of the South, Brown was a murdering

Lincoln posed for this photograph in 1861, shortly before he became President of the United States.

National Archives

Jefferson Davis of Mississippi, a former soldier, congressman, senator, and Secretary of War, became President of the Confederacy on February 18, 1861.

villain. Worse, he proved that what they feared was true. So this was what the Yankee abolitionists wanted—an uprising of the slaves, with bloodshed from one end of the South to the other! And so, while John Brown's body lay in the grave, his spirit moved among men, stirring up even deeper feeling between the North and the South.

Like the nation itself, the political parties were hopelessly split in the 1860 election. The Democrats ran two tickets, one Northern, one Southern. The border states ran their own candidate. The Republican candidate was

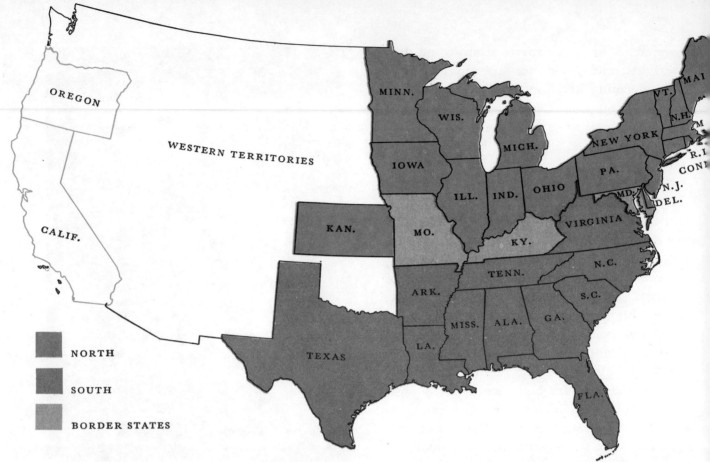

The division of the states in May, 1861, after the start of the war. California and Oregon were with the North, but were too far away to be of much help in the fighting. The border states were still undecided.

Abraham Lincoln. He won the largest number of electoral votes, although he did not receive a majority of the popular vote.

Lincoln was a moderate on the slavery issue. He believed that the Federal government did not have the power to interfere with slavery in the states where it already existed. But the Republican party represented the industrial North and was a threat to the still agricultural South.

When the election returns came in, the South Carolina legislature was in session. The palmetto-tree flag of the state was unfurled; the flag of the United States was rolled up and put away. South Carolina was preparing to leave the Union. On December 20, 1860, a state convention voted for secession. The people celebrated this great and fearful event with the ringing of bells, the drinking of champagne, and a display of fireworks.

Other states soon followed South Carolina's example. On February 8, delegates from South Carolina, Mississippi, Alabama, Geor-

gia, Florida, Louisiana, and Texas met at Montgomery, Alabama. There they set up a new nation, the Confederate States of America. Jefferson Davis of Mississippi, a former Senator and Secretary of War, was elected President.

Meanwhile, Lincoln was preparing to move from Springfield, Illinois, to Washington. With his own hands he tied up the family trunks and labeled them "Executive Mansion, Washington." On February 11, he began the twelve-day journey, and on March 4 he stood on the steps of the Capitol, delivering his inaugural address. The Union, he said, would remain "unbroken." But he warned the South: "In your hands, my dissatisfied fellow-countrymen, and not in mine, is the momentous issue of civil war."

In April, the guns roared at Fort Sumter.

The strength of the two sides as the war began is shown in these graphs. Blue areas represent the North; gray areas, the South; green, the border states. The North was much stronger in almost every way.

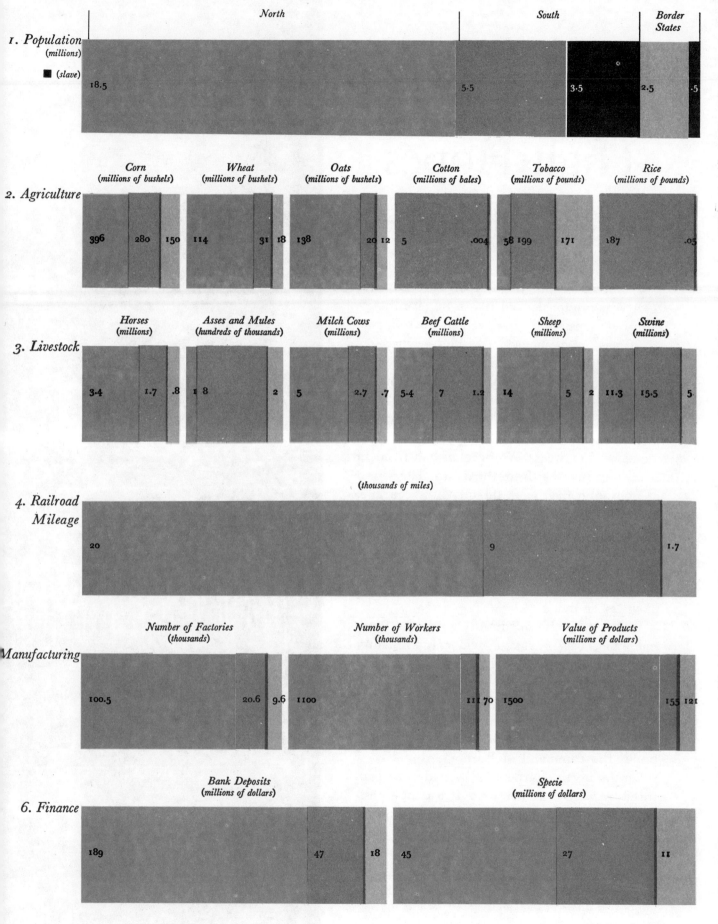

1. Population
(millions)
■ (slave)

North   South   Border States

18.5   5.5   3.5   2.5   .5

2. Agriculture

Corn (millions of bushels)			Wheat (millions of bushels)			Oats (millions of bushels)			Cotton (millions of bales)			Tobacco (millions of pounds)			Rice (millions of pounds)		
396	280	150	114	31	18	138	20	12	5		.004	58	199	171	187		.05

3. Livestock

Horses (millions)			Asses and Mules (hundreds of thousands)			Milch Cows (millions)			Beef Cattle (millions)			Sheep (millions)			Swine (millions)		
3.4	1.7	.8	1	8	2	5	2.7	.7	5.4	7	1.2	14	5	2	11.3	15.5	5

4. Railroad Mileage

(thousands of miles)

20   9   1.7

5. Manufacturing

Number of Factories (thousands)			Number of Workers (thousands)			Value of Products (millions of dollars)		
100.5	20.6	9.6	1100	111	70	1500	155	121

6. Finance

Bank Deposits (millions of dollars)			Specie (millions of dollars)		
189	47	18	45	27	11

29

High Hopes and a Battle

A MONTH AFTER the fall of Fort Sumter, Washington looked like a huge military camp. Troops were quartered in government buildings, warehouses, stables — wherever room could be found. The Capitol itself served as a barracks, and tents cluttered the public squares.

The swarming regiments were a welcome sight, in spite of the crowding and the inconvenience. For weeks Washington had lived in fear of an invasion from the South. The sound of marching men gave the city new courage. At the same time, it created a false hope. People thought the war would soon be over. One easy thrust into Virginia would collapse the Confederacy and restore the Union. Then the country could go back to the ordinary business of living.

It was not quite so simple. Across the Potomac, too, was a vast armed camp. Strung along the river were Southern troops facing the capital from key points only a mile or two away. Behind them, twenty-five miles from Washington, the main forces of the Confederacy were gathered at Manassas Junction, under the command of Beauregard.

To the north, Harpers Ferry had been captured by another Rebel force. It was in a position to control the rich Shenandoah Valley of

"On to Richmond!" was the cry as the Army of the Potomac paraded down Pennsylvania Avenue in Washington, rank upon rank. In the background the unfinished dome of the Capitol rose against the sky.

Virginia and strike at Washington from the northwest. Still other Confederate troops were stationed on the Virginia Peninsula, to prevent Union forces from landing on the shores of Chesapeake Bay and marching on Richmond. Before Washington could be really safe, the North had to seize the Virginia shore across the Potomac. Until it was in Union hands, no move could be made against Richmond.

One night near the end of May, Union troops quietly crossed the Potomac. Some went by boat; others marched across the bridges that spanned the river. The outnumbered Confederates retired without a fight.

One Union contingent occupied and fortified Arlington Heights, a high point just two miles from President Lincoln's office. Other troops moved downstream to Alexandria in order to keep the Potomac open to traffic. The occupation of the sleepy little town was routine, except for one brief, tragic incident. Elmer Ellsworth, the twenty-four-year-old colonel who had become famous as the commander of the Zouaves, dashed to the roof of a hotel and cut down a Confederate flag. Returning downstairs, he was shot and killed by the secessionist hotelkeeper. The news spread fast. The entire North mourned the Union's first martyr of the war.

Union troops occupied Newport News and Fort McHenry, at the head of Chesapeake Bay, without a shot being fired. But a few days later, a Union detachment set out from the fort to capture a Confederate camp. At a little place called Big Bethel, the Federals were routed. It was a skirmish of no importance, but it disturbed and angered the North, still smarting from the fall of Sumter.

The people of the North demanded action. Rebel Richmond was only a hundred miles from Washington. They saw no reason why their splendid new army should not march immediately on the Confederate capital. Few of them knew, however, that the splendid army was no army at all. It was simply a mass of unconnected companies and regiments, far from ready to fight.

The kind of action Northerners wanted came in the hills of western Virginia. General George B. McClellan drove a contingent of Confederates out of a mountain stronghold at Philippi early in June. It was a tiny victory, but the newspapers made it look like a big one. McClellan went on to smash a force of 4,500 men at Rich Mountain, driving the scattered Rebels back into the Shenandoah Valley. The action cleared the western part of the state and paved the way for its admission to the Union, two years later, as the new state of West Virginia.

The North cheered the news of McClellan's victories. After Sumter, Baltimore, and Big Bethel, the events in western Virginia were like a tonic. The cry of "On to Richmond" swept the North. No one would listen to the old commanding general, Winfield Scott. He knew it would take a long time to build a victorious army. His plan called for the blockade and encirclement of the South. But this meant a long war, and the idea of a long war was unpopular.

President Lincoln, too, wanted a quick and easy victory, yet he soon saw that the war could not be won by 90-day soldiers. Early in May he called for 42,000 volunteers to serve for three years. The three-year men began to arrive in Washington by late June, and Lincoln ordered an invasion of Virginia as soon as possible.

The commander of the troops around Washington, General Irvin McDowell, drew up a plan of attack on the main Confederate army at Manassas. Beauregard had only some 20,000 men at Manassas. But near Winchester in the Shenandoah Valley, there were 9,000 more Confederates under General Joseph E. Johnston. If Beauregard could be reinforced by these troops, his disadvantage would be greatly lessened.

Johnston had been holding Harpers Ferry, but had abandoned it to superior Union forces commanded by General Robert Patterson. Patterson, an aged regular army officer, had 16,000 men. When the plan to attack Manassas was drawn up, Patterson received orders to tie up the Confederate troops. Johnston must be prevented from helping Beauregard.

Long before McDowell issued the command to march on Manassas, Beauregard knew all about the Union's plans. In fact, they were no secret to anyone, in either the North or the South. The first thing Beauregard did was to ask for Johnston's troops. Richmond assured him that Johnston would get to Manassas as fast as he could.

The Union advance got under way late. It was not until July 16, a week later than he had planned, that McDowell marched his troops out of Washington. Cheering crowds lined the streets to watch the troops swing by in their colorful uniforms. Bands played and regimental flags flew proudly. A gay throng brought up the rear. Congressmen and government officials, fashionable ladies and plain citizens, trailed the troops in carriages and wagons or on horseback.

In two days the soldiers and their baggage trains covered only twenty miles. On July 18 they straggled into Centreville, facing a slow, winding little river known as Bull Run. Behind Bull Run, in a line eight miles long, Beauregard's army was entrenched. The first contact was made that same day. A Union division, probing one of the fords of the river, got too close to the Confederate lines. It was promptly driven back with losses. The tired Yankees were discouraged. They delayed their attack by a day—and the delay was fatal.

By the time McDowell got his weary forces into battle positions, Joe Johnston had arrived in Manassas with the bulk of his troops. More were on the way. Old Patterson had been given the slip. The Confederates were no longer greatly outnumbered. They now had 30,000 men. Furthermore, they were rested and they were dug in.

Beauregard planned to surprise the enemy by crossing the river and attacking the Union flank before the Federal troops had begun to move. But the boom of Northern guns, early that Sunday morning, told him that he was too late. McDowell's exhausted men had been awakened at two o'clock and thrown into action. The battle of Bull Run had begun. It was to rage throughout the day of July 21, 1861.

At first, a Northern victory seemed certain. The Union forces feinted twice at the Confederate center, then swung into a wide arc for their main attack on the enemy flank. The Southerners were pushed from one position to another, and it looked as though their line would break. But a brigade of Virginians stood firm. It was led by Brigadier General Thomas J. Jackson, a former professor at the Virginia Military Institute. As other Confederate units were wavering and falling back, Brigadier General Bernard Bee pointed with his sword.

"There is Jackson," he cried, "standing like a stone wall! Rally behind the Virginians!"

Bee's troops rallied. Fresh troops, just off the train from the Valley, joined the battle.

Two Union batteries that had kept up a deadly fire suddenly fell silent. A line of soldiers in blue had appeared. The gunners thought they were Northern reinforcements, but they were mistaken. Neither army had anything like a standard uniform, and the men in blue were Confederates. The Rebels opened fire at close range and captured the Northern batteries. The Union attack, which had come so near to success, collapsed. All the heart had gone out of it. The men began to head for the rear, and McDowell gave the order to withdraw. But the troops were too green to carry out the complicated maneuvers called for in the retreat of an entire army. Instead of a controlled withdrawal back to Centreville, they began to fall back in disorder. Still, it was no rout and there was no panic. That is, not until after the beaten army had crossed Bull Run. There, on the other side of the stream, were hundreds of civilians. They had ridden out from Washington in carriages, wagons, and buggies to watch the battle in Sunday picnic style.

As the retreating troops came across the river, the holiday crowd panicked. They stumbled into their carriages and swarmed over the highway to Washington. Soon the

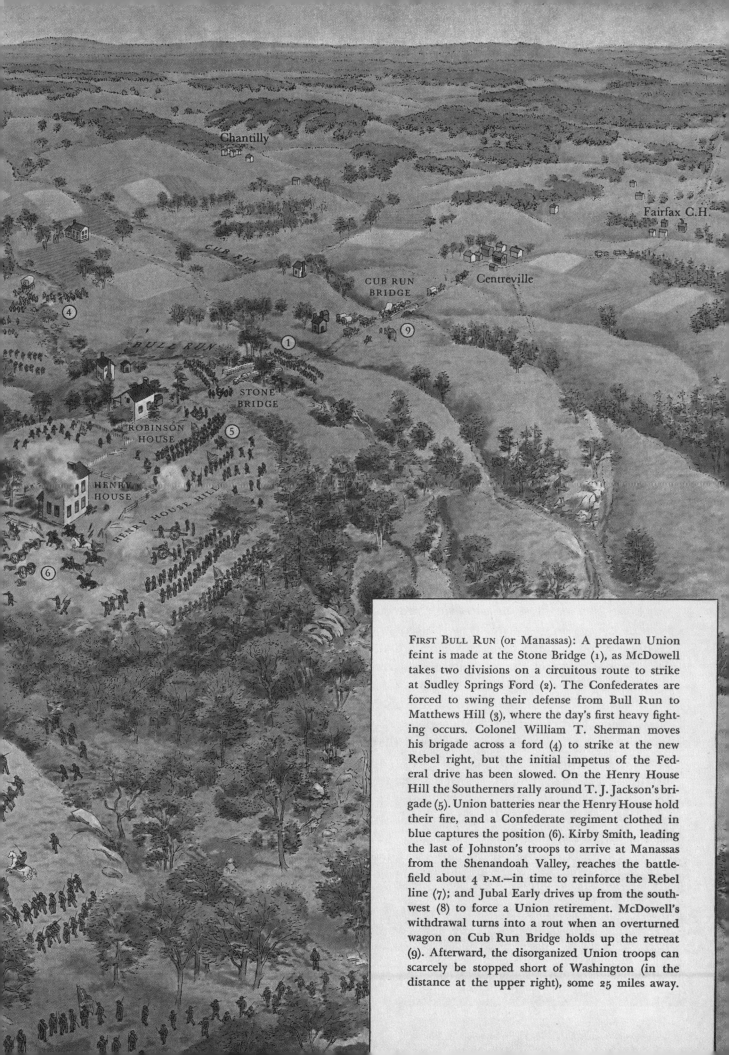

Chantilly

Fairfax C.H.

CUB RUN

CUB RUN
BRIDGE

Centreville

④

①

⑨

BULL RUN

STONE
BRIDGE

ROBINSON
HOUSE

⑤

HENRY
HOUSE

HENRY HOUSE HILL

⑥

FIRST BULL RUN (or Manassas): A predawn Union feint is made at the Stone Bridge (1), as McDowell takes two divisions on a circuitous route to strike at Sudley Springs Ford (2). The Confederates are forced to swing their defense from Bull Run to Matthews Hill (3), where the day's first heavy fighting occurs. Colonel William T. Sherman moves his brigade across a ford (4) to strike at the new Rebel right, but the initial impetus of the Federal drive has been slowed. On the Henry House Hill the Southerners rally around T. J. Jackson's brigade (5). Union batteries near the Henry House hold their fire, and a Confederate regiment clothed in blue captures the position (6). Kirby Smith, leading the last of Johnston's troops to arrive at Manassas from the Shenandoah Valley, reaches the battlefield about 4 P.M.—in time to reinforce the Rebel line (7); and Jubal Early drives up from the southwest (8) to force a Union retirement. McDowell's withdrawal turns into a rout when an overturned wagon on Cub Run Bridge holds up the retreat (9). Afterward, the disorganized Union troops can scarcely be stopped short of Washington (in the distance at the upper right), some 25 miles away.

Union troops fled in a panic at the first battle of Bull Run, ending hopes for an early end of the war.

road was a great tangle of military and civilian vehicles. It was the grandfather of all traffic jams.

The congestion was greatest on a bridge over a stream called Cub Run. A Confederate shell made a direct hit on the bridge. A wagon was knocked over, blocking the road completely. The confusion grew worse as soldiers and civilians tried to force their way through the jam. In the midst of the turmoil, there were shouts that the dreaded Confederate "black horse cavalry" was riding down on the mob. Newspapers and magazines had carried many stories about these horsemen, and now their name was enough to stir up fear. The raw recruits, who had fought so well, dropped their guns and ran. The army fell apart.

The Southerners were in not much better shape. They, too, were battle-weary and their forces scattered. Neither army could continue fighting that day, nor could they fight for many days to come.

Both the North and the South were shocked by the casualties, although later they would seem moderate. The Federals lost 2,896 men in killed, wounded, and missing, the Confederates 1,982. Some of the missing were men whose experience in battle gave them enough fighting for a lifetime. They simply headed for home. Others who went home, but with permission, were troops whose ninety-day enlistments ran out on the day of the battle. One whole regiment walked off the battlefield because its time was up.

Northerners listened to news of the defeat with disbelief. How could their army of splendid volunteers have been routed by the Rebels? Yet, as the truth sank in, they awakened to reality. There would be no glorious parade to Richmond with bands playing and flags flying. They knew that a terrible war—long, hard, bitter, and bloody—lay ahead.

In the South, the battle of Bull Run had the opposite effect. Many Southerners saw a quick and easy victory ahead. Hadn't the battle proved that one Rebel could lick ten Yankees? A number of soldiers went home, believing that the single battle had already ended the war.

But the North's mood of discouragement

soon gave way to a new spirit of unity. Lincoln wrote out a program of action. The blockade of the South must be maintained; the areas now under the Union flag must be held; above all, the shattered army must be rebuilt. Congress passed measures to strengthen the war effort, and thousands of three-year volunteers swamped the recruiting offices.

The first step in the program was taken as early as July 22, the day after Bull Run. On that day a telegram from the President was delivered to General George B. McClellan, who had made a name for himself in the fighting in western Virginia. The message ordered the young general to Washington to take command of the army, or what was left of it.

Other changes were made. McDowell's command was reduced to the defense of the Virginia side of the Potomac. Old Patterson, who had been outwitted by Johnston, was retired. Some generals were shifted to new posts.

McClellan rode into the capital like a hero. He rounded up the stragglers, restored discipline, and began training the new troops pouring into Washington. He saw that food, munitions, and equipment were properly distributed. Mountains of provisions rose in warehouses. Within two months after Bull Run, the new army had grown to a force of 168,000, four times the size of the enemy beyond Manassas.

The Army of the Potomac had been created.

Soon after the battle of Bull Run, army camps were set up around the city of Washington. Regiments of raw recruits, like those shown below, drilled in the dust of newly cut fields.

Confederate Museum

The North's First Victories

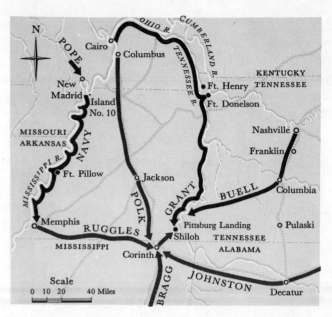

The first Federal moves in 1862, aimed at taking the Mississippi Valley, and the South's countermoves

FOUR DAYS after the battle of Bull Run, General John Charles Frémont arrived in St. Louis. He was there to take command of the Union forces in the West. A large part of Missouri was overrun by bands of Southern guerrillas. They operated at night, tearing up railroad tracks, burning bridges, and generally making trouble. St. Louis itself was full of Rebel sympathizers who were plotting to seize the city. In southwestern Missouri about fifty thousand troops of the Confederacy were in a position to strike. Still others were waiting at the river town of New Madrid, more in western Tennessee. They were a serious threat to the still neutral border states, Kentucky and Tennessee.

Frémont had another and even bigger problem. The Confederates had massed about ten thousand men within striking distance of Cairo, Illinois. Situated at the point where the Ohio enters the Mississippi River, Cairo was vital to the North. There were few spots in the United States as important. It was the key to any invasion of the South down the valley of the Mississippi.

Frémont had only twenty-three thousand men under his command. About a third of them were ninety-day volunteers who were about to go home. Arms and equipment to outfit the new troops were hard to come by. Altogether, it was a situation that would have

A Rebel gunner painted this picture of his battery at the Elkhorn Tavern, during the battle of Pea Ridge.

worried the greatest general in the world—and Frémont was far from great.

He was horrified to learn that Cairo was held by a mere six hundred men under arms. In a matter of days, Frémont managed to send thirty-eight hundred reinforcements. He made another important move, although at the time no one knew how really important it was. He put the troops at Cairo under the command of a little-known brigadier general, Ulysses S. Grant. He also started the construction of a fleet of gunboats that were to prove decisive in the river warfare that would come later. Aside from these things, Frémont did little. He was replaced by Henry Wager Halleck.

The new commander was a flabby, moon-faced regular army officer. He had written a textbook on warfare and was known throughout the army as "Old Brains." Halleck had little fighting spirit and moved cautiously. To make things worse, command over the forces in the West had been split. General Don Carlos Buell was to direct operations in eastern Kentucky and all of Tennessee. Two valuable months, November and December, were lost in long-distance wrangles between Halleck in his headquarters, Buell in his, and General McClellan, who had just been made general in chief, in Washington.

The Rebels had almost fought their way out of Fort Donelson when they were turned back by the Federals.

Southern troops were already on the move. Early that fall, General Leonidas Polk guessed that the Yankees were thinking of occupying Kentucky. He decided to beat them to it. He took two important points on the Mississippi, Hickman and Columbus, and fortified them. Grant, who by then had strengthened the garrison at Cairo, occupied Paducah, on the Tennessee and Cumberland rivers. As a result of the Southern seizure of Hickman and Columbus, Kentucky dropped its neutrality and came squarely into the war on the Union side.

The Confederacy then made General Albert Sidney Johnston over-all commander in the West. Shortly after he arrived in Kentucky, a good part of the state was taken over by the South. Johnston made a strong point out of Columbus. He mounted heavy guns to control the river and set up a garrison of some twenty thousand troops. He extended his line eastward through Kentucky, with about twenty thousand men in and around Bowling Green. In addition, he securely anchored his line on the east, near the Tennessee border.

One of the ablest of the professional soldiers who had joined the Confederacy, Johnston knew what he was doing. He was getting himself into position to maintain control over the Mississippi, the Cumberland, and the Tennessee rivers. The Cumberland and the Tennessee were important military highways. The Cumberland led to Nashville, the capital of Tennessee. The Tennessee River ran all the way to the deep South, and was essential for moving men and supplies. The Mississippi, the Father of Waters, was the greatest prize, as both sides well knew. "The Mississippi is the Backbone of the Rebellion," Lincoln wrote in 1861, "it is the key to the whole situation."

As 1862 began, the war for the rivers started in earnest, although General Halleck had to be prodded into it. One of those who pushed for action was his commander at Cairo, General Grant. Another was General George H. Thomas, attached to Buell's command.

Grant touched off a fight first. He took three thousand troops by steamer fifteen miles downstream, landing them at the tiny Missouri hamlet of Belmont. There, several Confederate regiments were driven out of their camp in a sharp fight. They returned soon after, forcing Grant to retreat.

Thomas followed up soon afterward, beating the Confederates at Mills Springs, Kentucky. It was a small battle, but it had important results. For one thing, it broke one end of the Confederate line. For another, it forced the hand of General Halleck. Grant urged Halleck to let him attack two Confederate river forts—Fort Henry on the Tennessee, and Fort Donelson on the Cumberland. A few days after the victory at Mills Springs, Halleck authorized Grant to move on Fort Henry.

Early in February, Grant started down the river from Cairo with fifteen thousand men and a squadron of the recently invented ironclad gunboats. The boats were under the command of Flag Officer Andrew Foote, who was to play a large part in the new and different kind of warfare. Grant and Foote had worked out a bold plan of battle. First they had to capture Fort Henry on the Tennessee. Then Grant was to make a forced march overland to Fort Donelson, fifteen miles away on the Cumberland River.

The combined land-and-water attack on Fort Henry was carried out without a hitch. After one hour and twelve minutes, the Rebel flag came down.

Grant slept little his first night inside Fort Henry. His mind was busy with his plan to thrust quickly at Fort Donelson. The very next day he set out with his staff and a small band of cavalry in the direction of Donelson, to get the lay of the land. Foote and his gunboats had returned to Cairo. From there they would make the long trip down the Tennessee and then up the Cumberland, to Fort Donelson.

In ten days all was ready. Grant had received reinforcements. A group of gunboats moved on Confederate concentrations as far south as Muscle Shoals, Alabama. The sailors ripped up the rails and destroyed the bridge of the only railroad connecting Columbus and Bowling Green. This would make it harder for the Confederates to get additional troops into Fort Donelson when the attack came.

In spite of the careful preparations, Fort Donelson was a tougher nut to crack than Fort Henry. For one thing, the Confederate general, A. S. Johnston, saw that the fall of Fort Henry threatened the center of his battle line. He pulled his troops out of Bowling Green, sending 15,000 of them by forced march to Fort Donelson. He sent the rest of the troops in Bowling Green to Nashville, to protect the city from a possible attack by Buell.

Union mortar scows shelling Island No. 10, a Confederate post on the Mississippi River.

41

Hundreds of Yankee soldiers lost their lives at the Hornet's Nest (center), during the battle of Shiloh.

The location of Fort Donelson also made it difficult to capture. It was on high ground, with powerful guns that could sweep the river. The weather, too, was against Grant. The river was swollen, delaying Foote's arrival. The first night the troops took up positions against the fort was cold, wet, and miserable. But the next day the sun rose, bright and warm, and soon the men were cheered by the sound of the ship's guns. Their cheer did not last long. The heavy guns within the fort blasted back at the ships, forcing them to withdraw. The fighting raged the whole day, and with night came the bitter cold. Wounded men who could not walk in, or who could not be found, lay on the cold ground. Hundreds were frostbitten, and some froze to death.

By February 16, the story had changed. The Union forces, which had received reinforcements, hemmed in the fort. The Confederates tried to fight their way through Grant's line. Just as they were about to succeed, they were turned back, losing their last chance to escape. Sometime after midnight, a letter was sent to General Grant under a flag of truce. It came from General Simon Bolivar Buckner, one of Grant's pre-war army friends, and asked for terms of surrender. Grant replied, "No terms except unconditional and immediate surrender can be accepted."

News of the victory stirred the entire North. Grant's firm reply to Buckner made him famous. People felt that at last the Union had found a general and was on the march.

Another Union victory, at Pea Ridge in northwestern Arkansas, sent the North's hopes still higher. The Southern forces were decisively beaten in a two-day battle, after having been chased all the way from southern Missouri. This rid Missouri of all Confederate troops. Guerrilla warfare would continue, but the Union's grip on the state was secure.

The Confederates knew that they were in serious trouble. Johnston could do nothing but retreat. He gave up Nashville, leaving a large amount of military supplies to fall into Union hands. Beauregard, who had been sent west to be second in command to Johnston, withdrew the garrison from Columbus. New Madrid, on the Mississippi, was also lost.

Meanwhile, Grant was moving up the Tennessee with about 45,000 men, and Buell was marching down from Nashville with 25,000 more. Grant was anxious to push on against

the enemy, but again Halleck stood in his way. "Old Brains" had been given full command in the West, and because of him there was one delay after another. They gave Johnston and Beauregard time to unite their forces at Corinth, Mississippi.

By early April, Grant had his men at Pittsburg Landing. Buell's men had not yet arrived, but they were on their way. Pittsburg Landing was a small riverboat settlement. It was a few miles from the country meeting house known as Shiloh Church, a little more than twenty from the main Confederate force at Corinth.

The Federal encampment surrounded Shiloh Church. In the quiet countryside, with the peach trees blossoming, war and death seemed far away. Grant and his division commanders felt that it would be bad for morale to have the men entrench.

43

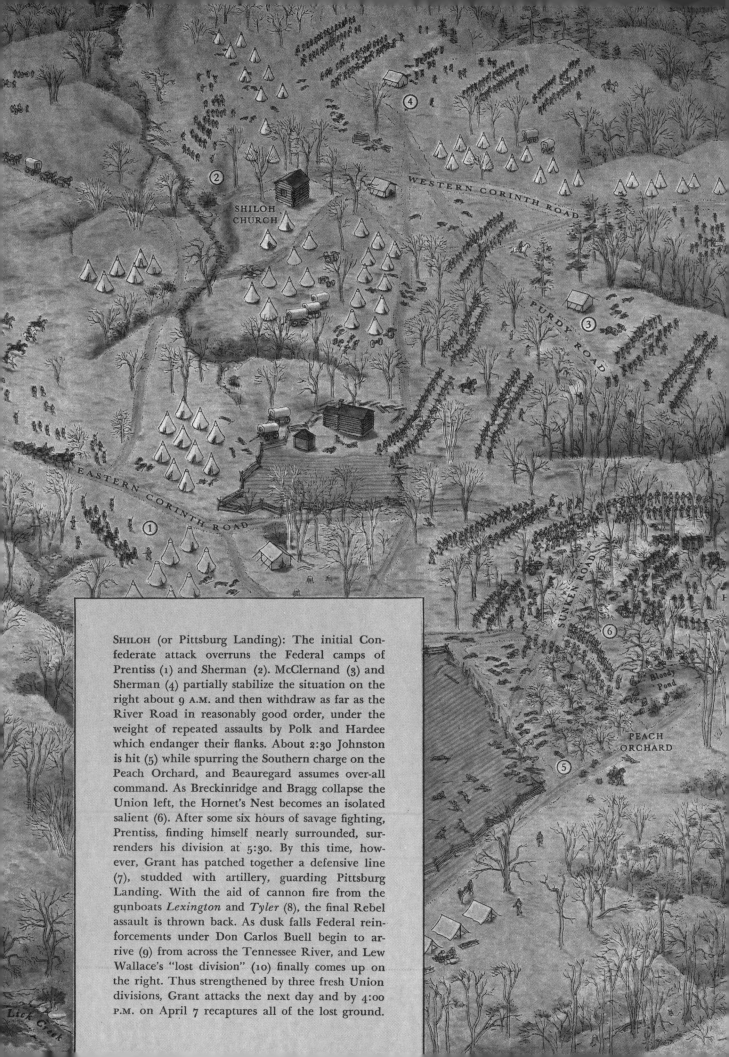

SHILOH (or Pittsburg Landing): The initial Confederate attack overruns the Federal camps of Prentiss (1) and Sherman (2). McClernand (3) and Sherman (4) partially stabilize the situation on the right about 9 A.M. and then withdraw as far as the River Road in reasonably good order, under the weight of repeated assaults by Polk and Hardee which endanger their flanks. About 2:30 Johnston is hit (5) while spurring the Southern charge on the Peach Orchard, and Beauregard assumes over-all command. As Breckinridge and Bragg collapse the Union left, the Hornet's Nest becomes an isolated salient (6). After some six hours of savage fighting, Prentiss, finding himself nearly surrounded, surrenders his division at 5:30. By this time, however, Grant has patched together a defensive line (7), studded with artillery, guarding Pittsburg Landing. With the aid of cannon fire from the gunboats *Lexington* and *Tyler* (8), the final Rebel assault is thrown back. As dusk falls Federal reinforcements under Don Carlos Buell begin to arrive (9) from across the Tennessee River, and Lew Wallace's "lost division" (10) finally comes up on the right. Thus strengthened by three fresh Union divisions, Grant attacks the next day and by 4:00 P.M. on April 7 recaptures all of the lost ground.

OWL CREEK

SNAKE CREEK

10

N

SHILOH

First Day: April 6, 1862

RIVER ROAD

7

Pittsburg
Landing

9

8

LEXINGTON

TENNESSEE RIVER

Dav

When a nervous colonel tried to warn William Tecumseh Sherman, a division commander, of suspicious enemy movements, Sherman glared at him.

"Take your damn regiment back to Ohio," Sherman said. "There is no enemy nearer than Corinth."

But already the Confederates were on the move, for Johnston had realized that his only hope was to strike before Buell's army reached Shiloh. At six o'clock of a Sunday morning, on April 6, 1862, the battle of Shiloh began. The massed Confederates, three lines deep, came booming out of the woods. A Union officer ran back to camp shouting, "The Rebels are out there thicker than fleas on a dog's back!"

The attack took the Yankees completely by surprise. After the first panic, the Union forces steadied, then gave way slowly. In the peach orchard, bullets clipped the blossoms, scattering the pink petals. Cannon bellowed, their shells plunging and bounding with screeching hisses. Everything was confusion, terror, noise, blood. Actually, Shiloh was a fight between two mobs of armed boys. Most of the soldiers on both sides had never been in battle before; a sizable number did not even know how to work their rifles.

Grant galloped all over the shot-torn field, "paying no more attention to the missiles than if they had been paper wads." His right and left wings were falling back; neither Buell's men nor a division under General Lew Wallace had arrived. But some Federals led by Benjamin Prentiss were standing firm at a sunken road. Grant ordered them to hold "at all hazards" while he tried to build a defensive line.

So deadly was the fire laid down by Prentiss' troops that the Rebels called the position the "Hornet's Nest." Instead of continuing to advance on a wide front, almost the entire Confederate army concentrated its firepower on the one spot. Sixty-two cannon raked the position at close range. For nearly six hours the men in the Hornet's Nest fought savagely, throwing back at least twelve assaults. At five-thirty, Prentiss was forced to surrender. Only 2,200 men—half of his original force— were still alive. The rest were killed, wounded, or missing.

A Union vessel rams a Confederate craft in the savage naval battle at Memphis.

Most of Grant's troops had fallen back to Pittsburg Landing. Here they were protected by artillery and the guns of two ships anchored just offshore. The fought-out Confederates made one more charge, but they were beaten back. As the sun began to go down, Buell's men arrived, ferried by steamboat from the east bank of the Tennessee. The first day of the battle of Shiloh was over.

A soft spring rain fell that night, but there was little rest in either camp. When morning came, Grant had 25,000 fresh troops to throw into the battle. Besides Buell's force, Lew Wallace's division had arrived. The Confederates could get no reinforcements and were exhausted from the night-long bombardment. Beauregard was now in command. Johnston had been wounded in the fighting around the Hornet's Nest. Carried to a blossom-filled ravine, he had bled to death before a doctor could reach him.

Again, on the second day of Shiloh, the fighting was savage. The Confederates, outnumbered, were forced to fall back. By midafternoon, they began an orderly retreat. The Union troops were too weary to pursue them, and they reached Corinth by evening. The bewildering, bloody battle ended with tremendous losses on both sides. The Union had lost 13,000 men, the Confederates 10,000.

Northerners were shocked by the terrible casualty list, and criticized Grant violently for being taken by surprise. Nevertheless, the Union forces had won a battle of great importance. The South had failed to regain western Tennessee, and after Shiloh Confederate fortunes in the West went downhill all the way. The South lost Island No. 10, a strongly fortified point on the Mississippi. Memphis, Tennessee, fell after Union gunboats destroyed a Confederate river fleet in its harbor. And, before the month was over, New Orleans, the "Queen City of the South," was attacked.

With its 175,000 inhabitants, New Orleans was the Confederacy's largest city. Its thriving trade made it the richest as well. River steamers and ocean packets lined the wharves that were strung along the broad Mississippi.

Into New Orleans came food, guns, and all kinds of supplies needed to wage war. Much of the South's trade with Europe, especially in cotton, passed through its port.

Two forts—Jackson and St. Philip—near the mouth of the Mississippi, guarded New Orleans against attack from the Gulf of Mexico. Confederate military experts—and many in the North—believed that it was impossible to capture New Orleans from the sea. An elderly but still spry Union naval officer, David Glasgow Farragut, believed otherwise.

On a misty morning in April, Farragut's squadron of warships lay off Forts Jackson and St. Philip. With the squadron were nineteen mortar vessels—converted schooners, each with a tub-shaped mortar—commanded by Captain David Dixon Porter. For a week the mortar boats tossed shells into the forts, until 17,000 rounds had been fired. Still the forts stood, and Farragut decided to risk steaming past them.

In the blackness of two in the morning on April 24, the ships started upriver. The forts opened up with their guns. In the words of an eyewitness, the bombardment was like "all the earthquakes in the world, and all the thunder and lightnings...going off at once." The Confederates also had some armed river boats, and they sent blazing rafts downstream to set the Union ships afire. Farragut blasted back at the enemy. The river was covered with heavy smoke, lit by the red flares of the rafts and the sharp flashes of the guns.

Suddenly the Union ships were past the forts, with only moderate damage. They sank or drove ashore the Confederate vessels and plowed on to occupy New Orleans. Hopelessly cut off, the forts surrendered. Ben Butler came in with troops to take possession of the forts and the city, and the mouth of the great river was in Federal hands.

A few days later, Baton Rouge and Natchez surrendered. By midsummer of 1862, the South's hold on the Mississippi was limited to Vicksburg and Port Hudson.

(Next page) David G. Farragut's fleet ran past enemy forts and boats to win New Orleans for the Union.

The South Outwits the North

ALL WAS QUIET along the Potomac in the autumn of 1861. After Bull Run, the Confederate command had felt that the next move in Virginia was pretty much up to the Yankees, and the Yankees would not be ready to make a move for months to come. At Manassas, the Confederate army had built long lines of entrenchments. In some of them were mounted wooden guns, which looked like the real thing from a distance. Stonewall Jackson had been sent to the Shenandoah Valley with a division of infantry and a small cavalry unit. Rebel patrols had edged forward to the hills overlooking Washington on the south bank of the Potomac. Farther downstream, batteries of Southern guns blockaded the river.

Around Washington, in a ring of camps, was the Army of the Potomac. Things seemed about the same as they had been in early spring, before the disaster at Bull Run. But

McClellan had 150 huge mortars in place near Yorktown, but the Rebels withdrew before they fired a shot.

there was, actually, a big difference. General George B. McClellan had built a real army. It was well trained, well equipped, and ready for action.

The young commander of the Army of the Potomac was extremely popular with his troops. Often they would be called out for reviews, with McClellan himself riding the lines to inspect the newly organized brigades and divisions. The men were taught to cheer whenever he appeared, but they needed little urging. McClellan made them feel like soldiers. In return, they gave him their complete confidence and deep affection.

During the first months of his command, McClellan was a hero to the entire North. The newspapers spoke of him as the "Young Napoleon" who could do no wrong. "The people call upon me to save the country," he wrote to his wife. "I must save it, and cannot respect anything that is in the way."

As time went on, however, people began to wonder. The great Army of the Potomac trained, drilled, marched, and paraded. But when would it fight? Every day the army issued a bulletin: "All quiet on the Potomac." Yes, all was quiet—much too quiet. What happened at Ball's Bluff made matters even worse.

Ball's Bluff was a wooded hill on the south bank of the Potomac, a little more than thirty miles from Washington. Confederate infantry was camped in the area. In October, McClellan ordered several regiments to cross the river and see what the Rebels were doing. The Union troops were routed, and some of the dead floated down the river past the Washington waterfront. Among those killed was Colonel Edward Baker, the commanding officer of the Northern force. He had been a United States Senator from Oregon. The whole affair had little military importance, but Congress made a great fuss about it.

This was still not enough to threaten McClellan's position. In fact, he rose still higher. In November Winfield Scott resigned, and Lincoln made McClellan general in chief of all the armies. The President feared that being general in chief as well as commander of the

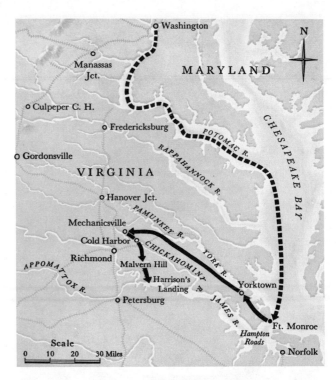

The map traces McClellan's advance by water down Chesapeake Bay, his campaign on the Peninsula, and his withdrawal to Harrison's Landing on the James.

Army of the Potomac might be too much for one man. With complete confidence in himself, McClellan said, "I can do it all."

Lincoln defended the general against the criticism that came from Congressmen and members of the Cabinet. He did his best to provide the men and arms McClellan demanded. He kept visiting McClellan's headquarters. He asked questions, gave suggestions, and even volunteered his own plan for an attack on Manassas.

McClellan brushed it aside. The army needed more men and further training. One big reason for McClellan's caution was the reports he was getting from Allan Pinkerton. A famous detective, Pinkerton had been put in charge of military intelligence. He made fantastic mistakes, estimating Confederate strength at double or triple its actual size. But McClellan believed him and was convinced that the South had 100,000 men at Manassas.

December came, and with it heavy rains and mud that kept the army from moving. On top of that, McClellan came down with typhoid fever. He was in bed for three weeks,

Major General George B. McClellan

during which everything came to a complete halt. Lincoln was deeply discouraged. One day, in the office of Quartermaster General Meigs, he said, "General, what shall I do? The people are impatient. Chase [the Secretary of the Treasury] has no money, and he tells me he can raise no more. The General of the Army has typhoid fever. The bottom is out of the tub. What shall I do?"

At Meigs' suggestion, Lincoln met with the ranking generals of the army and several members of the Cabinet. Lincoln is supposed to have remarked that if McClellan had no use for the army, he would like to borrow it. At any rate, everyone agreed that the army should move on Manassas. The news reached McClellan, whose health quickly improved. He drew up a plan of his own. He told no one about it, not even the President.

Lincoln was determined to press the war against the South. Late in January he wrote an order for a general advance of the armies, to begin February 22. Now McClellan was forced to act. But he was unwilling to make a direct attack on Manassas through the win-

McClellan rides at the head of his staff in this painting of the Federal camp at Cumberland Landing.

ter mud. Instead, he offered his own plan. He would move the army by steamboat down the Potomac River and Chesapeake Bay to the Virginia Peninsula. He would land about fifty miles from Richmond, then march overland to storm the Confederate capital.

Lincoln hesitated. He objected strongly to leaving Washington without protection. Nevertheless, he approved the plan. Some of the men in the Cabinet were strongly opposed to it. They no longer trusted McClellan and believed he was for the South at heart. They said openly that he might prove to be a traitor, willing to let the enemy win the war.

McClellan learned from Lincoln that his loyalty was being questioned. Leaping to his feet, he demanded an apology. Lincoln did apologize, explaining that he was merely repeating charges made by others. But a short time later he removed him from the job of general in chief, leaving him in command of the Army of the Potomac. The reason Lincoln gave was that McClellan could not direct the armies on another front while he was leading a field campaign.

March 18 was the date set for the army to start moving. But General Joe Johnston, who commanded the Confederates in Virginia, moved first. Leaving his heavy gun emplacements along the Potomac, Johnston evacuated Manassas and the Bull Run line. The Confederates now occupied the area below the Rappahannock River where the Union forces were supposed to land unopposed. So McClellan moved his troops instead to Fort Monroe, at the tip of the James River Peninsula.

Lincoln and Secretary Stanton were still worried about Washington. If a Union army were moving overland toward Richmond, it would always stand between Washington and the main Confederate army. Under McClellan's plan, the capital would be dangerously open to capture. They refused to take chances. They removed an entire army corps from McClellan. Under command of General McDowell, it was to cover the area between Washington and Fredericksburg. They also set up a separate command in the Shenandoah Valley under Major General Nathaniel P. Banks. And they put General Frémont in command in western Virginia, with instructions to begin moving east. McClellan started up the Peninsula with only 90,000 men instead of the 130,000 he had expected to have. At

Foul weather and bad roads slowed the advance of the Union forces in the Virginia Peninsula campaign.

Yorktown, McClellan found a Confederate force entrenched behind a chain of earthworks. They were under the command of Major General John Bankhead Magruder. "Prince John," as Magruder was called, had only 15,000 troops. His orders were to hold off the Union army long enough for Johnston to get all his men down the Peninsula. Magruder was well known as an amateur actor, and he put on quite a show for McClellan's benefit. He marched his small number of troops back and forth, up hill and down, so that they seemed to be a large army.

Even after Johnston's men reached Yorktown, the Confederates were outnumbered. Johnston remarked that "no one but McClellan would have hesitated to attack." But McClellan had been fooled by Magruder's trickery. He believed the Southern line was "one of the most extensive known to modern times." He prepared to lay siege to Yorktown, and as a result lost an entire month. At last he brought up his big guns.

Library of Congress

Lieutenant General Thomas J. "Stonewall" Jackson

Johnston realized that he was in danger. On May 4—the day before the Union was ready to open a crushing bombardment—he quietly began to fall back. The Union troops pursued the retreating Rebels. A steady rain fell, and both armies had to struggle with horses, wagons, and guns that stuck in the muddy roads. On May 5, the Confederates slowed McClellan's advance by fighting a bloody rearguard action at Williamsburg. Then the two armies plodded on.

Although bad weather made the going rough, McClellan was coming closer and closer to his goal—Richmond, the Confederate capital. Even so, he was worried. He still believed Pinkerton, who reported that Johnston had nearly 120,000 troops. Not knowing that the Confederates had less than half that number, McClellan demanded reinforcements. He sent word to Washington that he must have the support of McDowell's divisions.

Lincoln and the War Department ordered McDowell to join the Army of the Potomac. Before the order could be carried out, they had other troubles. These troubles were caused by "Stonewall" Jackson.

Brigadier General J.E.B. Stuart

Cook Collection, Valentine Museum

Jackson had become famous at Bull Run, but he was far from being a picture-book soldier. He was once described as a "seedy, sleepy-looking old fellow, whose uniform and cap were very dirty." He was a bold and brilliant fighter, with a fierce will to defeat the Yankees. He drove his men as hard as he drove himself.

While McClellan approached Richmond, Jackson slashed through the Shenandoah Valley toward Washington. A Federal army under General Frémont was edging in through the mountains on the west. Jackson, with a much smaller force, beat back Frémont. Then he turned east, where there was another Union army led by General Nathaniel Banks. At Front Royal, on May 23, Jackson smashed a part of Banks' force. Two days later he turned north again. He hit other units of Banks' army at Winchester, chasing the defeated troops toward the Potomac River.

By this time Jackson had 17,000 men, and they threw a scare into Washington. Alarms were sent to all state governments. Northern newspapers carried big headlines: "WASHINGTON IN DANGER." Lincoln canceled McDowell's orders and sent him against Jackson. Besides protecting the capital, he hoped the three Union armies could trap Jackson in the Valley. But Jackson's men, marching light, with only muskets and blankets, were not so easy to trap. Jackson reversed his direction and moved south. Traveling swiftly, he slipped between the armies of Frémont and McDowell. He surprised a division under General James Shields at Port Republic. His delaying action finished, Jackson now joined Lee to bolster Richmond's defenses.

Jackson's campaign had tied up 50,000 Union troops. It also held up the Union assault on Richmond. McClellan, moving closer to the Confederate capital, did not dare to attack without reinforcements. He kept waiting for McDowell—but McDowell never came.

By May 28, McClellan was about five miles from Richmond. To get at the city, he had to cross what he called the "confounded Chickahominy" River. One part of his army was on the north side of the stream, the other part on the opposite shore, at Fair Oaks. On May 31, the Confederates attacked, driving back the Yankees. The fight was bloody, but it decided nothing, for on the next day the Union troops won back the lost ground.

The Confederates suffered heavy losses at Fair Oaks. The larger Northern force might have counterattacked after the second day's battle with a good chance of success. But McClellan was still convinced that he was greatly outnumbered. He dug in, bombarding Washington with pleas for more troops.

One thing did happen at Fair Oaks that would have an important effect on the story of the Confederacy. During the fighting, General Joe Johnston was seriously wounded. He was replaced by General Robert E. Lee, who was given command of the newly named Army of Northern Virginia.

Lee was the son of "Lighthorse Harry" Lee, a Revolutionary War hero. A professional soldier, he had already had a promising career in the Federal army before the war. Lee was opposed to slavery and secession. But he believed the North had no right to use force against the South, and he could not fight against his native state, Virginia. He turned down Lincoln's offer to be field commander of the Union army. He resigned his commission and joined the Confederates, who made him a general. As military adviser to President Jefferson Davis, he spent many months at a desk. He had seen little action.

Handsome, gentle, understanding, Lee was looked upon by his men as almost a saint. At the same time he was a fighter of skill, daring, and imagination. He was the South's greatest general; in fact, he was later called the greatest soldier since Napoleon.

Soon after he took his new post, Lee wanted to know the exact position of the enemy. He sent one of his generals, J.E.B. Stuart, to find out. With 1,200 men, "Jeb" Stuart rode completely around the Union army in a four-day scouting trip. He was pursued by a Federal cavalry unit led by his own father-in-law. He took 165 prisoners and lost only one man.

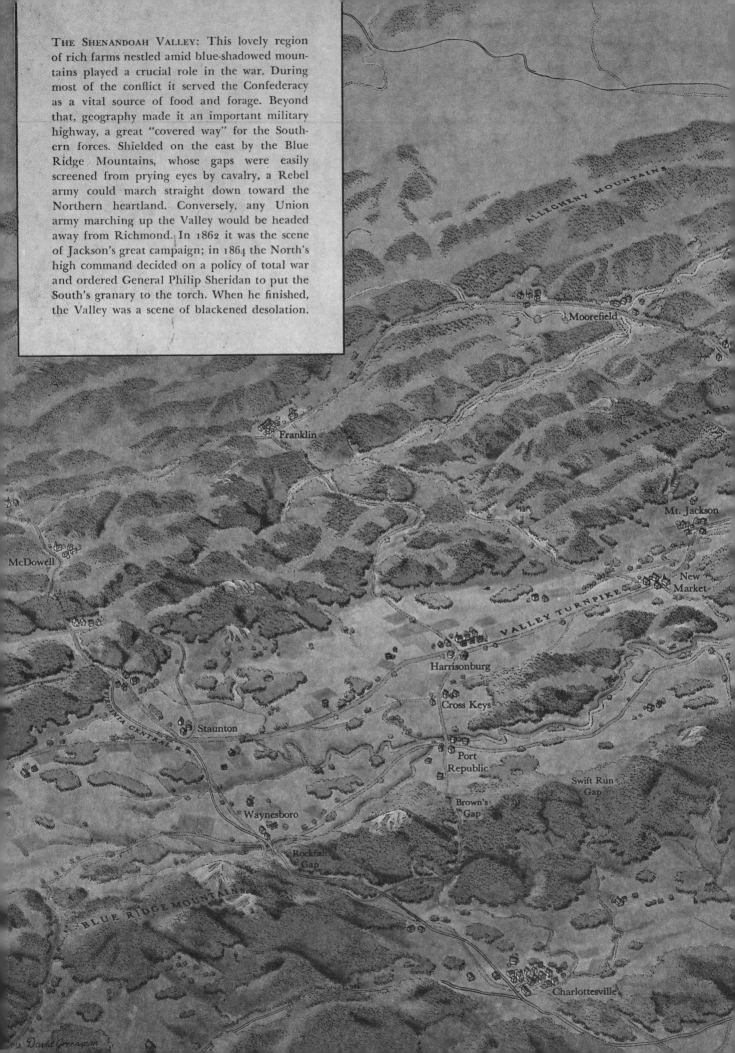

THE SHENANDOAH VALLEY: This lovely region of rich farms nestled amid blue-shadowed mountains played a crucial role in the war. During most of the conflict it served the Confederacy as a vital source of food and forage. Beyond that, geography made it an important military highway, a great "covered way" for the Southern forces. Shielded on the east by the Blue Ridge Mountains, whose gaps were easily screened from prying eyes by cavalry, a Rebel army could march straight down toward the Northern heartland. Conversely, any Union army marching up the Valley would be headed away from Richmond. In 1862 it was the scene of Jackson's great campaign; in 1864 the North's high command decided on a policy of total war and ordered General Philip Sheridan to put the South's granary to the torch. When he finished, the Valley was a scene of blackened desolation.

ALLEGHENY MOUNTAINS

Moorefield

Franklin

SHENANDOAH MOU

Mt. Jackson

McDowell

New Market

VALLEY TURNPIKE

Harrisonburg

Cross Keys

VIRGINIA CENTRAL R.R.

Staunton

Port Republic

Swift Run Gap

Brown's Gap

Waynesboro

Rockfish Gap

BLUE RIDGE MOUNTAINS

Charlottesville

David Greenspan

THE VALLEY

McClellan's 4,300 wagons and ambulances ford Bear Creek on the retreat from Richmond.

Stuart came back from his famous ride with the information Lee needed. Just as he suspected, the right wing of the Union army lay exposed to attack on one side of the Chickahominy River. As Lee began to plan his next move, "Stonewall" Jackson arrived from the Shenandoah Valley. The Confederate army was now at its peak strength of 85,000 men. Lee decided to strike.

Again "Prince John" Magruder was given the job of fooling McClellan. He marched his 20,000 men about as he had in Yorktown. McClellan telegraphed Washington that the Rebels had an overwhelming force 200,000 strong. Meanwhile, Lee was massing his troops on the north side of the river. They faced Porter's force of 30,000 men. The rest of the Union army was on the other side of the river.

On June 26, Lee hurled his troops against Porter, starting the first of the famous Seven Days' Battles. All day the fighting went on around Mechanicsville. At last the massed artillery of the Union army stopped the Rebel attack, and Porter regrouped his men at Gaines' Mill.

Porter's new position was very strong. His infantry was ranged in lines across a slope, with the artillery on the plateau behind them. Between the Yankees and the enemy was a sort of moat of swampy ground. The battle began at noon on June 27, and throughout the afternoon Porter's troops shattered the Confederate charges.

As shadows lengthened across the fire-torn field, Lee ordered a three-mile-wide assault. General Hood's Texans broke through the Yankee center. A gallant charge by the 5th U. S. Cavalry failed to close the gap, and Por-

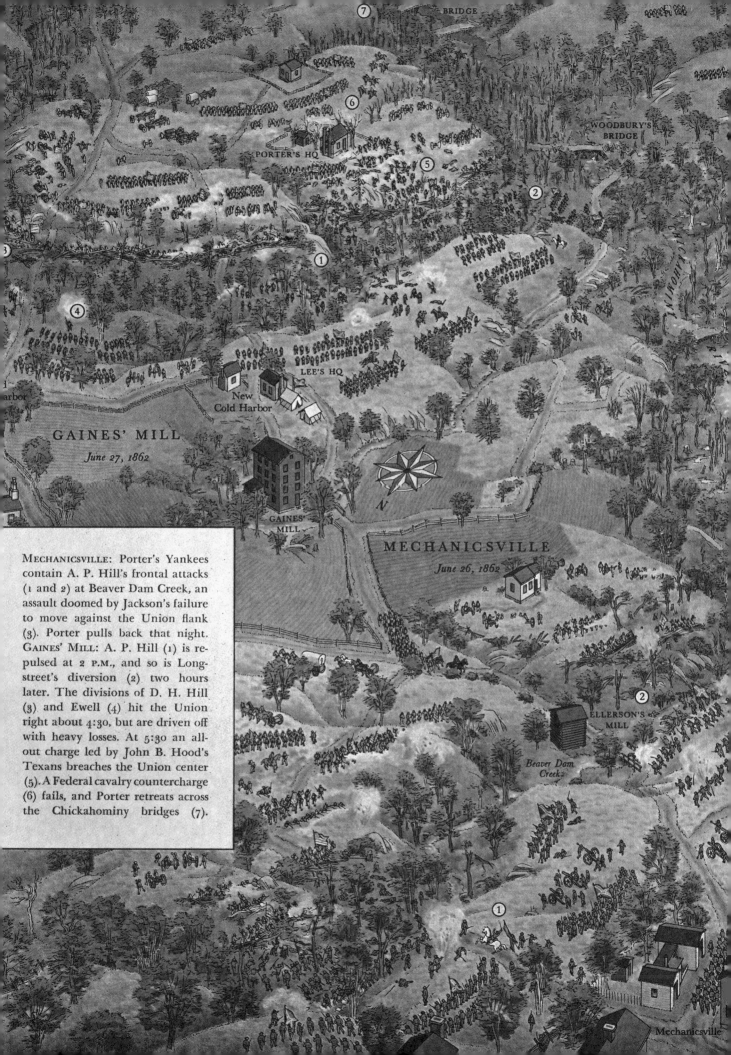

MECHANICSVILLE: Porter's Yankees contain A. P. Hill's frontal attacks (1 and 2) at Beaver Dam Creek, an assault doomed by Jackson's failure to move against the Union flank (3). Porter pulls back that night. GAINES' MILL: A. P. Hill (1) is repulsed at 2 P.M., and so is Longstreet's diversion (2) two hours later. The divisions of D. H. Hill (3) and Ewell (4) hit the Union right about 4:30, but are driven off with heavy losses. At 5:30 an all-out charge led by John B. Hood's Texans breaches the Union center (5). A Federal cavalry countercharge (6) fails, and Porter retreats across the Chickahominy bridges (7).

BRIDGE

WOODBURY'S BRIDGE

PORTER'S HQ

LEE'S HQ

New Cold Harbor

GAINES' MILL

June 27, 1862

GAINES' MILL

MECHANICSVILLE

June 26, 1862

ELLERSON'S MILL

Beaver Dam Creek

Mechanicsville

ter withdrew across the river. Having cut McClellan's supply line, Lee wrote Davis that night: "We sleep on the field and shall renew the contest in the morning."

McClellan then ordered a general retreat down the Peninsula. To reach a new supply base at Harrison's Landing on the James River, he had to march south across White Oak Swamp. There was confused fighting when Lee tried to cut the Union column. Day after day, as the Army of the Potomac fell back, Lee attacked furiously. His aim was to head off the retreat, turn back the enemy, and destroy the Northern army. But, in one bloody engagement after another, he failed to win a really decisive victory.

At Savage's Station, on June 29, Magruder struck at McClellan's rear guard. He had to break off the action when "Stonewall" Jackson could not come to his support. On June 30, Lee planned to hit the Federals south of White Oak Swamp. Two-thirds of his army would make a flank attack. The other third, under Jackson, would slash at McClellan's rear. Again things went wrong. The flank attack, at Frayser's Farm, was made by only two divisions. Although they fought fiercely in hand-to-hand combat, it was no use. Jackson gave them little help. Besides, the Yankee supply and artillery train had already passed the spot about five hours before.

McClellan fell back to Malvern Hill. While his men dug in, he telegraphed Washington: "I shall do my best to save the army. Send more gunboats."

It was up to General Porter to hold the 150-foot-high hill. He had plenty of infantry, both in place and in reserve. More important, he had plenty of fieldpieces—about a hundred of them, standing hub-to-hub. He also had long-range siege guns, and gunboats with heavy batteries on the James River.

One of Lee's generals, D. H. Hill, studied the enemy's position. He said, "If General McClellan is there in strength, we had better let him alone."

Lee did not agree. He felt that one more push might be all the Union army could stand. On July 1 he gave orders for an attack, the greatest of the Seven Days' battles. It turned out that General Hill was right. In a short time, the Federal guns had silenced every Southern battery within range.

Through a mix-up in orders, wave after wave of Confederate infantry charged up the hill. Each time they were smashed by the massed Federal guns. As General Hill said later, "It was not war, it was murder." About 5,500 Confederates fell on the slopes of Malvern Hill that day. The next morning, a horrified Union officer looked at the bodies strewn over the ground. He said, "A third of them were dead or dying, but enough of them were alive and moving to give the field a singular crawling effect."

The terrible Seven Days were over. Altogether, Lee had lost 20,000 men in killed and wounded, to the Union's 16,000. But in spite of his losses, he had won a victory which the Confederacy had to have. Lee fell back to Richmond, to rest his men and refit his battered army. The Federals marched the eight miles from Malvern Hill to Harrison's Landing. They, too, needed rest and new equipment. They had even abandoned field hospitals, with 2,500 sick and wounded.

McClellan's army had fought magnificently, and he had led them well—but in retreat. He could not or would not attack. Even at the end of the Seven Days, he still had 86,000 troops. If he had counterattacked after Malvern Hill, he might yet have smashed the smaller Confederate army and marched back to Richmond. As it was, the North would not have a chance to take the Confederate capital for three long years. Lee's daring had lifted the siege of Richmond and driven back the Union's larger forces. The way was now clear for him to take the offensive and strike at the North.

McClellan dug in at Harrison's Landing and asked Washington for 100,000 more troops. The newspapers now made fun of him, calling him McNapoleon. There could be no doubt about it—he had been outthought and outfought.

MALVERN HILL

July 1, 1862

JAMES RIVER

MALVERN HOUSE

PORTER'S HQ

TO HARRISON'S LANDING

WEST HOUSE

CREW HOUSE

FRAYSER'S FARM: Longstreet and A. P. Hill (1) attack Mc-Call's Union division, capturing McCall himself before being stopped. They then hit Kearny (2) but again are halted. Jackson fails to advance on Long Bridge Road (3), permitting the Federal army to escape to Malvern Hill on the Quaker Road (4). MALVERN HILL: Union artillery knocks out the Rebel guns; then shatters Confederate infantry attacks on the Federal center (1) and left (2), aided by fire from the gunboats (3). McClellan retreats (4) to Harrison's Landing.

WILLIS CHURCH

NELSON HOUSE

QUAKER ROAD

FRAYSER'S FARM

FRAYSER'S FARM

June 30, 1862

LONG BRIDGE ROAD

David Greenspan

The War at Sea

A Northern recruiting poster, calling for seamen

ONE DAY IN August of 1861, a cantankerous man in New York wrote a long letter to the President of the United States. He was John Ericsson, a brilliant inventor and marine engineer who had emigrated to the United States from Sweden.

"The writer," the letter said, "offers to construct a vessel for the destruction of the rebel fleet at Norfolk and for scouring the Southern rivers and inlets of all craft protected by rebel batteries." Ericsson wanted no pay for his services. They would be his contribution to the Union cause.

Perhaps Lincoln did not get to see the letter, for it went unanswered. Ericsson then wrote to the Navy Department, repeating his offer to the President. He added that the vessel he had in mind would have a revolving gun turret, something that had never been built before. It would "split the rebel fleet at Norfolk into matches in half an hour."

This letter, too, went unanswered. For weeks Ericsson fumed, and he had good reason to be concerned. He had heard rumors that the Confederates were converting a fifty-gun steam frigate, the *Merrimac*, into an ironclad of revolutionary design. The warship had been left behind when the Union was forced to evacuate the Norfolk navy yard. If even half the rumors were true, the *Merrimac* would be able to destroy any ship in the Union navy.

As it turned out, there were other Northerners who were also concerned about the *Merrimac*. Somehow they learned about Ericsson's plans. In late September he had a caller—

The U.S.S. Kearsarge *sinks the Rebel raider* Alabama.

Cornelius Scranton Bushnell, a Connecticut manufacturer and a close friend of Secretary of the Navy Gideon Welles. After a long talk, Ericsson gave Bushnell a dust-covered box containing the model of the *Monitor*, the ship he proposed to build. It was a strange-looking contraption. One naval officer who later saw it said, "It is the image of nothing in the heavens above, or the earth beneath, or the waters under the earth."

A few days later, Bushnell brought the model to Lincoln at the White House. The President was impressed. The next day he and Bushnell showed the model to the Navy Department's Committee on Ironclads. Some members of the committee thought Ericsson's idea was a good one; others thought it ridiculous. Then they asked Lincoln his opinion.

"All I can say," Lincoln remarked, "is what the girl said when she put her foot in the stocking: 'It strikes me there's something in it.'"

That settled it. Ericsson was told to build the *Monitor*. After work was started on the vessel, officials of the Navy Department asked

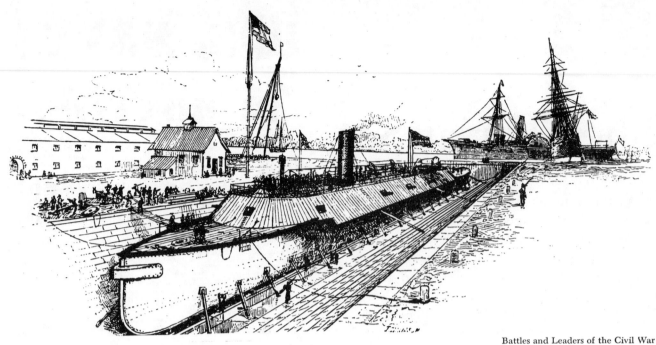

Battles and Leaders of the Civil War

The Northern frigate Merrimac *was outfitted by the Rebels at Norfolk as the ironclad* Virginia.

him to finish it as soon as possible. The reason was that they had learned more about the *Merrimac*.

Later, in February, a Negro woman came to Washington carrying important news for Secretary Welles. At his home, she left a letter about the rebuilding of the *Merrimac*, written by a mechanic who had worked on its construction.

The letter contained information about the *Merrimac*—her size, her speed, the thickness of her armor, and many other details. It also indicated that the ironclad was almost ready to put to sea. Welles and his admirals now knew that the *Merrimac* would be a hard ship to beat. Her three-inch armor and her ten guns that could handle 150-pound shot were better than anything they had. They feared that she could demolish the Union fleet, which was then anchored off Hampton Roads, the sea approach to Norfolk.

The first appearance of the *Merrimac* was off Hampton Roads at noon on March 8, 1862. A Union lookout on the warship *Congress* sighted her through his spyglass. He shouted, "That *thing* is coming down!"

No one on the *Congress* or the sloop *Cumberland*, anchored nearby, had been expecting an attack. On both ships men were swabbing the decks. The crew's laundry hung from the lower rigging, drying in the sun. The officers soon saw that the "thing" was steaming toward their ships. They ordered the decks cleared for action and the crews to take their battle stations.

As the *Merrimac* approached, the *Congress* fired the first shot. To the dismay of her gunners, the shell bounced harmlessly off the ironclad's side. The *Merrimac* then let loose a broadside at the *Congress*. All but one of the crew at Gun Number Ten were either killed or disabled, and shells came crashing through the oak planking.

After raking the *Congress* with a deadly fire, the *Merrimac* made straight for the *Cumberland*. With the throttles of her engines wide open, she rammed the *Cumberland's* starboard bow. The wooden hull of the Yankee ship was crushed like an eggshell. She began to go down, pounded by shell after shell. As a newspaper account of the battle said, "The scene became most horrible. The cockpit was filled with the wounded it was impossible to bring up.... The decks were slippery with blood, and arms and legs and chunks of flesh were strewed about."

The *Cumberland* sank, and 120 of her crew were killed or drowned. The *Congress*, set aflame by shells from the *Merrimac*, was forced to run up the white flag of surrender. Then the Confederates turned their attention to the *Minnesota*, another Federal warship. They drove her aground, but the outgoing tide kept them from getting close enough to destroy her. Evening was coming on, and the *Merrimac* steamed back to her anchorage in Norfolk Harbor. The victory at Hampton Roads was a triumph for the ironclad; no navy in the world could any longer depend on wooden ships.

The *Merrimac* itself was a triumph—a triumph of the South's engineers. When the Confederates had seized the Norfolk navy yard, they had found the *Merrimac* scuttled. After raising the hulk, they saw that the upper works had been destroyed by fire. The imaginative engineers went on to construct a new and strange kind of fighting ship.

The *Merrimac's* hull was cut down to the berth deck. A citadel—a protected main struc-ture—was built on the midships section. It had slanting sides, with ports for ten guns. The walls were made of pitch pine and oak two feet thick, and were covered with two-inch iron sheathing. An open grating over the top of the citadel allowed light and air to reach the gun deck. An armored pilothouse was built forward, and a four-foot iron beak for ramming was fastened to the bow.

When the *Merrimac* left the dry dock, she looked like a turtle with a smokestack on top. Her engines were not in good condition, and she could not move very fast. She was one of the unhandiest vessels to steer that was ever put afloat. But in all the navies of the world, there were not more than two ships that could have given her a fight. (The French had one ironclad frigate, and the British another; all the rest of the world's warships were of wood.)

News of the *Merrimac's* victory reached Washington on the morning after the battle. Secretary Stanton was almost in a panic. Lincoln kept going to the White House windows,

On her first attack, the Merrimac *burned one Union ship, sank another, and drove a third aground.*

to see if the *Merrimac* was coming up the Potomac. But the Union's own ironclad, the *Monitor*, had been launched in New York on January 30. She had arrived at Hampton Roads just as the *Merrimac* steamed away.

The *Monitor* was just as odd-looking as the Confederate vessel. She had a long, flat hull, and amidships was a revolving iron turret that mounted two 11-inch guns. Aft of this was a smoke pipe, and forward there was a

stubby iron pilothouse. People said she resembled a tin can on a shingle, or a cheesebox on a raft.

On the very morning that Lincoln was staring fearfully out of the White House windows, the *Monitor* and the *Merrimac* met in battle. For four hours they battered each other. Neither was badly damaged; neither could win a decisive victory. "The two ironclad vessels," said the report to the Union

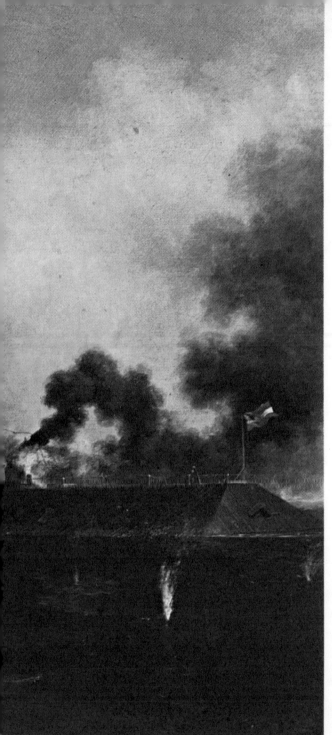

The great naval duel between the ironclads Monitor *(left) and* Merrimac *revolutionized warfare at sea.*

Cabinet, "fought part of the time touching each other, from 8 A.M. to noon, when the *Merrimac* retired....The *Monitor* is uninjured and ready at any moment to repel another attack."

The battle ended with the *Merrimac* retiring to a safe spot in the Elizabeth River. The *Monitor* did not try to follow, nor did she ever attempt to force a finish fight. The *Merrimac* destroyed no more Union warships,

but she kept the Federals out of the James River. The fact that she existed was one of the reasons McClellan moved up the Virginia Peninsula so slowly. When the Union forces occupied Norfolk, she was left without a home port. She drew too much water to go up the James River to Richmond, and she was too unseaworthy to go out into the open ocean. There was only one thing the crew could do, and on May 10 they scuttled her.

There was no doubt that the *Monitor* and the *Merrimac* revolutionized warfare on the water. The North built a number of other ironclads of various types. They included some of the same type as the *Monitor*, and heavily armed, shallow-draft gunboats for river fighting.

The South could not hope to match the North in naval power. It was short of mechanics, short of metal, short of factories. It had to get along as best it could with whatever was at hand. Even so, the South built some ironclads, and it tried all sorts of new devices. Among them were mines made of old beer-kegs, and crude submarines. The Confederate Navy Department did very well, considering what little it had to work with.

At the start of the war, the South had no navy at all. The North had a navy, but some of the ships were out of commission, some were old-fashioned sailing craft, and some were scattered in foreign waters. More important, most of the ships were the wrong kind for the job they had to do—blockading the South.

Shortly after the fall of Fort Sumter, the North proclaimed a blockade of all Southern ports. The aim was to keep ships from bringing in badly needed supplies. To do this, the Union had to seal off 189 Confederate harbors and river mouths along 3,500 miles of coast line. Besides, the navy had to control such rivers as the Mississippi and the Tennessee. It also had to be prepared to strike at fortified seaports, and to join the army in attacks all the way from Cape Hatteras to the Rio Grande.

The Union's ships had been designed for fighting on the high seas, not for blockade duty. The navy was forced to get together one of the most curious fleets ever seen on the waters of the globe. Anything that would float and carry a gun or two would do. Most of them would never have to fight; they did their work simply by being on the scene. At the very least, they gave the Union time to build new and specially designed vessels.

Craft of every possible kind were put into service, armed, and sent steaming down to take their stations off Southern ports. There were ferryboats, excursion steamers, whalers, tugs, fishing schooners, old clippers. Altogether, they were a strange and wonderful collection of floating oddities.

In the end, they were successful. But before the blockade was completely effective, great and small battles were fought. One of the earliest took place off the coast of North Carolina. Confederate forts guarded Hatteras Inlet, the entrance to Pamlico Sound. In August, 1861, Union warships captured the forts. Infantry, carried on transports, occupied the position. Later that winter a Northern fleet moved on Port Royal, South Carolina. The port's two forts surrendered after being bombarded by powerful Union guns. Troops were put ashore, and Port Royal remained a Union naval base until the end of the war.

One of the most important Union victories was at New Orleans. Throughout the war, attacks were made up and down the Confederate coast. Some were successful; others failed. Among the places attacked were Norfolk, New Bern, Roanoke Island, Fort Pulaski, Jacksonville, St. Augustine, Mobile, Galveston, and Charleston.

Charleston was not a Union success. The

A bird's-eye view of the battle for Port Royal. Union vessels moved in circles, shelling Forts Beauregard (right) and Walker (left) in turn. A reporter wrote that, after the bombardment started, "the rising of the dust on shore...looked as if we had suddenly raised...a grove of poplars."

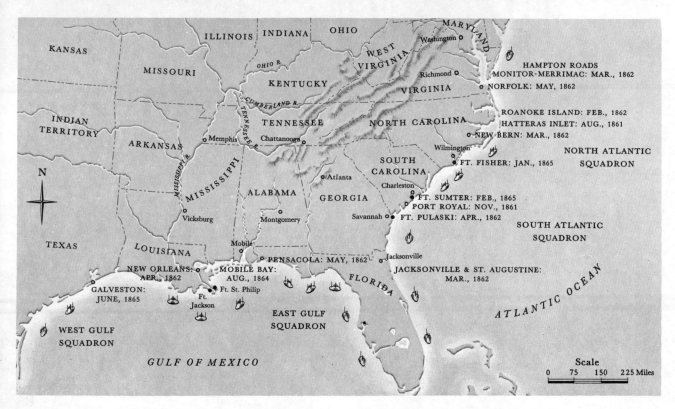

KANSAS
MISSOURI
ILLINOIS INDIANA OHIO
MARYLAND
Washington
WEST VIRGINIA
KENTUCKY
Richmond
VIRGINIA
HAMPTON ROADS
MONITOR-MERRIMAC: MAR., 1862
NORFOLK: MAY, 1862
INDIAN TERRITORY
ARKANSAS
TENNESSEE
Memphis Chattanooga
NORTH CAROLINA
Wilmington
ROANOKE ISLAND: FEB., 1862
HATTERAS INLET: AUG., 1861
NEW BERN: MAR., 1862
NORTH ATLANTIC SQUADRON
MISSISSIPPI
ALABAMA
Atlanta
GEORGIA
SOUTH CAROLINA
Charleston
FT. FISHER: JAN., 1865
FT. SUMTER: FEB., 1865
PORT ROYAL: NOV., 1861
FT. PULASKI: APR., 1862
SOUTH ATLANTIC SQUADRON
Vicksburg Montgomery
Savannah
TEXAS
LOUISIANA
Mobile
NEW ORLEANS: APR., 1862
MOBILE BAY: AUG., 1864
PENSACOLA: MAY, 1862
Jacksonville
JACKSONVILLE & ST. AUGUSTINE: MAR., 1862
GALVESTON: JUNE, 1865
Ft. Jackson
Ft. St. Philip
FLORIDA
ATLANTIC OCEAN
WEST GULF SQUADRON
EAST GULF SQUADRON
GULF OF MEXICO
N
Scale
0   75   150   225 Miles

The map above shows how the Northern blockade slowly closed Confederate ports. The dates indicate when the Union seized various points along the coast.

Hagley Museum

city was the birthplace of secession and also a strategic port. In the North, as a Union naval officer wrote, "the desire was general to punish that city with all the rigors of war." On April 7, 1863, eight ironclads were sent into the harbor. The guns of Fort Sumter, occupied by the Confederates, boomed out. "It seemed as if the fires of hell were turned upon the Union fleet," an eyewitness said. One ship was "riddled like a colander," and the harbor became "a circle of fire not to be passed." The ironclads were forced to retreat.

In August, the Union tried again. The Federal navy's big guns pounded Sumter into ruins. And still Charleston held out. When Sumter's batteries were silenced, Confederate infantrymen replaced the artillery. They used rifles, grenades, fire bombs, and even bricks to stop the Yankees. Then all the forts in the harbor opened fire. The Union fleet had been led into a trap, and once more it was forced to retire. Sumter remained in Confederate hands.

A year later, at Mobile, Alabama, the story was different. Protected by twin forts, Mobile

(Next page) Farragut watches the ironclad Tennessee brush past his flagship in the battle of Mobile Bay.

This inaccurate sketch of the tiny Rebel sub Hunley *shows too many men and the drive shaft unlinked to the propeller. She carried nine men, who went down with the sub in the explosion that sank a Union ship.*

had long been a safe harbor for Confederate blockade-runners. Admiral Farragut, who had taken New Orleans, was determined to capture Mobile. At dawn on August 12, 1864, he roused his crews. He gave them sandwiches and coffee, promising that they would have breakfast inside Mobile Bay "at the regular hour."

With the wooden ships of his fleet lashed together in pairs, he steamed into the narrow entrance of the bay. Shot after shot crashed into the admiral's flagship *Hartford*. The Rebel fire mowed down the men, "deluging the decks with blood, and scattering mingled fragments of humanity so thickly that it was difficult to stand on deck." The lead vessel was soon in trouble. The *Hartford* went into the lead, in spite of Confederate mines. By 8:35 the flagship was well in the bay, and breakfast was served to the crew.

Then the Rebels brought up the *Tennessee*, one of the most powerful ironclads afloat. With two other Federal ships, the *Hartford* rammed the ironclad again and again. At ten o'clock the *Tennessee* surrendered. Mobile Bay was closed to the Confederacy.

The Union fleet attacking Fort Fisher, which defended Wilmington, North Carolina.

The Confederate raider Nashville *burns a captured merchant vessel.*

This left Wilmington, North Carolina, as the South's chief port for the blockade-runners. On January 15, 1865, a Union army-navy team took Fort Fisher. Wilmington, too, was bottled up. The South's flow of supplies from overseas became only a trickle.

Before the Union closed the Southern ports, blockade running was a thriving business. Many of the ships were captured, but a great number got through. Profits were enormous. If a ship made only one or two voyages before being caught, she returned a profit to her owners. At one time, 1,650 vessels were running the blockade, bringing in great quantities of arms and ammunition. They brought in luxury goods as well, to be sold at fantastic prices. At last the Confederacy passed a law stopping the import of some luxuries. It ruled that half the space on every vessel must be reserved for government goods.

To make up for its lack of naval vessels, the South also carried the war at sea halfway around the world. Confederate raiders roamed the seven seas, searching for Union merchant ships. The best of them were built in England. Often they flew the Stars and Stripes of the North, or the British Union Jack. They would swoop down on Yankee merchantmen, destroying ships and cargoes.

The raider that did the most damage was the *Alabama*, commanded by Raphael Semmes. After two years at sea, she had destroyed fifty-eight vessels valued at $6,547,000. In June of 1864, she put in at Cherbourg, France, for repairs. When the Federal ship *Kearsarge* put in at the same port, Semmes challenged her to a duel. On the morning of June 19, the two vessels began firing broadsides at each other. In two hours, the Confederates surrendered to the well-trained Yankees. Semmes threw his sword overboard and jumped into the sea. He was picked up by a British yacht. The *Alabama* went to the bottom, ending the great days of Confederate commerce raiding.

The raiders were no more than an expensive nuisance to the North. They could not decide the course of the war. That was done by the land armies, which fought great and terrible battles. But the navies of both sides played their part in the struggle. Most important was the action of the Union navy in blockading the South. The Confederacy grew weaker and weaker as it was cut off from the supplies it could not manufacture itself.

The Confederates
Invade the North

THE SUMMER of 1862 was a dismal one for the North. In the spring, after months of planning, the Army of the Potomac had moved toward Richmond. But the Peninsular Campaign had failed. No victorious Union army had occupied the Confederate capital. Instead, McClellan's defeated troops had fallen back to Harrison's Landing.

Convinced that McClellan was unwilling to fight, Lincoln set about finding new commanders for the Union army. For general in chief, he chose Major General Henry Halleck. It

looked like a good choice. The Union forces had won successes in the West, which was Halleck's territory. The actual fighting had been done by Grant and other generals, but, as far as anyone in Washington could tell, the credit belonged to Halleck.

Lincoln had no way of knowing that Halleck lacked the spirit that won wars. "Old Brains" was excellent at military routine, and he had read all the books on strategy and tactics. At heart, however, he was just a shuffler of papers.

Another Western general, John Pope, was

The Bull Run battlefield, as seen looking west from Bald Hill. Figure 1 is Thoroughfare Gap; Figure 2, the Confederate lines. Figure 4 is the State House, used as a Union hospital. Trapped by Lee, the Federals lost about 15,000 men in the second battle fought here.

given command of the new Army of Virginia. This was the force of about 50,000 men that had been held back in northern Virginia and the Shenandoah Valley because of "Stonewall" Jackson. Pope had won some victories in the West and had not hesitated to brag about them. His fellow officers called him a "bag of wind" and said he lied about his battle record. Still, no one could deny that he liked to fight—and Lincoln needed fighting generals. "A liar," Lincoln said, "might be brave and have skill as an officer."

Pope got off to a bad start with his men. He made a speech hinting that they were not as good fighters as the soldiers in the West. His new troops never forgave him, but he was too conceited to take notice of their contempt.

When Halleck arrived in Washington, Pope was moving down toward Richmond along the line of the Orange and Alexandria Railroad. "Old Brains" saw that the situation could be dangerous. Pope's and McClellan's forces outnumbered Lee's, but they were far apart. Lee was squarely between them, and he could easily deal with one, put it out of action, and then deal with the other. Halleck found that McClellan was reluctant to have the Army of the Potomac advance on Richmond, and he ordered it back to Washington. It seemed sensible to him to unite McClellan's force with Pope's, and then start another drive on Richmond. The trouble was that it would take a long time to move all of General McClellan's troops back to the Washington area.

75

A Negro family, fleeing from slavery, crosses the Rappahannock River into the Northern lines.

This time was a gift to the Confederates, and General Lee took advantage of it at once. He sent "Stonewall" Jackson north to hold up Pope's advance. Pope, looking for a fight, was at Cedar Mountain when Jackson struck on August 9. The Union's advance unit was driven back to the Rappahannock River. Pope decided to stay there until McClellan joined him.

But Lee had other plans for Pope. He knew that if Pope and McClellan got together, they would be too strong for him. His only hope was to beat Pope first. He figured that McClellan would stay put, so he left only token forces to face him, and moved north toward Pope. Then, taking an enormous risk, Lee boldly split his own forces. One half, under Jackson, he sent on a wide sweep through the Bull Run Mountains. The other half, under General James Longstreet, he kept with him. He also sent "Jeb" Stuart to tear things up in the Federal rear.

Stuart raided Pope's headquarters. He took $350,000 in cash and Pope's dress coat. More important, he took the Union general's dispatch book. This showed the positions of the Federal army, giving Lee valuable information.

Meanwhile Jackson's men swung far to the left, marching sixty-two miles in forty-eight hours. They fell upon the Union supply base at Manassas Junction, about twenty miles to the rear of Pope. They cut the rail lines leading north, destroyed whatever supplies they could not take, and swiftly left.

Pope set out in search of Jackson, but he could not quite find where he was. Hidden by woods and hills, Jackson's 25,000 troops were digging in on the old battlefield of Bull Run. They were setting the trap planned by Lee.

CAMPAIGN OF SECOND BULL RUN: *After pillaging Pope's stores at Manassas Junction (1) on August 26, Jackson moves toward Centreville (2), pursued by Heintzelman and Reno (3). Jackson slips away and digs in (4) near Groveton on August 28. That evening he attacks King (5), revealing his position. Sigel (6) countermarches, followed by Porter (7). As the various Federal columns converge on Groveton, Longstreet (8) advances to join Jackson.*

76

SECOND BULL RUN CAMPAIGN

*Evening, August 28—
Dawn, August 29, 1862*

Thoroughfare Gap ⑧

Hay Market

Sudley Springs

Gainesville

⑤

④

Bull Run

Groveton

HENRY HOUSE HILL

STONE BRIDGE

MANASSAS GAP R.R.

New Market

② Centreville

⑥

MANASSAS SUDLEY ROAD

Broad Run

Milford

③

ORANGE & ALEXANDRIA R.R.

⑦

Bristoe Station

Manassas Junction

①

ECOND BULL RUN

Second Day: August 30, 1862

SUDLEY CHURCH

JACKSON'S HQ

GROVETON — SUDLEY ROAD

UNFINISHED RAILROAD

① ⑥

MANASSAS — SUDLEY ROAD

MATTHEWS HILL

MATTHEWS HOUSE

③

WARRENTON TURNPIKE

POPE'S HQ

② STONE HOUSE

YOUNG'S BRANCH

ROBINSON HOUSE

HENRY HOUSE HILL

TO CENTRE

HENRY HOUSE

④

BALD HILL

⑤

reenspan

78

On August 28, Jackson struck at a Union force at Groveton. The vicious fight ended in a draw, but the Confederate trap was sprung. Pope was lured into an attack that would become one of the great battles of the war. It was the Second Battle of Bull Run, fought on the two days of August 29 and 30, 1862.

On the morning of the first day, Pope hurled his forces at the Confederates. Outnumbered by the 62,000 Federal troops, the Southerners fought back fiercely. At the end of the day they still held their position, but Pope believed he had won a victory.

He had no idea that Lee had brought up the second half of the Confederate army. Thirty thousand men under General Longstreet were drawn up on the left of the Federals. They lay in wait as Pope renewed his attack at two o'clock in the afternoon of the second day. The Yankees drove against Jackson on a two-mile front, stretching his line to the breaking point. His men threw rocks at the attackers when their ammunition ran out.

Still Longstreet waited. Not until the last Yankee reserves had been thrown against Jackson did he take action. Then he launched his counterattack. An artillery barrage smashed at the left side of the Union forces. Rebel infantry, "screaming like demons emerging from the earth," fell upon the surprised Yankees as Longstreet's five divisions rolled against the Union flank.

A thin line of Federals fought desperately to give Pope time to bring up reinforcements. As Pope tried to halt Longstreet on the left, Jackson hit him on the right. The whole Union line bent like a horseshoe. A handful of Yankees made a stand on Henry House Hill, allowing the rest of the army to retreat to Centreville.

SECOND BULL RUN (or Manassas): *Pope begins the second day's action with an assault (1) on Jackson. Then Longstreet's artillery (2) stuns the Union left, followed by a flank attack (3 and 4) which captures Bald Hill. As the Federals form a new defensive line (5) on the Henry House Hill, Jackson strikes their right wing (6). This patchwork line holds long enough for the rest of the Federal army to escape via the Stone Bridge to Centreville.*

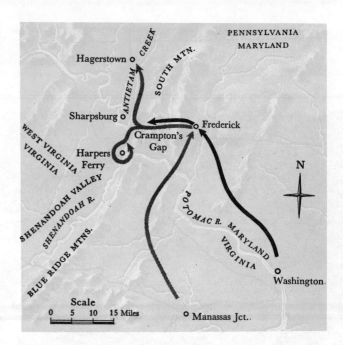

The gray lines indicate the path of Lee's invasion of the North. He divided his forces to take Harpers Ferry. The black line indicates McClellan's pursuit.

Lee attacked again the next day at Chantilly, and Phil Kearny, one of the North's best generals, was killed.

Casualties at Second Bull Run were heavy on both sides. The Union lost 1,724 killed, 8,732 wounded, and 5,958 missing. The South's losses were 1,481 killed, 7,627 wounded, and 89 missing. But the figures do not show how complete a victory it was for the Confederacy, and how terrible a defeat for the Union. Pope was recalled and sent west to fight Indians.

Again Lincoln was bitterly disappointed. There was only one man he could turn to now—George B. McClellan. "Little Mac" had the qualities the North needed after Second Bull Run. He was a good organizer, and he held the loyalty of the troops. When word reached the soldiers that McClellan had replaced Pope, one soldier reported that there was "such a hurrah as the Army...had never heard before...."

McClellan wrote his wife: "Again I have been called upon to save the country." He rallied the men, and by early September nearly 90,000 of them were on the march. This time they marched, not into Virginia, but northwest—for, on September 5, Lee had crossed the Potomac into Maryland.

Harpers Ferry, with the Potomac River at right, the Shenandoah at left. In foreground is Maryland Heights.

Lee had good reasons for invading the North. To the north lay lands untouched by battle and rich in crops. Lee also thought he could bring Maryland, a border state, into the Confederacy. Then he could threaten the cities of Washington, Baltimore, and Philadelphia, and perhaps end the war in a short time. And so he led 50,000 tough fighting men, the cream of his army, into Maryland.

Lee's troops were dirty, tattered, hungry. Hundreds of them wore no shoes. An eyewitness said, "They were the dirtiest men I ever saw, a most ragged, lean, and hungry set of wolves. . . . Yet there was a dash about them that the northern men lacked. . . . They were profane beyond belief and talked incessantly."

As he had before, Lee divided his army. He sent "Stonewall" Jackson to capture the Federal arsenal at Harpers Ferry, with its huge store of supplies. A large force under General Longstreet went north to Hagerstown, Maryland. Smaller units were posted in various places to guard against McClellan's advance.

Lee was forced to change his plans almost at once. He was given no hero's welcome by the people of Maryland. They looked upon his lean and hungry troops as invaders who had come to plunder the land. Even the most enthusiastic of the secessionists failed to rally to the Confederate flag.

That was bad enough, but something else happened that was even worse. On the morn-

ing of September 13, a Union private was rest-ing near Frederick, Maryland. He noticed an envelope in the grass. As he picked it up, out dropped a few cigars and a piece of paper. After dividing the cigars among his comrades, the private idly examined the paper. It was a copy of Lee's orders to his generals, outlining his plans. Before the end of the day, the paper was in the hands of General McClellan.

For the Union command, it was an enormous stroke of luck. The paper showed exactly where the enemy was and what he intended to do. McClellan was jubilant. Waving the paper be-fore the eyes of one of his officers, he said, "Here is a paper with which, if I cannot whip Bobby Lee, I will be willing to go home. If I don't crush Lee now, you may call me whatever you please."

And indeed, if McClellan had moved fast, he could have crushed Lee. But he did not move fast. Within twenty-four hours, Lee knew about the lost orders. He began to pull together his scattered forces, ordering them to join him at Sharpsburg, Maryland. Then he fell back be-fore McClellan's slow approach.

The first meeting of the two enemy armies came on September 14, at two passes in the South Mountains. Small Confederate units held off McClellan's advance, winning Lee precious

Two Ohio regiments capture a fence at Turner's Gap on South Mountain.

ANTIETAM

September 17, 1862

TO POTOMAC RIVER

LEE'S HQ

TO HARPERS FERRY

Sharpsburg

8

ANTIETAM CREEK

6

BURNSIDE'S
BRIDGE

7

David Greenspan

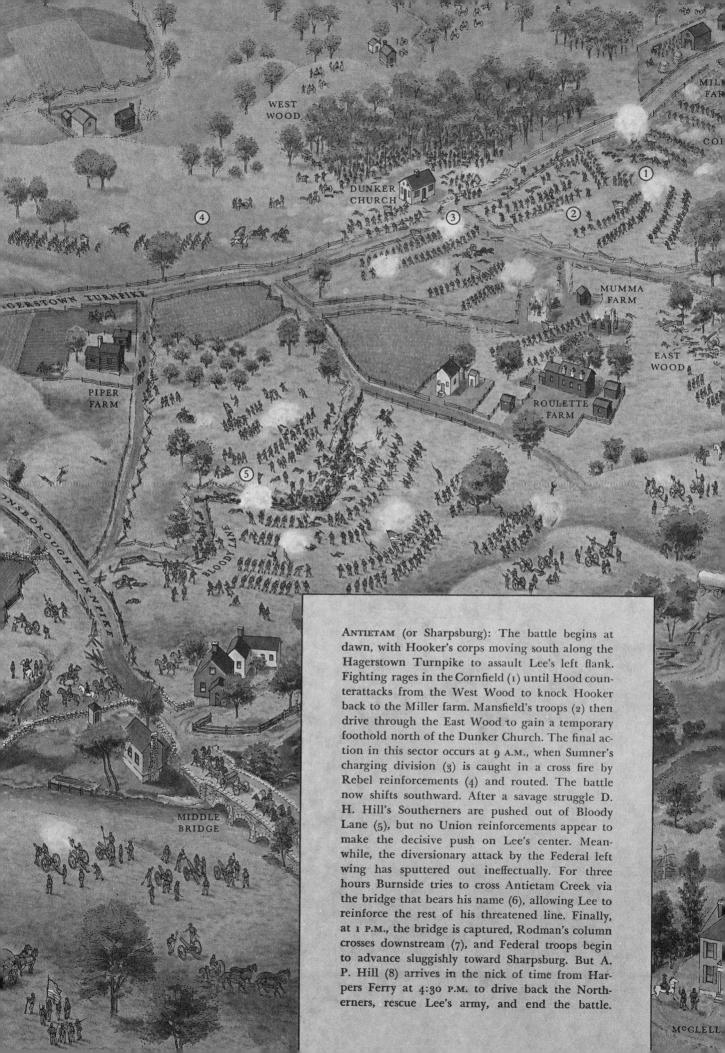

WEST WOOD

DUNKER CHURCH

④

③

②

①

MUMMA FARM

MIL FA

M°CLELL

CO

EAST WOOD

HAGERSTOWN TURNPIKE

PIPER FARM

ROULETTE FARM

⑤

BLOODY LANE

NSBOROUGH TURNPIKE

MIDDLE BRIDGE

ANTIETAM (or Sharpsburg): The battle begins at dawn, with Hooker's corps moving south along the Hagerstown Turnpike to assault Lee's left flank. Fighting rages in the Cornfield (1) until Hood counterattacks from the West Wood to knock Hooker back to the Miller farm. Mansfield's troops (2) then drive through the East Wood to gain a temporary foothold north of the Dunker Church. The final action in this sector occurs at 9 A.M., when Sumner's charging division (3) is caught in a cross fire by Rebel reinforcements (4) and routed. The battle now shifts southward. After a savage struggle D. H. Hill's Southerners are pushed out of Bloody Lane (5), but no Union reinforcements appear to make the decisive push on Lee's center. Meanwhile, the diversionary attack by the Federal left wing has sputtered out ineffectually. For three hours Burnside tries to cross Antietam Creek via the bridge that bears his name (6), allowing Lee to reinforce the rest of his threatened line. Finally, at 1 P.M., the bridge is captured, Rodman's column crosses downstream (7), and Federal troops begin to advance sluggishly toward Sharpsburg. But A. P. Hill (8) arrives in the nick of time from Harpers Ferry at 4:30 P.M. to drive back the Northerners, rescue Lee's army, and end the battle.

time. On September 15, Jackson captured Harpers Ferry. He took about 11,000 prisoners, and set out at once to join Lee.

On that same day, after a ten-hour march, Lee arrived in Sharpsburg. His 18,000 troops took position on a ridge overlooking Antietam Creek and prepared to fight. Later in the day, McClellan's 87,000 men began to appear on the opposite side of the Antietam. Again McClellan's caution lost him the chance to crush the enemy. He spent the entire day of the sixteenth going over his battle plans. By nightfall, Lee's force was doubled by Jackson's arrival. Another Rebel division, under General A. P. Hill, was moving up quickly from Harpers Ferry.

A gentle rain fell during the night, and September 17, 1862, dawned foggy and gray. The Army of the Potomac was spread over acres of cornfields and woodlands, ready to attack. As General Longstreet said, it was "an awe-inspiring sight."

With the first streak of light, the Federals began a massive assault on the Confederate left. A great wave of rifle and artillery fire leveled the cornfields. Southern soldiers were mowed down as if they themselves were so many rows of stalks. A furious counterattack by General Hood's Texans kept the Yankees from breaking the Rebel line. "Fighting Joe" Hooker's crack Union corps struck again, and the Confederate dead strewed the field among the fallen corn.

For hours the battle raged over the forty acres of Farmer Miller's cornfield. Neither side could gain a clear advantage. It was a nightmare of attack and retreat, attack and retreat, attack and retreat. Then Southern reinforcements were thrown into a breach in the Confederate line. They stopped a Yankee charge, saving the left side of the Rebel defense. Hood's division, in his own words, was "dead on the field." The fighting shifted to other parts of the great battlefield, but the story was the same.

Several times during the day the massed Federal power might have defeated the Southerners. Each time McClellan missed his opportunity. He made his worst mistake when the Confederate center collapsed along Bloody Lane. McClellan had considerable fresh reserves he could have sent into action. Later in the day, Burnside's Federals finally crossed Antietam

A Yankee officer rallies his men at Perryville, as reinforcements move up to meet the Rebel assault.

Southern dead by the fence of Farmer Miller's cornfield, at Antietam

Creek on the Rebel right and launched an assault on Sharpsburg. But A. P. Hill's division had arrived from Harpers Ferry at exactly the moment they were most needed. They went crashing into the left flank of the Yankees. To add to the North's confusion, many of Hill's men wore blue uniforms they had picked up at Harpers Ferry. The whole Union left wing was knocked back to the heights along Antietam Creek.

The battle and the long day—the bloodiest of the war—were over. A Confederate soldier remembered that "the sun seemed almost to go backwards, and it appeared as if night would never come." Altogether, about 23,500 men had fallen, with the casualties evenly divided between both sides. From the blasted fields, still smoldering and smoking, rose the pitiful cries of thousands of wounded men.

The next day, September 18, the two exhausted armies watched each other. Lee held his battle lines, expecting another attack. The attack never came; McClellan had no fight left in him. He did not even try to pursue Lee when, that night, the Confederates retreated across the Potomac to Virginia.

While the Yankees had been battling Lee in the East, things had gone wrong for the Union in the West. At the bottom of the trouble was the fondness of the Union commander, General Halleck, for making war by the book. He had learned from military textbooks that it is best to occupy enemy territory. That is precisely

85

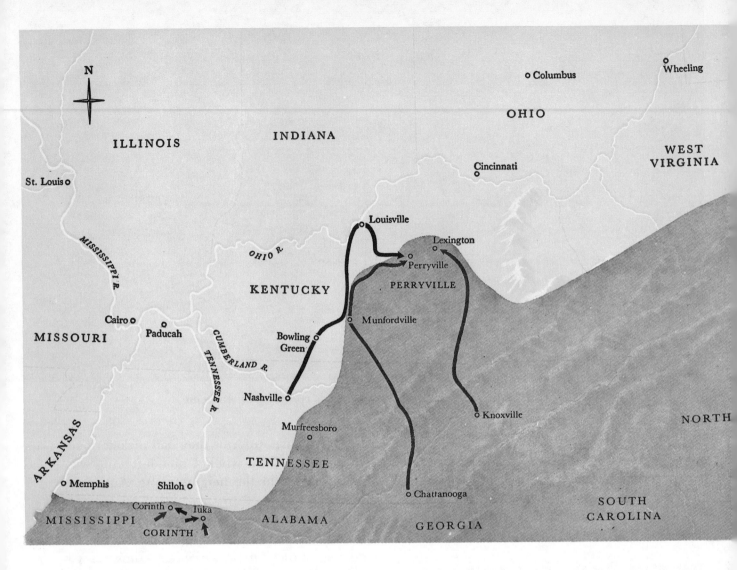

what he did after the capture of Corinth. With his army of more than 100,000 men, he could have beaten any force the Confederates could have sent against him. Everything seemed to be in his favor, and victory was practically guaranteed—if he had continued to attack.

Instead, he split his army. Grant was given the job of holding Memphis and western Tennessee. Don Carlos Buell was sent eastward to occupy Chattanooga. On the way, he was to rebuild and protect the railroad lines. This took so much time that he never did reach Chattanooga. By August, the war in the West was at a standstill. Halleck had been ordered to Washington. Grant and Buell were now independent commanders.

The main Confederate army in the West was commanded by General Braxton Bragg. He was a "spit and polish" kind of general, strict with

his men, but he understood strategy. When he saw how scattered the Union forces were, he ordered "rapid movements and vigorous blows." His chief aim was to capture the important border state of Kentucky.

First, Bragg sent General Kirby Smith moving northward from Knoxville. By the end of August, Kirby was in Lexington, Kentucky. With 12,000 troops, he controlled the central part of the state. Bragg then marched his 30,000 men northward from Chattanooga.

General Buell suddenly found that the enemy had side-stepped right around him. He dropped his work on the railroad and started in pursuit of Bragg. He was too late to save the Union garrison at Munfordville, where 4,200 men surrendered on September 17.

Bragg was north of Buell, in position to cut the Union's supply line to Louisville. He ex-

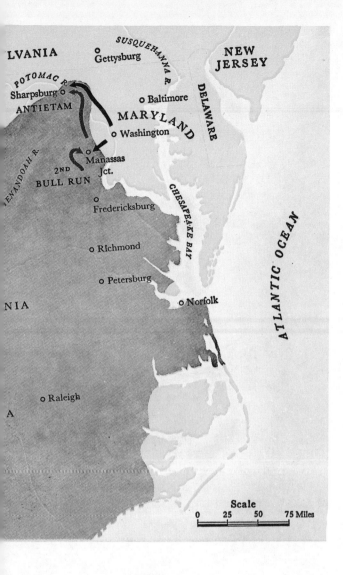

here. In fact, Buell did not even know a battle was going on until it was almost over.

The Yankees were moving eastward from Louisville, trying to catch up with Bragg before he joined forces with Smith. Buell had no idea that the Rebels were in the vicinity. It happened that Kentucky had been having a long dry spell, and water was scarce. The soldiers of Buell's leading column, under a new general named Philip Sheridan, were thirsty. They found water at Doctor's Creek near Perryville—but they had to fight for it. Some of Bragg's troops, just as thirsty, had got there first.

The fighting began with a skirmish, and then spread. Bragg, who did not realize that he was outnumbered three to one, punched hard at the Union left with two divisions. At first they were successful. They were finally halted by Sheridan, who was proving himself to be a good fighting man. Half of Buell's army took no part in the battle, which ended in a draw.

Neither side had reason to be proud of its commanding general. Bragg felt that he had done all he could in Kentucky, and began to fall back toward Tennessee. Buell made only a leisurely attempt to pursue him, much to the anger of the Union's War Department. He was soon replaced with William S. Rosecrans. Before the month was out, both armies were back in Tennessee.

In military terms, very little was decided at Perryville and Antietam. It seemed as if the 31,000 men who fell in the two battles had been sacrificed for nothing. And yet these battles were as important as any fought in the entire war. The Confederate drives, by Lee in the East and Bragg in the West, had failed completely. Never again would the South take the lead as it did during the months of autumn, 1862. The ability of General Lee would keep the Confederates ahead in the East for nearly a year after Antietam. In the West, there would be a series of empty victories and costly defeats from which the South would never recover.

pected Smith's troops to join him for an all-out push on Louisville. But Smith failed to appear. Bragg was forced to swing east toward Lexington, leaving the Federals a clear path to Louisville. As the Confederates tramped across Kentucky, they made a surprising discovery. It was the same discovery Lee had already made in Maryland. The border states were not enthusiastic about being liberated by the South.

Meanwhile, there was action in northeastern Mississippi. A Confederate striking force tried to keep Grant tied down. Two hard fights took place, at Iuka and Corinth. Grant and William S. Rosecrans were able to stop the attack and still send troops to aid Buell.

On October 8, the armies of Buell and Bragg blundered into each other at Perryville. The battle that followed was a curious one. Neither commanding general had intended to fight

The War Drags On

AFTER THE battle of Antietam, the North and the South began to fight a new kind of war. It was a terrible, grinding kind of war, in which words like "honor" and "glory" did not quite fit any more. And one of the chief reasons for the change was President Lincoln's Emancipation Proclamation.

During the late spring and early summer of 1862, Lincoln had considered freeing the slaves. He saw that the North must do more than fight for union. The government needed the full support of the anti-slavery men. To win such support, it would have to come out officially against slavery. Lincoln was already preparing the proclamation before McClellan's army left the Virginia Peninsula, but he could not make it public until the North won a victory. If he issued it after a string of Northern defeats, it would sound too much like a cry for help.

When the Confederate invasion of the North broke down, Lincoln felt that the time was right. On September 23, 1862, the newspapers carried a draft of the proclamation. It stated that on January 1, 1863, all slaves held in a state or part of a state which was in rebellion should be "then, thenceforward and forever free."

The Emancipation Proclamation was a curious document. It proclaimed freedom for all slaves in the states where the Federal government was no longer in control. It allowed slavery to continue in slave states which remained under Federal control. Abolitionists felt that it did not go nearly far enough, while border-state people and many Northern Democrats felt that it went altogether too far. But in the end it changed the whole character of the war and, more than any other single thing, made the defeat of the Confederacy certain.

The proclamation meant that the North was fighting for human freedom as well as for union. Because of this strong stand against slavery, European nations refused to join forces with the South. The United States was pledged to crush slavery by force, and there could be no turning back. The war could end only when the armies—and the civilians—of North or South were beaten to their knees.

Nathan Bedford Forrest, a Confederate general, once remarked that "War means fighting and fighting means killing." William Tecumseh Sherman, a Union general, said, "War at best is barbarism." The country was soon to learn the truth of their words.

Following the battle of Antietam, Lincoln prodded McClellan. He wanted the general to go after the retreating Confederate army and destroy it. McClellan replied that he could not, because his horses were too tired. Lincoln wired McClellan: "Will you pardon me for asking what the horses of your army have done since the battle of Antietam that fatigues anything?"

In November, Lincoln dismissed McClellan as commander of the Army of the Potomac and put General Ambrose E. Burnside in charge. Burnside was a handsome, likeable man, who would become more famous for his whiskers than for his military ability. He believed he was not fit for high command and did not want the job. Nevertheless, Lincoln appointed him, urging him to take action against the Confederate army in Virginia.

Andrew Humphrey leads his Pennsylvanians, in action for the first time, against a Confederate "sheet of flame" during the fierce fighting at Fredericksburg.

Burnside came up with a new plan. He would go east to Fredericksburg, cross the Rappahannock River there, and force Lee to fight somewhere between Fredericksburg and Richmond. Then he would drive on toward the Confederate capital. Lincoln approved the plan, but warned Burnside: "It will succeed, if you move rapidly; otherwise not."

At first Burnside moved rapidly enough. He brought his 122,000 men to the Rappahannock, reaching a point opposite Fredericksburg on November 17. Only a handful of Rebels held the town. If Burnside had acted quickly, he could have taken it with little trouble. But the river was rising after several days of rain. The pontoon bridges that Burnside had ordered failed to arrive. He had to wait two weeks for them.

The delay gave General Lee just the time he needed to pull his scattered forces together. In a few days, General Longstreet's corps was in Fredericksburg. Soon after, "Stonewall" Jackson, with the rest of the Confederate forces, marched hurriedly down from the Shenandoah Valley. By November 30, 78,500 Confederate troops faced the Yankees across the river.

Even after Burnside's pontoons arrived, he waited ten days to strike. On December 11 he started his army across the ice-choked river. All that day and the next, his men marched across on the pontoons. They took up positions along the river-bottom land below Fredericksburg and in the streets of the town. From the heights above the town, the Southerners looked down upon them. "Stonewall" Jackson, who was studying the situation, was asked what he planned to do. "We will give them the bayonet," he answered.

Although they were outnumbered, the Confederate forces had all the advantages. They were in strong positions on high ground, almost impossible to take. Burnside's attack, which came on December 13, had no chance of success. Time after time the Yankees charged at various points, only to be beaten back with heavy losses.

The worst slaughter took place in front of a hill called Marye's Heights. Burnside sent

Union bridge builders were targets for Mississippi sharpshooters in Fredericksburg.

wave after wave of troops against the Confederates, who were behind a stone wall along a sunken road. Longstreet was asked if he could hold this line against the Union attacks. He answered, "If you put every man now on the other side of the Potomac in that field to approach me over the same line, and give me plenty of ammunition, I will kill them all before they reach me."

Longstreet was not just boasting. The Union soldiers formed breastworks with the bodies of their fallen comrades. About 9,000 of them were shot down in front of Marye's Heights. Confederate losses were slightly over 1,500.

Across the river, Burnside paced up and down. "Oh those men!" he said. "Those men over there! I am thinking of them all the time." At the end of the day, he called off the attacks. In the words of a Union captain, "A cold, bitter, bleak December night closed upon that field of blood and carnage." Altogether, the Union lost more than 12,000 men in killed, wounded, and missing. The Confederates lost less than half that number.

The next day Burnside wanted to renew the attacks. There was nothing wrong with his personal courage, and he intended to lead the men himself. His officers persuaded him that any further fighting was hopeless, and on the night of December 14-15, he pulled his defeated army back across the Rappahannock.

The two armies faced each other from opposite banks of the river for several weeks. Then Burnside tried to move upstream. His plan was to cross beyond Lee's left flank and fight a new battle. But three days of steady, icy rain turned the unpaved roads into bottomless mud. In the end, the soldiers managed to pull themselves, their wagons, and their artillery out of the mud and came slogging back to camp. Burnside was removed from command. The Army of the Potomac would do no more fighting that winter.

While the Union troops in Virginia were retreating, their comrades in the West were beginning to move against the enemy. One of the main armies in the West, the Army of the Cumberland, had a new commander—William S. Rosecrans. He replaced Buell, who had failed to overtake Bragg during the Rebel retreat from Kentucky. Red-faced and outspoken, Rosecrans was liked by the men. He was a good fighter, but he had a hot temper and tended to become too excited at crucial moments.

General Grant was still in command of the troops in western Tennessee. His job was to hold Memphis and the important railroad network. The rail lines ran east and northeast from the city and north from the Mississippi border to the upper Mississippi River. His chief aim was to capture the Confederate stronghold at Vicksburg.

Early in November, 1862, Rosecrans advanced to Nashville. Once there, he began preparing for a move into eastern Tennessee. He took his time about it. Not until the day after Christmas did he order his troops to march. Divided into three columns, they went southeast toward the little town of Murfreesboro.

The Confederate Army of Tennessee, under General Bragg, had been encamped at Murfreesboro for a month. Bragg had taken a decisive position above the town. His troops were astride Stones River, a narrow stream that loops northward to join the Cumberland River. On the low hills east of Stones River, Bragg had posted a detached division under John C. Breckenridge, the former Vice-President of the United States. His main force was west of the river, behind a dense growth of scrub cedar.

On the evening of December 29, Rosecrans' army began arriving in the vicinity of Murfreesboro. By nightfall, two-thirds of his force was in position along the Nashville Turnpike, less than 700 yards from the Rebel line. By the next day, the rest of Rosecrans' troops had arrived. The Union force numbered 44,000 men, while the Confederates had 38,000.

All that day, and well into the night, the two enemy commanders worked out their battle plans. By a strange coincidence, the plans were identical. Rosecrans and Bragg each decided to hold with his right and attack with his left.

(Next page) A Union officer painted this picture of a Northern attack on the Rebel lines in front of Marye's Heights. About 9,000 Yankees were shot down here.

FREDERICKSBURG

December 13, 1862

BURNSIDE'S HQ

STAFFORD HEIGHTS

RAPPAHANNOCK

①

Fredericksburg

CANAL

Ditch

PLANK ROAD

HANOVER STREET

STONE WALL

⑤

SUNKEN ROAD

MARYE'S HOUSE

MARYE'S HEIGHTS

David Greenspan

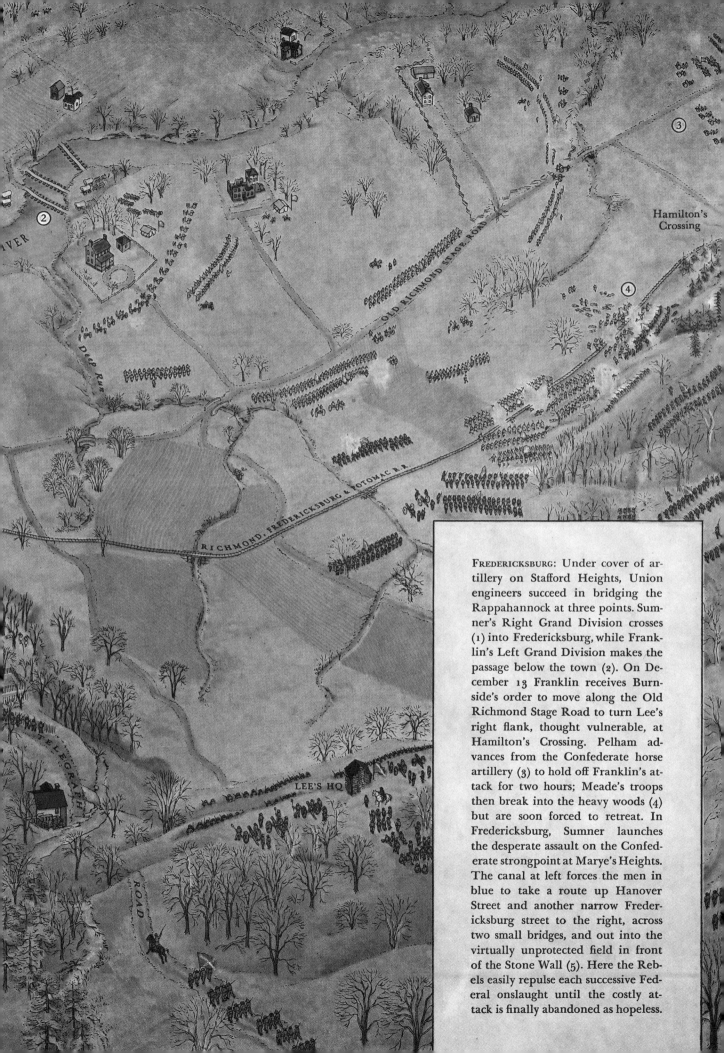

③

Hamilton's
Crossing

②

④

OLD RICHMOND STAGE ROAD

Deep Run

RICHMOND, FREDERICKSBURG & POTOMAC R.R.

TELEGRAPH

LEE'S HQ

ROAD

FREDERICKSBURG: Under cover of artillery on Stafford Heights, Union engineers succeed in bridging the Rappahannock at three points. Sumner's Right Grand Division crosses (1) into Fredericksburg, while Franklin's Left Grand Division makes the passage below the town (2). On December 13 Franklin receives Burnside's order to move along the Old Richmond Stage Road to turn Lee's right flank, thought vulnerable, at Hamilton's Crossing. Pelham advances from the Confederate horse artillery (3) to hold off Franklin's attack for two hours; Meade's troops then break into the heavy woods (4) but are soon forced to retreat. In Fredericksburg, Sumner launches the desperate assault on the Confederate strongpoint at Marye's Heights. The canal at left forces the men in blue to take a route up Hanover Street and another narrow Fredericksburg street to the right, across two small bridges, and out into the virtually unprotected field in front of the Stone Wall (5). Here the Rebels easily repulse each successive Federal onslaught until the costly attack is finally abandoned as hopeless.

Nervous reserves waiting to join the fighting at Fredericksburg watched operations on the wounded.

At dawn on December 31, the Confederates moved against the Union right flank. They moved precisely, and caught some of the Yankees cooking breakfast. The Union troops put up a stiff fight, but the Confederates pressed on strongly. The Union right swung back like a door on a hinge. By ten in the morning, the line stood at almost right angles to what it had been when the attack came.

Confederate cavalry, pursuing the fleeing Union troops, captured Federal ammunition trains. By eleven o'clock, Union troops were forced to retire with empty cartridge belts. Some were ordered to "Fix bayonets and hold your ground!" One regiment had no bayonets and was ordered to club the enemy with its muskets.

Rosecrans tried to rally his troops and get a counterattack under way. When an officer asked for reinforcements, Rosecrans ordered him to "contest every inch of ground." The tireless general still hoped to cross Stones River and attack the lightly held Confederate left. Inspecting a ford in the river, he asked the officer in charge if the position could be held. "I will try, sir," replied the officer. Rosecrans repeated the question. "I will die right here," said the officer. Rosecrans asked the question a third time. "Yes, sir!" said the officer, and Rosecrans was finally satisfied.

By four in the afternoon, Rosecrans had reformed his lines. He held his positions, throwing back the Confederate charges. But he was unable to mount an attack, and the battle petered out. Bragg was sure the Union army would pull back to Nashville the next day. He wired Richmond: "God has granted us a Happy New Year."

New Year's Day, 1863, was cold and clear. Bragg watched the enemy on the opposite side of the river. The Yankees were re-forming their lines, but to Bragg it looked as though they were preparing to leave. The next day he was surprised to see that the Union army was still there. Late in the afternoon, he suddenly or-

Murfreesboro

S HQ
31

WILKINSON TURNPIKE

WIDOW
SMITH
HOUSE

GRISCOM
HOUSE

EMBER 31ST

①

Overall's Creek

MURFREESBORO (or Stones River): At dawn on December 31 Bragg launches his sledge-hammer attack near the Widow Smith House, catching some of the Federals at breakfast (1). This assault completely turns the Union right, an entire corps being driven back some three miles before rallying on the Nashville Turnpike. As succeeding waves of Confederates crash through the scrub cedar, men under Phil Sheridan fight valiantly (2) but are forced to retire for lack of ammunition, which has been held up by Rebel cavalry forays at far left. Imperturbable George H. Thomas, whose very glance seemed to freeze would-be skulkers in their tracks, falls back and begins to form a new Union line (3), at right angles to the original one. Astride the railroad tracks, Colonel William B. Hazen's artillery stubbornly holds its original position—the only Union detachment to do so—at the center of the line (4). The first day's battle draws to a close with the Federals formed in a salient around Rosecrans' Headquarters (5). On January 2 Breckinridge is ordered to make a charge across an open field (6), vulnerable to Union artillery at the river's edge. Only when Union reinforcements are hurried across the river (7) is this final Confederate assault halted.

Federals retreating before a Rebel charge at Murfreesboro on December 31, 1862

dered Breckenridge's division to attack. Across 500 yards of open ground, the Southerners charged. As the Union artillery opened fire, frightened rabbits scurried off in all directions. A Rebel soldier called out, "Go it, cotton-tail; I'd run too if I hadn't a reputation."

Within twenty minutes the Confederates fell back, after losing about 1,800 men. That evening Bragg learned that Union reinforcements had arrived. Discouraged, he retreated thirty-six miles to the south, where he stayed all winter. Rosecrans did not try to pursue him. He moved his troops into Murfreesboro, and six months would pass before they would fight again. No one quite knew who had won the battle between the two armies. The casualties had been shocking. The Union had lost 13,000 men, the Confederates, nearly 12,000—in each case, more than a fourth of the army's total strength. Few Civil War battles ever cost more or meant less.

If the Union was to get anything at all out of the fighting in the West, it would have to come from Grant. And for a long time it did not

seem that his luck was going to be better than anybody else's.

Things started out well enough for Grant. In November he advanced down the line of the railroad. He set up a supply base at Holly Springs, twenty-four miles south of the Tennessee-Mississippi border. Grant's plan was to make a double attack aimed at Vicksburg, which controlled the Mississippi River. General Sherman, supported by the navy, was to sail his troops down the Mississippi and attack Vicksburg itself. Meanwhile, Grant was to attack the town of Grenada, Mississippi, a Confederate strong point. He expected to tie up so many Rebel troops that Sherman would have no trouble taking Vicksburg.

It was a good plan, but within a few weeks it was wrecked by the Confederates. Rebel cavalry under General Van Dorn swung in behind Grant, capturing the $1,500,000 supply base at Holly Springs. At the same time, another force under General Forrest rode up into western Tennessee. Forrest cut railroads and telegraph lines. He captured enough weapons, horses, and equipment to outfit the new recruits who joined him. He caused great confusion deep in the Federal rear, and Grant was brought to a standstill. Grant could get no word of any of this to Sherman, who was on his way to Vicksburg with 30,000 men.

A drenching rain fell as navy boats put Sherman's troops ashore north of Vicksburg. The Yankees fanned out in the swamplands below the Confederate fortifications on the bluffs. They attacked at Chickasaw Bayou on December 29, the same day that Rosecrans arrived at Murfreesboro. Crushed by artillery fire, they lost more than 1,700 men. The only sensible thing they could do was withdraw.

The war in the West, like that in the East, was stalled—but Grant was not a man to stand still for long. After moving his men down the Mississippi from Memphis, he studied the situation at Vicksburg. There seemed to be four possible ways to take the city. One involved cutting a canal to bypass Vicksburg; the second, cutting a channel for the same reason; the third, attacking Vicksburg's fortifications from the side; the fourth, bringing up troops by water through a fearfully complicated network of streams.

Grant tried each of these schemes, and each of them failed. As spring came on, he sat in his headquarters, staring at the cigar smoke that surrounded him. While he smoked, he worked out still another way to attack Vicksburg. If this also failed, his army would probably be lost, and with it the war. If it succeeded, the North would at last be on the road to victory. Whatever happened, everything was up to him.

Not until after the Emancipation Proclamation in 1863 did Lincoln call for the enlistment of Negro regiments. They served under white officers, and a number of them saw combat action.

The South's Last Bid

IN THE spring of 1863, the Northern grip on the Confederacy was slowly tightening. There was, of course, still a chance that the South might upset everything. But the Union's Army of the Potomac was ready for any Southern threat—thanks to its new commander, General Joseph Hooker.

"Fighting Joe," as he was called, was a handsome, dashing, boastful soldier with a good battle record. An officer of the regular army, he had been appointed to his new command in January. He surprised everyone by being a fine organizer and executive. He saw to it that his men got enough to eat and lived in decent camps. He turned his cavalry corps into an outfit that could give "Jeb" Stuart a real fight. Even more important, he gave his soldiers confidence.

Hooker himself had plenty of confidence—too much, Lincoln suspected. Hooker once said that the question was not whether he could take Richmond, but simply when he would take it. This sounded a little too optimistic. He made another over-optimistic remark when he presented the plan for his spring campaign. "May God have mercy on General Lee," Hooker said, "for I will have none."

As a matter of fact, things did seem favorable for the Union. Hooker had more than 120,000 well-trained, well-equipped troops. The South, on the other hand, was beginning to suffer from a shortage of men and supplies. General Lee had hardly more than 60,000 men in and around Fredericksburg. They did not have enough guns, ammunition, food, or clothing.

Lee and Jackson meet at dawn on May 2, 1863. That night Jackson was mortally wounded by his own men.

Late in April, the Army of the Potomac moved out of its camps to meet Lee and attack Richmond. McClellan had tried to take Richmond from the east; Burnside had tried it from the north. Hooker had a different plan. He would make a wide sweep to his right and come in on Lee from the west. This called for a long hike along the Rappahannock River, and crossings of that river and its tributary, the Rapidan. After that, he would have to march down the south bank of the two streams through a tangled woodland known as the Wilderness. If Hooker could do all this quickly, he would be on good fighting ground behind Lee's lines.

Leaving one wing of his army at Fredericksburg to deceive Lee, Hooker crossed the Rapidan on the night of April 29. The next day he was at the small crossroads of Chancellorsville. The Union troops were just twelve miles from Lee's Fredericksburg lines and well behind them, but they were still in the Wilderness. Lee saw that he was in danger and moved quickly. He left part of his army at Fredericksburg and marched hard for Chancellorsville with 45,000 men.

On May 1, Hooker's army started toward Fredericksburg. The moment it ran into Rebel fire, Hooker pulled back to Chancellorsville. He had not expected Lee to strike so soon, and his nerve failed. "I just lost confidence in Joe Hooker," he later admitted.

Hooker placed O. O. Howard's XI Corps on his extreme right, as far from the enemy as possible. When Lee learned that this corps was unprepared for an attack, he made the most daring decision of his military career. Outnumbered 70,000 to 45,000, he nevertheless sent "Stonewall" Jackson with 26,000 men on a

CHANCELLORSVILLE

Second Day: May 2, 1863

RAPPAHANNOCK RIVER

RIVER ROAD

TURNPIKE

TO SALEM CH...

Chancellorsville

HOOKER'S HQ

ORANGE PLANK ROAD

FAIRVIEW CEMETERY ⑦

Mott's Road

②

⑧

N WERT OUSE

HAZEL GROVE

⑥

FURNACE ROAD

CATHERINE FURNACE

①

JACKSON

Lewis Creek

David Greenspan

CHANCELLORSVILLE: At first light on May 2 Jackson begins a flank march (lower right) across the Union front. Sickles glimpses the tail of this column, moves forward from Hazel Grove, and attacks (1). His minor success convinces Hooker that the Confederates are in full retreat, and that Lee's probing attacks (2) are merely rear-guard actions. Jackson, meanwhile, has gone into position athwart the Union right flank, which faces south along the Turnpike. At 6 P.M. he drives forward (3), routing the XI Corps, his wide battle line overlapping the desperate Union attempts to form (4). The victorious Confederates sweep up the Turnpike, past the Wilderness Church and Dowdall's Tavern. Here remnants of the XI Corps make a last stand (5) and, reinforced with a few guns, delay Jackson's men long enough for the rest of the troops to make good their escape. Sickles falls back to Hazel Grove, where Union guns knock back a Rebel attack (6) threatening this key position. The fire of Hooker's massed artillery at Fairview Cemetery (7) finally halts the Southern advance. At 9 P.M. Jackson and his staff, returning from a reconnoitering mission to locate the new Federal positions, are fired on by a nervous Confederate regiment, and Jackson is fatally wounded (8).

long, concealed flank march in front of Hooker's army. Jackson was to attack Hooker's right wing, while the rest of Lee's army attacked the center. With the Union army between them, they would push it into a smaller and smaller area, and then destroy it.

By late afternoon of May 2, Jackson was set to strike at the XI Corps. Lee's information had been correct; the Corps was unprepared for an attack. Its position was made even worse by the hasty action of Daniel Sickles. Sickles was the commander of the Union center. When he saw what was the end of Jackson's column moving off through the woods, he thought the Confederates were retreating. He moved forward to attack, which had very little effect on the fighting. But it left the Federal right completely cut off from the other Union forces.

At six o'clock, Jackson's men burst from the forest in a wave a mile wide. Howard's XI Corps crumbled, the men fleeing down the road toward Chancellorsville. Lee believed he could now trap all of Hooker's men. He ordered an attack all along the line. The result was a fiery, confused battle in the smoky, moonlit night.

It was like no other battle in the entire war. A Northern soldier later recalled "the infernal and yet sublime combination of sound and flame and smoke, and dreadful yells of rage, of pain, of triumph, of defiance." Men milled around in the woods, in the clearings, on the roads. They attacked and retreated without knowing where they were or where they were going. Blindly they slashed and fired, not knowing whether their victims were friends or foes. Two Union detachments ran into each other in the dark and fought savagely until they discovered their mistake.

The Rebels made a similar mistake. At about nine o'clock, the men of a North Carolina regiment fired on what they thought was Yankee cavalry. Instead, it was "Stonewall" Jackson and his staff, returning from a scouting mission. Jackson reeled in the saddle, hit by three Confederate bullets. The strange battle went on for nearly three hours after the wounding of Jackson.

Oddly enough, when the next day dawned, Hooker was in position to turn the tables on Lee. His reinforced army outnumbered Lee's

Farragut's flagship Hartford *leads an unsuccessful attack on Port Hudson, which later fell to the Union.*

This four-gun Confederate battery was one of many that defended Vicksburg.

two to one, and it was squarely between the still divided Rebel forces. But Hooker did not even consider making an attack. He was a beaten man and could think only of defense. It was the Confederates who attacked, and Hooker was driven back to the Rappahannock.

As his infantry took up positions along the river, the big Union guns were wheeled into place. The general commanding the artillery told Hooker not to worry. He said, "I'll make 'em think hell isn't half a mile off!" He let loose a terrific barrage, beating back the Rebel charge. For the time being, Hooker was saved.

Hooker had already sent to Fredericksburg for reinforcements. To reach him, General John Sedgwick's 25,000 men had to battle 10,000 Rebels under General Jubal Early. The Confederate lines were at Marye's Heights, where Burnside had been stopped the previous December. Sedgwick took the heights after three charges, then set off for Chancellorsville. He never got there—because once again Lee acted boldly.

Leaving a few brigades to keep an eye on Hooker, Lee moved out to meet Sedgwick. They collided at Salem Church, halfway between Fredericksburg and Chancellorsville. After a day of hard fighting, the Yankees were forced to retreat. It was the final blow to Hooker's hopes for victory. On the night of May 5 he ordered a general withdrawal across the Rappahannock. "Fighting Joe" Hooker had had enough of fighting. He had failed to take advantage of an excellent start and several good chances. He had lost 17,000 men and had been defeated by an army half the size of his.

For the Confederates, it was a bitter victory, for it cost them one of their greatest generals. On May 10, "Stonewall" Jackson murmured, "Let us cross over the river, and rest under the shade of the trees." Then he died, of the wounds he had received from his own men. Lee said, "I have lost my right arm." The Army of Northern Virginia was never quite the same again.

With Hooker defeated, the next move in the East was up to Lee. He went to Richmond, where he held conferences with President Davis

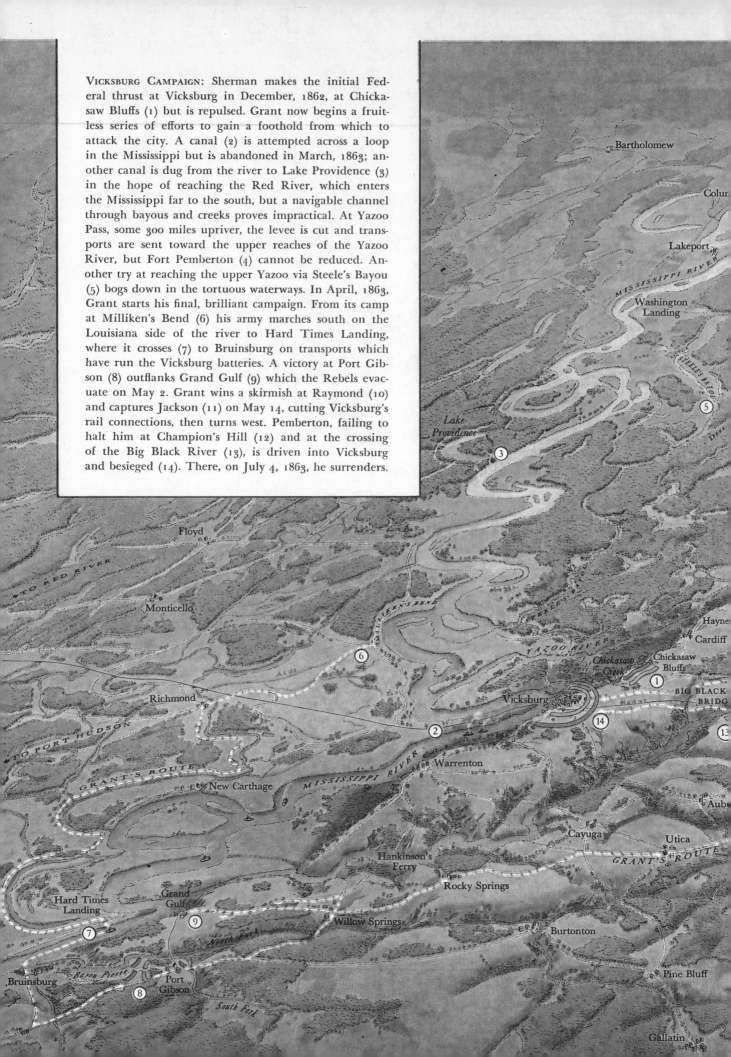

VICKSBURG CAMPAIGN: Sherman makes the initial Federal thrust at Vicksburg in December, 1862, at Chickasaw Bluffs (1) but is repulsed. Grant now begins a fruitless series of efforts to gain a foothold from which to attack the city. A canal (2) is attempted across a loop in the Mississippi but is abandoned in March, 1863; another canal is dug from the river to Lake Providence (3) in the hope of reaching the Red River, which enters the Mississippi far to the south, but a navigable channel through bayous and creeks proves impractical. At Yazoo Pass, some 300 miles upriver, the levee is cut and transports are sent toward the upper reaches of the Yazoo River, but Fort Pemberton (4) cannot be reduced. Another try at reaching the upper Yazoo via Steele's Bayou (5) bogs down in the tortuous waterways. In April, 1863, Grant starts his final, brilliant campaign. From its camp at Milliken's Bend (6) his army marches south on the Louisiana side of the river to Hard Times Landing, where it crosses (7) to Bruinsburg on transports which have run the Vicksburg batteries. A victory at Port Gibson (8) outflanks Grand Gulf (9) which the Rebels evacuate on May 2. Grant wins a skirmish at Raymond (10) and captures Jackson (11) on May 14, cutting Vicksburg's rail connections, then turns west. Pemberton, failing to halt him at Champion's Hill (12) and at the crossing of the Big Black River (13), is driven into Vicksburg and besieged (14). There, on July 4, 1863, he surrenders.

THE CAMPAIGN
AND SIEGE OF VICKSBURG

December, 1862 – July, 1863

On May 19, 1863, Grant made the first of two attempts to take Vicksburg by storm.

and the Confederate Cabinet. The decision was that Lee would invade Pennsylvania.

The whole thing was a gamble. The Confederates were betting that the magnificent Army of Northern Virginia could somehow win a battle on Union soil. A smashing victory would take the heart out of the North and might bring the war to an end. On the other hand, the risks would be many. The Southern army was certain to be outnumbered. The Yankees were bound to make a great effort to stop the Confederate thrust. Furthermore, the South did not have enough men and supplies for a long campaign. Lee would have to make a raid, rather than a regular invasion. If it did not succeed, the Confederacy might lose both its army and the war.

And yet, the South had to take the chance.

Dugouts behind the center of the Union lines that sealed off the city of Vicksburg during the siege

The fact was that no really good move was open to Lee. If he stayed in Virginia, the Army of the Potomac would attack again in a month or so. The attack might be beaten back, but at a cost the South could not afford. Virginia could not support Lee's troops much longer. "The question of food," Lee said, "gives me more trouble and uneasiness than everything else combined."

There was one more reason for Lee to march north. An invasion of Pennsylvania might cause the North to pull troops away from the West. And this was important, for in the West Grant was making a move as daring as Lee's own. He had at last hit upon a new scheme to take Vicksburg.

Grant's scheme was simple, but, also like Lee's, it was risky. He put it into operation in April of 1863. First he marched his army south, along the west bank of the Mississippi River. His men had to hack their way through the

111

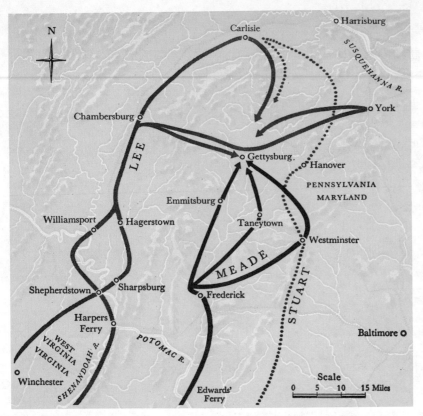

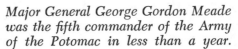

At one point in his invasion of Pennsylvania, Lee's army was spread out over 100 miles. Before concentrating at Gettysburg, some of his advance units were as far east as the Susquehanna.

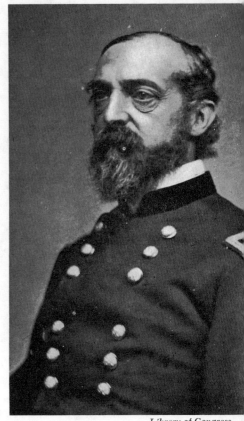

Major General George Gordon Meade was the fifth commander of the Army of the Potomac in less than a year.

thickets and rushes that covered the low, swampy land. Then they had to cross the river below Vicksburg on naval transports. If they succeeded, they would be on dry ground on the same side of the river as the enemy.

Grant's plan depended on the navy. Only the navy could silence the Rebel shore batteries and keep his army supplied. Luckily, the Union navy at Vicksburg was commanded by Rear Admiral David Dixon Porter, a brave, tough, tireless sailor.

On the night of April 16, Porter got his fleet under way. One by one the ships moved to the middle of the river, with not a light showing. The engines were turned off, and they floated silently downstream. As the lead gunboats approached Vicksburg, they were seen by Rebel sentries on the shore. The Confederates lit huge

bonfires to make the ships easier targets for their gunners. For an hour and a half the terrible cannonading went on, but Porter's fleet sailed past the batteries with only slight damage. A few nights later he ran more ships past the guns.

To confuse the enemy, Grant had ordered a cavalry brigade to make raids through central Mississippi. It was under the command of Benjamin H. Grierson, a former music teacher. He hated horses, having been kicked by one when he was a small child. When he had joined the army he asked to be put in the infantry. Because of a mix-up, he was placed in the cavalry, and he proved to be a fine officer. His men tore up railroads south of Vicksburg, upsetting Rebel troop movements.

As Grant prepared to cross the river below

Vicksburg, he ordered Sherman to make a mock attack at Haynes' Bluff, just above Vicksburg. General John C. Pemberton, who was in charge of the Vicksburg defenses, was completely fooled. He thought it was the main attack—and Grant's men crossed the river far downstream without trouble.

Grant pushed on to place himself between the two largest Rebel armies. One was at Vicksburg. The other, under General Joe Johnston, was at Jackson. By taking Jackson, Grant could cut off the railroad that supplied Vicksburg. As the Yankees marched on Jackson, Pemberton tried to cut the Union supply line. The Confederates soon discovered that there was no such line. The Yankees were traveling light and living off the country. Aside from ammunition, they carried only coffee, sugar, and salt. They found plenty of food in Mississippi, and gorged themselves on chicken, pork, and steak.

On May 14, the Rebels abandoned Jackson, the capital of Jefferson Davis' home state. Union troops occupied the city. Obeying Sherman's orders to "destroy everything public not needed by us," they took the place apart. They looted stores and houses, and set fire to foundries, machine shops, warehouses, factories, and arsenals.

Grant now turned toward Vicksburg. On May 16, he defeated Pemberton in a stiff fight at Champion Hill. The next day he routed the Confederate rear guard at the Big Black River. Johnston warned Pemberton: "If it is not too late, evacuate Vicksburg." It was too late. Pemberton was trapped.

He could, however, hold out for many weeks, as the Yankees were to learn. Twice, on May 19 and May 22, Grant tried to take the city by storm. Both times he was stopped with heavy losses. There was only one way to take Vicksburg—starve it out. He sent a force eastward to hold off Joe Johnston, and settled down to a siege. Johnston was building up his army, but he could never make it strong enough. He had perhaps 25,000 men, and Pemberton had 30,000. Grant was reinforced until he had 75,000, and he could handle both Pemberton and Johnston without too much trouble. By the first of June, Pemberton was locked up and

Johnston was helpless. It seemed likely that Vicksburg's fall would only be a question of time.

Grant's line of trenches, fifteen miles long in all, sealed off the city. A Rebel soldier said later that "a cat could not have crept out of Vicksburg without being discovered." Porter's fleet held the river. His guns and Grant's batteries lobbed shells into the city. The people took to cellars and caves, "packed in, black and white, like sardines in a box." It was spring, and one woman wrote in her diary: "In the midst of all this carnage and commotion . . . birds are singing . . . flowers are in perfection . . . and the garden bright and gay . . . all save the spirit of man seems divine."

To the Yankee soldiers, the siege seemed endless. They were bored, dirty, not too well fed, and many of them were sick. After a month of waiting for the Rebel garrison to surrender, they became impatient. Grant decided to try something different. He would dig a tunnel under the Vicksburg fortifications and blow them up. Working around the clock for days, his engineers burrowed in the ground. They then placed in the tunnel a huge quantity of explosives, attached to fuses. The plan was to set off the charge and then attack.

When everything was ready, the fuses were lit. Within a few minutes there was a tremendous explosion. After the smoke and dust had cleared away, a huge crater could be seen in the Rebel breastworks. Union troops charged into it, and the Confederates poured down a hail of grapeshot, canister, and bullets. So many men were lost that the crater was given up. Grant's troops settled back into their trenches to wait.

As the weeks went on, Vicksburg's food supply grew smaller and smaller. Some of the people had nothing to eat but mule meat and peas. At last, on July 3, Pemberton asked Grant for surrender terms. As the two generals discussed the terms, Yankee soldiers visited with the Confederates. A private noted that "several brothers met, and any quantity of cousins. It was a strange scene."

On July 4, Vicksburg surrendered. Five days

A. P. Hill's Rebel divisions swept in on Gettysburg from the west, early in the first day's fighting.

later Port Hudson, another Confederate strong point on the river, fell to the Union. The North controlled the entire length of the Mississippi; the South was split in two.

Meanwhile, in the East, the South had suffered another terrible defeat. Lee had started to move early in June, and by the end of the month he was in Pennsylvania. He learned that the Army of the Potomac was near Frederick,

Maryland, squarely on his flank. It had a new commanding general, George Gordon Meade. Meade was a hot-tempered, capable professional soldier. Lee knew the man, and said, "General Meade will make no blunder on my front."

Lee's troops were stretched out in a long line, running from Chambersburg nearly to Gettysburg. Gettysburg was a quiet little crossroads

On the second and third days of the battle the Union line was anchored on the hills in the background.

town. Except to the people who lived in the area, among the rolling hills, it had no importance whatever. But Lee wanted to gather his army together, and Gettysburg was the handiest place to do it. Neither he nor General Meade had any intention of fighting a battle there. The greatest single battle of the war came about by accident.

Lee's troops were living off the country, taking supplies wherever they could get them. One of the things they needed most was shoes. On the morning of July 1, 1863, General Harry Heth's division of A. P. Hill's corps set out for Gettysburg to find some shoes. On the Chambersburg Pike, a mile and a half from the town, they ran into Yankee soldiers. They were John Buford's cavalry, patrolling the roads of the area for Rebels.

GETTYSBURG

Second Day: July 2, 1863

Gettysburg

CULP'S HILL ⑦

⑧

CEMETERY HILL

MEADE'S HQ

ZIEGLER'S GROVE

CODORI HOUSE

CEMETERY RIDGE

⑥

⑤

SEMINARY RIDGE

ROGERS HOUSE

TROSTLE FARM

PEACH ORCHARD

③

WHEAT FIELD

WARFIELD HOUSE

EMMITSBURG ROAD

ROSE HOUSE

David Greenspan

GETTYSBURG: The action on the second day opens with a Confederate artillery barrage at 4 P.M. An hour later Hood's Rebel division sweeps in around the Union left flank, overruns Devil's Den (1), and begins the ascent of the undefended Little Round Top, which dominates the entire Federal position. Warren hastens troops to the crest, and they repulse Hood's men after a bitter struggle (2). As the battle shifts steadily northward, Longstreet sends in McLaws, who shatters Sickles' salient (3), embracing the Peach Orchard and the Wheat Field, and advances toward a gap in Meade's line (4). Artillery is rushed forward to hold together the battered Union line until reinforcements arrive. At the Trostle Farm, Barksdale's Mississippians manage to take a Yankee battery (5), but Barksdale is mortally wounded and his brigade wrecked. The Rebels strike at the Union center (6), where they meet stiff resistance, including a doomed counterattack by the 1st Minnesota, and are stopped. At dark Ewell demonstrates against the Federal right, but fails to take the strong position on Culp's Hill (7). In the day's final action Jubal Early gets two Rebel brigades in among the Union batteries on Cemetery Hill (8), but they are not strong enough to resist counterattacks and are driven off.

Three small boys were picking raspberries nearby. Young Billy Bayly and his friends watched the start of the great battle. Later, Billy wrote of their experience:

"The discharge of a cannon . . . made us jump, as it seemed to be just beyond the bushes concealing us. This was instantly followed by a rapid succession of discharges, and we three boys broke for the open and back to the black-smith's shop. . . . We perched ourselves on the topmost rail of the road fence and drank in the melody of the battle."

The three boys saw the Yankee cavalry dismount to trade shots with the Rebel infantry. They saw, too, the arrival of reinforcements. Billy later recalled the scene:

"But our gallery seats, although good for the whole show, began to have features of discomfort when we noticed up the road, coming over the nearest hill, great masses of troops and clouds of dust; how the first wave swelled into successive waves, gray masses with the glint of steel as the sun struck the gun barrels, filling the highway, spreading out into the fields, and still coming on and on, wave after wave, billow

after billow after billow. We waited not until we could 'see the whites of their eyes' but until they were a few hundred yards between us and the advance column, and then we departed. . . ."

Buford's men held out for two hours until General John Reynolds' infantry corps arrived. Reynolds rushed into action, shouting, "Forward! for God's sake, forward!" He threw back the Rebel attack, then was killed by a sharp-shooter's bullet. Confederate reinforcements were pouring into the line faster than those of the Yankees.

Howard's XI Corps, which had been so badly mauled at Chancellorsville, came marching up. At the same time, "Stonewall" Jackson's old corps, now under General Richard Ewell, bore down from the north and east. Lee had not wanted to fight here, but he now ordered the Confederate line forward. The XI Corps collapsed, and the Federal right wing with it. The Federal left wing, facing the Confederates west of town, was uncovered.

A brigade of Union infantry and some artillery tried to make a stand along Seminary Ridge. In the words of a gunner, "for seven or

This painting shows the Confederate high tide at Gettysburg, with troops surging through the Union line.

eight minutes ensued probably the most desperate fight ever waged between artillery and infantry at close range without a particle of cover on either side . . . bullets hissing, humming and whistling everywhere; cannon roaring; all crash on crash and peal on peal, smoke, dust, splinters, blood, wreck and carnage indescribable.''

Soon the entire Union line gave way. The soldiers fled through Gettysburg to high ground beyond, where there was a rise called Cemetery Hill. By the time they managed to pull their forces together, it was dusk. If the Army of the Potomac was to make a stand at Gettysburg, these men had to hold out. But they could not hold out if they lost the hill.

Lee realized this. He ordered Ewell to take Cemetery Hill "if possible." Jackson would have understood the meaning behind those words. Lee was always polite. What he really meant was: "Take the hill without fail." But Ewell was no Jackson. He did nothing. When his patrols reported that the Union line had been reinforced, he called off the attack. For the moment, the Union army was safe. General

Meade soon arrived to take personal command, making his headquarters in a tiny farmhouse on the rear slope of Cemetery Ridge.

That night Lee told his officers, "We will attack . . . in the morning as early as practicable."

As the battle went into its second day, Meade's position was a strong one. His line, three miles long, was shaped like a fishhook. At one end there were two hills—Round Top and Little Round Top. At the other end was a rise called Culp's Hill. His center ran the length of Cemetery Ridge. The Confederate line, which was five miles long, was roughly parallel.

As strong as Meade's line was, it had one great weakness. If the Confederates could take any one of the hills, it would be extremely difficult to keep them from taking the others. It would be just as difficult for the Union center to hold out.

Meade understood this very well. On the morning of July 2, he prepared to meet an attack from Lee. He believed Lee would try to take Culp's Hill, on the Union right. It was a good guess, but it did not go far enough. Lee planned to strike at both ends of the Union line.

General James Longstreet was assigned to make the attack on Little Round Top, on the Union's left. He took his time about it, and he was not ready until late afternoon. As it turned out, the delay helped the Confederates. Daniel Sickles' corps held the Union left. Sickles thought he knew more about fighting than Meade. He moved his troops to the slightly higher ground a half mile in front of Cemetery Ridge, an open position from which they could not possibly defend Little Round Top.

Meade ordered Sickles to return to his former position. Before the order could be carried out, the Confederates attacked. Amid a heavy bombardment, they came pounding in on Devil's Den at the foot of Little Round Top. They broke through the Union line and began scrambling up the rocky slopes. If Little Round Top were lost, the entire Union line on Cemetery Hill would be exposed to a deadly fire.

119

Meade's wagon trains approaching the Potomac, long after Lee's escape from Gettysburg.

Fresh Yankee troops pushed forward, fighting the Rebels toe to toe. As one soldier put it, "The lines at times were so near each other that the hostile gun barrels almost touched." When the defenders of the hill ran out of ammunition, they fixed bayonets and charged. They saved Little Round Top—but only for a while.

In a peach orchard and a wheat field just below Little Round Top, fighting raged. Here men went at each other hand-to-hand, with bayonet and rifle butt. Shellfire splintered the trees, and the grain was trampled flat. The fighting in orchard and field seesawed back and forth all afternoon, until a Confederate charge drove the Yankees up the slope. Sickles' leg had been shattered, and his corps was broken to bits.

Near the wheat field, at the foot of Little Round Top, was a boulder-covered area known as the Devil's Den. It seemed like a fitting name that day. Men fired at each other from behind the rocks. The wounded and the dying crept into the crevices, trying to save themselves.

By taking the wheat field and the peach orchard, the Confederates tore a gap in Meade's line. They hammered at the Union center, only to be stopped by the Yankee artillery. The big guns, jammed to the muzzles with canister, blasted the charging Rebels. The Federals tried a counterattack, but were halted with enormous losses.

By now it was nearly dark, and the thunder of battle on the Union left died down to a mutter. An occasional volley crackled, with the gunfire looking like lightning in the smoking haze. But the fighting was not yet over for the day. Lee had ordered Ewell to make a demonstration—a show of force to mask the main attack. It was to be made against the Union right, at Cemetery and Culp's hills.

As Longstreet had attacked on the Union left, Ewell's artillery had begun a barrage. His guns were soon silenced by the heavier Union fire. Ewell was anxious to make up for his failure to take Cemetery Hill the day before. He ordered his infantry forward. He sent one division to take Culp's Hill, which was held by a single Union brigade. But the Federals were protected by sturdy log barricades and they beat off four separate attacks.

As the assault lost steam, two Confederate brigades pushed up a ravine between Culp's Hill and Cemetery Hill. The Northern line was thin here, and the Southerners captured several batteries in bitter hand-to-hand fighting. A Union counterattack in the gathering darkness drove them out of the ravine.

So ended the second day at Gettysburg. Lee had failed to turn either Union flank, and the ground he had gained was hardly worth the terrible cost. That night Meade called a meeting of his generals. They agreed that they would neither retreat nor attack. They would wait and see what Lee intended to do. As the meeting broke up, Meade called General John Gibbon aside. Gibbon commanded the division holding the center of Cemetery Ridge. "If Lee attacks tomorrow," Meade said, "it will be in your front."

At daylight on July 3, the Rebels again attacked Culp's Hill. By ten-thirty, it was plain that the hill could not be taken. A strange quiet settled over the battlefield. The Yankees watched the Confederates move their cannon into position a mile west of Cemetery Ridge. Finally about 150 of them were aimed at the center of Meade's line.

At one o'clock the Rebel guns opened fire on Cemetery Ridge. Luckily for Meade, they were firing just a little too high. The Union guns fired slowly in return. The gunners were saving their ammunition for the big Rebel push.

It came soon enough. Six Confederate brigades, plus George Pickett's fresh division—15,000 men in all—moved forward. A Union eyewitness saw "an overwhelming resistless tide of an ocean of armed men sweeping upon us . . . on they move, as with one soul, in perfect order . . . over ridge and slope, through orchard and meadow and cornfield, magnificent, grim and irresistible."

The Confederate infantrymen came on, steadily and quietly. Union artillery fire shook their ranks, and then both sides exploded in a tremendous clash. The Rebel flanks were smashed in. The spearhead, however, drove on to the clump of trees and the stone wall at the Union center—soon to be known simply as the Angle. The battle noise was "strange and terrible, a sound that came from thousands of human throats . . . like a vast mournful roar."

Lee was trying to do what could not be done —to batter down Meade at his strongest point. Wave after wave of infantry, only 1,400 yards apart, rolled across the battlefield. Three brigades under General Pickett's command were given the fearful job of breaking through Meade's line. They made a glorious and heroic charge, but it failed.

Suddenly the battle was over. Union reinforcements came swarming into the line, and the Confederates withdrew. Watching the survivors return, Lee said, "All this has been my fault."

The next day, July 4, a rain "washed the blood from the grass." After resting a day, Lee began his long retreat to Virginia. Meade followed him slowly, catching up at the Potomac. Lee dug in, and Meade was too cautious to attack with his badly mangled army. By July 14 Lee was over the river, his dream of victory in the North dead forever.

More than 7,000 men had died on the bloody ground of Gettysburg; 44,000 were wounded and missing. The Union had lost 23,000 men, the Confederacy 5,000 more—which meant that Lee had lost nearly a third of his whole army. The Rebel wounded jolted southward in a seventeen-mile-long train of springless wagons. Gettysburg and the nearby towns were swamped with wounded. A Quaker nurse wrote, "There are no words in the English language to express the sufferings I witnessed today."

Many of those who died in the battle, both Northerners and Southerners, were buried at Gettysburg. The United States government set aside seventeen acres on Cemetery Hill for a military cemetery. The battlefield was cleaned up, and on November 19, 1863, the cemetery was dedicated. Edward Everett, a well-known orator, made a speech that lasted two hours. Abraham Lincoln had been asked to make a "few appropriate remarks." He spoke ten sentences that would be long remembered as the Gettysburg Address.

The Armies

THE SOLDIER in the Civil War was a good fighter, but he was different from the highly trained soldier of the European armies. He was an amateur. Unlike most European countries, the United States had no standing army when the Civil War broke out. There was only a tiny professional force to garrison the coastal forts and to protect settlers in the West from Indian attacks. Drafting men for army service was unheard of. That would not come until late in the war.

The Civil War soldier, at least in the beginning, went off to war because he wanted to go. Right after Fort Sumter, war looked like a great adventure. The waving flags, the brass bands, the loud-voiced orators made it seem like a wonderful thing to be a soldier. Thousands of young Northerners and Southerners hurried to enlist, feeling that they were lucky to have the chance. Many of them were afraid the war would be over before they could get into action.

Later, after experiencing the boredom of camp life and the horror of battle, their feelings changed. But in the spring of 1861, few Americans in either the North or the South had any understanding of what war was about. Just as few had any knowledge of camp life. In the South, for example, a young aristocrat might volunteer as a private and turn up in camp with a body servant and a full trunk of clothing. Northern volunteers often arrived at camp with knapsacks weighing as much as a hundred pounds, containing overcoats, extra uniforms, bear oil for their hair, and all kinds of gifts from their families and friends.

The volunteers did not take easily to discipline. Discipline was especially bad in the Western regiments. An Indiana soldier ex-

Collection of Mrs. John Nicholas Brown

plained: "We had enlisted to put down the rebellion and had no patience with the red-tape tom-foolery of the regular service. Furthermore, our boys recognized no superiors except in the line of legitimate duty. Shoulder straps waived, a private was ready at the drop of a

hat to thrash his commander; a feat that occurred more than once."

Fist fights were common between officers and men. In the Confederate army, it went even further. Officers were sometimes challenged to duels by privates who did not like the way they

To aid the Union's recruiting drive, an imaginative artist drew this picture of confident Yankee Doodles marching down the road to Dixie. At the start of the war, young men of both sides were eager to volunteer. One soldier wrote in 1861, "So impatient did I become for starting that I felt like ten thousand pins were pricking me in every part of the body, and started off a week in advance of my brothers."

were ordered about. One reason for the trouble was that company and regimental officers were either elected by the soldiers or appointed by the state governor because of politics. The officers were, or wanted to be, personally liked by their men. Some had political ambitions. They were not likely to bear down very hard, and if they did the privates were not likely to take it very well. On top of this, neither the North nor the South had anything resembling officer-candidate schools. Most officers had to learn their jobs while they were doing them.

In camp, discipline was imperfect, and on the march it was seldom tight enough to prevent straggling. But in battle it was often very good. The soldiers learned that to win battles they had to obey orders.

They never did learn to like military drill. An Illinois soldier wrote that the drill sergeant was the "most exasperating and yet most useful

Confederate Museum

institution of the early army...." His own sergeant, like many of the others, was a German. The sergeant bawled out orders: "Eyes vront! Toes oudt! Leetle finger mit de seam de bantaloons! Vy shtand like a _____ haystack? You neffer make a soldier."

All privates were taught the fundamentals—how to stand at attention, how to pick up and shoulder a rifle, and so on. More important, they had to be taught how to get from a marching formation into a fighting formation. A division moving along a country road would usually march in a column of fours, about eight feet wide and a mile long. Reaching the battlefield, the division had to change its shape completely. It might have to become six feet long and a mile wide. It might have to form a series of lines, each line one or more regiments in width. Or it might throw its regiments into boxlike shapes, with two companies marching abreast as it moved from a road onto a battlefield.

If the ground was rough and badly wooded, the ten companies of a regiment might go for-

A bearded Yankee poses with his sword.

ward in ten parallel columns. Each column would be two men wide and forty or fifty men deep. The fighting line they made might lie at any angle to the original line of march. Once in action, the line might have to shift to the right or the left, to advance or retreat, or swing on a pivot like an immense gate. These movements had to be made up hill and down, through underbrush, woods, swamps, gullies. And they had to be made under fire, with the words of command almost impossible to hear in the terrible racket.

Troops that could not do these things could not fight efficiently, as the first battle of Bull Run proved. To do them well required an immense amount of drill. Few generals ever considered that their men had had enough. The soldiers thought otherwise. One wrote to his family that he found drill "harder work than farming." It was just as hard for the officers as it was for the men. Except for the West Pointers, the officers knew little more about military matters than the raw recruits. Often they stayed up at night studying military textbooks.

Oddly enough, the average regiment did not get a great deal of target practice. The ordinary American was supposed to be a backwoodsman who knew how to handle a rifle. That had never

The artist Winslow Homer showed the boredom of camp life in the painting titled Home, Sweet Home.

Drummer boys sounded the calls in army camps.

N. S. Meyer, Inc.

been entirely true, and it was certainly not true by 1861. More of the Southern recruits had actually lived under frontier conditions and really knew how to shoot. It gave the Confederacy a slight advantage.

The musket in use during the Civil War caused trouble for the troops on both sides. It looked like the old infantry musket, but it was quite different. Although the new musket was still a muzzle-loader, its bore was rifled instead of smooth. This gave it far greater accuracy and range than the old smoothbore. It was a far more deadly weapon.

When the old smoothbore muskets had been in use, firing lines that were much more than a hundred yards apart could not do much damage to each other. Troops that were to make an attack would be massed together, elbow to elbow. When the order to charge was given, they would make a run for it. If there were enough of them, and they ran fast enough, they could not be seriously hurt by enemy fire. Once they got in close, they settled things with the bayonet.

The new rifled musket could kill at distances up to half a mile. When the soldiers were on the defense in trenches, which they learned to dig early in the war, a direct attack on them was almost impossible. The casualty lists in the Civil War were huge, because battles were fought with the new muskets in the same way they had been fought with the old muskets. It took the generals a long time to learn that a new way of fighting was needed. Meanwhile, a tremendous number of men were killed and wounded.

Artillery was also improved in its ability to kill during the Civil War. All of the cannon were muzzle-loaders, but guns with rifled barrels were coming into use. The rifled cannon could hit harder and reach farther than the smoothbore. It could knock out a battery of smoothbores without being hit in return. The three-inch rifled cannon, made of iron, could fire a ten-pound cone-shaped shot instead of the ordinary round cannonball. It had immense penetrating power.

But the old smoothbore—a brass gun of four and one-half inch caliber, firing a twelve-pound round shot—remained in use throughout the war. It was especially useful in wooded, hilly country, where so many of the battles were fought. Its range of slightly less than a mile was about all that was needed. For close work against infantry, it was better than the rifled cannon. It was murderous when it fired canister—a tin can full of lead slugs. The can flew apart when the gun was fired, and the slugs were sprayed in all directions. The effect was like that of a huge sawed-off shotgun.

There were also several other types of artillery for special purposes. One of these was the squat mortar. It had a higher angle of fire than most field cannon, and was used against fortifications and prepared field positions. Siege guns were also used at times. They were too heavy to be used in ordinary battles, but they were brought up to be used against fortifications. They were powerful enough to knock down masonry walls.

Civil War artillery was not easy to work with, and often extremely dangerous. The large pieces were hauled by horses, the smaller ones by the men themselves. They could get stuck in the mud, or overturn on rough ground. Loading the cannon was difficult. The shot was loaded into the muzzle, most of the time while the gun was still hot and smoking. Setting off the guns was dangerous to the gunners. It was even more dangerous to infantry in position in front of the guns. Shell fuzes were often defective, and the shot would go off too soon, killing friends instead of the foe. The big siege guns tended to be weak in the breech. Every now and then one of them would explode when fired.

The artillery was one branch of the army in which the North had the advantage. It had more factories to supply the guns. The Union army was larger than the Confederate, and could assign more men to the artillery. Also, coming from an industrial section of the country, the Yankees had more skill with cannon than the Rebels.

When it came to cavalry, however, the South outclassed the North. Many Rebel recruits were expert horsemen. "Jeb" Stuart's troopers could have taught tricks to circus riders. Most Northern cavalrymen had to be first taught how to stay in the saddle. Not until 1863 could the Army of the Potomac send out troopers who came anywhere near matching Stuart's men.

In the West, the Confederates had Nathan Bedford Forrest. He was an untaught genius who was probably the best cavalryman in the war. He used his troops like mounted infantry, in much the same way as a modern general uses motorized infantry. Forrest's aim, as he himself said, was "to git thar fust with the most men." (He did *not* say "git thar fustest with the mostest.") Once at the field of battle, his men dismounted, tied their horses to trees, and fought on foot.

Except for troopers like Forrest's, cavalry did not play a large part in the war. It was used mainly for scouting the enemy and screening the movements of its own army. Although troopers fought one another when they met, they seldom fought infantry. Infantrymen looked down on the horsemen. A common saying among the foot soldiers was: "Who ever saw a dead cavalryman?"

A much smaller branch of the armies, though an important one, was the corps of engineers. It built bridges, opened roads, laid out fortifications, kept railroads in repair, and was in charge of the pontoons that were used to get the troops across rivers. The engineers also assisted in stringing wires for the newly invented telegraph. For the first time in warfare, generals at the front could be in instant communication with their bases. The South had the best engineer officer of them all—General Robert E. Lee.

No one knows exactly how many men served in the armies of the North and the South. The best estimate is that the Union had about 1,500,000 three-year enlistments, the Confederacy about 1,000,000.

Altogether, 617,000 men lost their lives; 359,000 were Union soldiers, 258,000 were Confederates. These figures include deaths from disease as well as battle casualties.

The Civil War soldier fought at a time when weapons had become more deadly than they had ever been in the past. It was also a time when not too much was known of the science of medicine. The soldier got the worst of it in two ways. When he fought, he was likely to be pretty badly hurt. When he stayed in camp, he lived under conditions that were very likely to make him sick. In either case, he had almost no chance to get proper medical care. It was nobody's fault. Both the Federal and the Confederate governments did their best, but the best was not very good. There was simply no such thing as good medical care during that period.

Battle wounds were almost certain to become infected, and the death rate from wounds was very high. The wounded who lived often lost arms or legs. Army hospitals, especially the emergency centers near the fighting lines, were unbelievably bad.

(Next page) Conditions at the Confederate camp at Corinth, Mississippi, were not quite as shown in this picture. Many soldiers died here of disease.

If a wounded man did not die at a field hospital, he would be sent to a general hospital to the rear. These were usually crowded, not only with the wounded, but with the sick. Diseases contracted in camps and on the march killed more men than enemy fire during the war. Soldiers were struck down by typhoid, dysentery, pneumonia, malaria, and many other diseases. Medical science knew neither the cause nor the cure, but the main cause was living conditions in the camps. Sanitation was poor; water supplies were often contaminated. For every death from combat, three soldiers in the Confederate army died of disease. In the Union army, it was two and one-half to one.

As the war went on, the care of the sick and the wounded became a little better. The poet Walt Whitman became a male nurse after visiting his wounded brother. He wrote articles about conditions in the army hospitals, as did others. Groups of citizens in both the North and the South tried to help. In Washington, Clara Barton, who would later found the American Red Cross, organized a medical care program. Sally Tompkins did the same in Richmond. Civilian volunteers supplied medicines, rolled bandages, and worked in hospitals and camps.

Even without sickness, life in the camps was often dreary. A common complaint in both armies was the boredom between battles. A Pennsylvania boy wrote, "The first thing in the morning is drill, then drill, then drill again. Between drills, we drill and sometimes we stop to eat a little and have a roll call."

The long stretches in winter quarters were particularly hard on the soldiers. A Yankee de-

The uniforms designed for Ellsworth's company of Zouaves

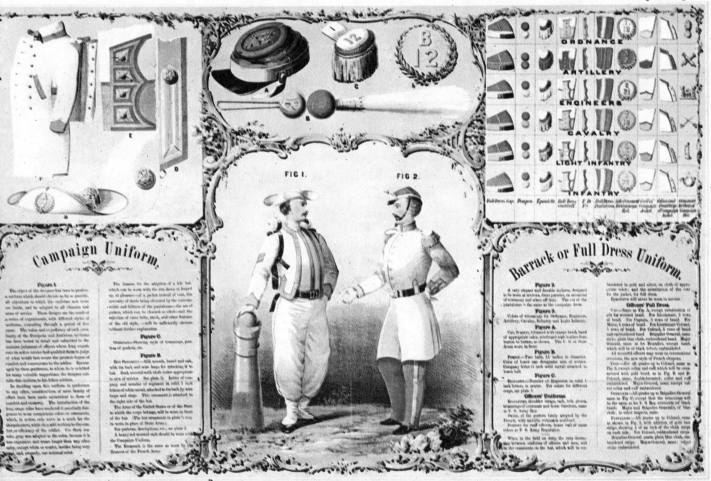

the Union dead. Northern troops were better clothed, but on the march their uniforms were far from regulation. An observer, writing about the infantry, said, "The more they serve, the less they look like soldiers and the more they resemble day-laborers who have bought second-hand military clothes."

To help pass the time, the soldiers sang. They left the patriotic songs to the folks back home. They preferred ballads like *Tenting To-night* and *Just Before the Battle, Mother*. They sang of their sweethearts, in songs like *Aura Lee, Lorena*, and *The Yellow Rose of Texas*. Besides singing, soldiers amused themselves with all kinds of horseplay. The Union troops liked a fairly new game called baseball.

Army food was poor, consisting mainly of hardtack, salt pork, and coffee. Soldiers on the march lived off the land as much as possible, usually at the expense of farmers and other civilians. They could buy a few things from the

A song sheet of the Civil War

scribed the life: "After breakfast there is little for the well men to do. The forenoon is spent in poke, poke, poking around till the appetite says it is dinner time." And a Southerner wrote: "Oh, how tiresome this camp life is . . . One everlasting monotone, yesterday, today, and tomorrow."

Confederate soldiers suffered more from hunger and disease than their enemy, but they had great staying power. As late as May, 1864, one of them wrote: "As for myself, I am getting pretty tired of it, but am not ready yet for a while to say Enought. I think I can stand thru three more years yet and I think before that time the enemy will get middling tired of it."

Regulations specified the uniform for the Confederate troops, but it was rarely seen. They wore whatever they could get their hands on. Sometimes they received clothing in packages from home; sometimes they scavenged among

Rebel troops seldom wore the regulation uniform, as shown by the dress of these captured Confederates.

M. and M. Karolik Collection, Boston Museum of Fine Arts

More than 1,000 Union officers were confined in Richmond's Libby Prison, a former tobacco warehouse.

sutler's wagon, but foraging was cheaper. The most skillful foragers were the men who marched with Sherman from Atlanta.

Hungry Rebels were also good foragers. During the invasion of Pennsylvania, one of them wrote: "Fowls and pigs and eatables didn't stand much chance." Confederate troops short of food foraged even in their own territory. The Governor of North Carolina complained, "If God Almighty had yet in store another plague worse than all the others, I am sure it must have been a regiment or so of half-armed, half-disciplined Confederate Cavalry."

After hard fighting, the troops were sometimes given weekend passes to visit the nearest town. There, as a Southerner wrote, they would "visit the Theaters maybe get on a big Whope & Paint the thing red." Punishment for drunkenness and gambling was usually light. For breaking camp discipline, it was more severe. Some offenders were tied to tree limbs by their wrists, with bayonets gagged in their mouths. Thieves were stripped of their uniforms, had their heads shaved, and were drummed out of camp. For desertion, the penalty was death. During the war, 141 Union men were executed.

Chicago Historical Society

As punishment for stealing from a wounded friend, this Union soldier is being drummed out of camp.

132

The number would have been higher if Lincoln had not, as he said, taken "the risk on the side of mercy."

The lot of the ordinary soldiers was hard, but that of the prisoners of war was worse. Thousands died of starvation, disease, and brutality in the prison camps of both the North and the South. Conditions became even more miserable after the prisoner exchange system broke down in 1864. The camps were fearfully overcrowded, without adequate sanitation, and, especially in the North, without sufficient heat in winter.

The most terrible prison was at Andersonville, a Georgia hamlet in the midst of a pine forest and swampy marshes. In the summer of 1864, about 32,000 Union prisoners were crowded into the stockade that surrounded the camp. In six months almost 13,000 died.

Prisoners were never well fed. Late in the war, the South could scarcely feed its own soldiers and civilians, let alone prisoners. The food ration at Andersonville during that time was a pint of coarse corn meal and a tablespoon of peas a day.

Northerners were horrified by the stories they heard of Andersonville. After the war was over, the camp commander, a Swiss immigrant named Henry Wirz, was put on trial. He was found guilty of conspiracy to impair the health and destroy the life of prisoners. Still claiming he was innocent, he was hanged in November of 1865.

The Northern prison camps were probably no better than those in the South. Jefferson Davis made bitter charges against the treatment of Confederate prisoners. He accused the Federal government of "the most revolting inhumanity." He said that Southerners, "unprepared for the cold of a northern winter, have been conveyed . . . to the most northern and exposed situation that could be found by the enemy." As a matter of fact, two of the main Union prisons were in places that had a cold climate. One was in Illinois, the other in Ohio.

The North held a total of 220,000 Confederate prisoners during the war; 26,436 of them died. The South held a total of 126,950 Union prisoners; 22,576 of them died. Neither side wanted to be cruel; it was the war itself that was brutal, heartless, and inhuman.

Nearly 32,000 Union prisoners were held in the 26-acre stockade at Andersonville, Georgia.

Marching to Chattanooga, the Federals under General Rosecrans (waving sword) cross the Tennessee River.

The River of Death

AFTER GETTYSBURG, Lee and Meade were careful to keep a safe distance between their armies. Lee did not have the strength to make a real campaign, and Meade was little better off. The two moved up and down around the Orange and Alexandria Railroad, sparring for position. Neither wanted a stand-up fight. There were skirmishes, a little fighting between cavalry units, and now and then sharp clashes between parts of the armies. But nothing really important took place. As the summer gave way to fall, it became clear that there would not be a really big campaign in Virginia before 1864.

In Mississippi, too, there was little action. After the capture of Vicksburg, Grant wanted to go driving on. He was sure that nothing could stop him from sweeping through southern Mississippi and Alabama. But the officials of the War Department in Washington had other ideas. They still believed that the important thing in this war was to occupy Southern territory. Grant was forced to scatter his troops. Instead of fighting, the soldiers went on garrison duty, occupying cities and guarding railroad lines.

In middle Tennessee, Rosecrans with the Army of the Cumberland faced Bragg with the Army of Tennessee. The two armies had been in camp for six months since the battle of Murfreesboro, and they were less than forty miles apart. By spring, Rosecrans was ordered to break camp. Lincoln was especially anxious for the troops to move. He wanted them to take control of eastern Tennessee, where there were many people who favored the Union. First, Rosecrans was to seize Chattanooga, which was an important rail center. That would make it

134

possible for the Federals to occupy Knoxville and all of eastern Tennessee.

Rosecrans delayed. He had 60,000 men, while Bragg's Army of Tennessee had 47,000. But the Confederates held a good defensive position about fifty miles northwest of Chattanooga. Rosecrans felt that he did not have enough men to do the job. Not until the end of June did "Old Rosy," as his men called him, give the order to advance. But when he did move, he moved brilliantly and with speed.

Bragg's army was around the town of Tullahoma. Instead of attacking him directly, Rosecrans went around him. First he moved as if he were going to swing around Bragg's left flank. Then he quickly reversed himself and went in the opposite direction. Before Bragg knew what was going on, the Union troops were at the rear of his right flank. Rosecrans bluffed an attack, then slipped off on another flanking movement. Completely puzzled, Bragg had to retreat. The Confederates fell back all the way to Chattanooga.

For more than a month Rosecrans tried to find the best way to get at Bragg. Early in August, he found it. He made an unexpected crossing of the Tennessee River thirty miles west of Chattanooga. At Bridgeport, Alabama, he set up his supply base. He marched his troops into a mountain valley, and there was nothing between him and Chattanooga but Lookout Mountain.

Again Rosecrans decided not to make a direct attack. He went southeast, going through a series of gaps in Lookout Mountain. He was heading for the Western and Atlantic Railroad, which ran from Chattanooga to Atlanta. Once he cut off the railroad, Bragg would not be able to get supplies. Afraid to make a stand without reinforcements, Bragg withdrew from Chattanooga to northern Georgia, and Union troops occupied the city.

Rosecrans had forced Bragg out of Tennessee without a fight. He had completed a daring and almost bloodless campaign. The only trouble was that he did not know he had completed it.

Hand-to-hand fighting in the lines at Chickamauga, as Union reinforcements rush up at the left. The Federals were routed, but Confederate General Bragg allowed them to escape.

CHICKAMAUGA

Second Day: September 20, 1863

KELLY HOUSE

POE HOUSE

BROTHER HOUSE

THOMAS' HQ

SNODGRASS HILL

SNODGRASS HOUSE

TO ROSSVILLE AND CHATTANOOGA

① ④ ⑤

David Greenspan

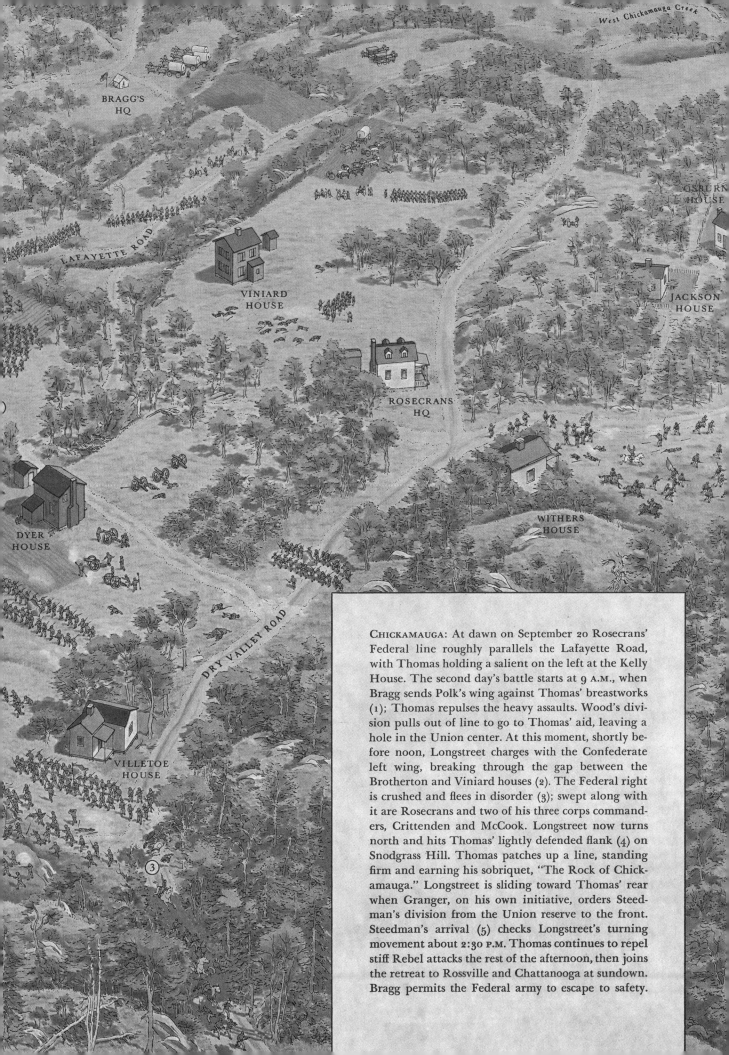

West Chickamauga Creek

BRAGG'S
HQ

LAFAYETTE ROAD

VINIARD
HOUSE

OSBURN
HOUSE

JACKSON
HOUSE

ROSECRANS
HQ

DYER
HOUSE

WITHERS
HOUSE

DRY VALLEY ROAD

VILLETOE
HOUSE

③

CHICKAMAUGA: At dawn on September 20 Rosecrans'
Federal line roughly parallels the Lafayette Road,
with Thomas holding a salient on the left at the Kelly
House. The second day's battle starts at 9 A.M., when
Bragg sends Polk's wing against Thomas' breastworks
(1); Thomas repulses the heavy assaults. Wood's division pulls out of line to go to Thomas' aid, leaving a
hole in the Union center. At this moment, shortly before noon, Longstreet charges with the Confederate
left wing, breaking through the gap between the
Brotherton and Viniard houses (2). The Federal right
is crushed and flees in disorder (3); swept along with
it are Rosecrans and two of his three corps commanders, Crittenden and McCook. Longstreet now turns
north and hits Thomas' lightly defended flank (4) on
Snodgrass Hill. Thomas patches up a line, standing
firm and earning his sobriquet, "The Rock of Chickamauga." Longstreet is sliding toward Thomas' rear
when Granger, on his own initiative, orders Steedman's division from the Union reserve to the front.
Steedman's arrival (5) checks Longstreet's turning
movement about 2:30 P.M. Thomas continues to repel
stiff Rebel attacks the rest of the afternoon, then joins
the retreat to Rossville and Chattanooga at sundown.
Bragg permits the Federal army to escape to safety.

He might have stopped for a while in Chattanooga, to renew his supplies and let his hard-marching army catch its breath. Then he could have advanced down the railroad line. Instead, he tried to keep on going.

As the three Union army corps moved through the mountain passes, they became widely separated. This did not worry Rosecrans, who believed that the Confederates were in full retreat. But Bragg was no longer retreating. He was at La Fayette, Georgia, about twenty-five miles from Chattanooga. At last he was getting reinforcements. Troops were arriving from Knoxville and Mississippi. He was even getting two divisions from the Army of Northern Virginia, led by James Longstreet.

When Bragg began moving in for a counterattack, Rosecrans suddenly realized he was in danger. He quickly gathered his scattered troops together. On September 18, they reached Chickamauga Creek, about twelve miles below Chattanooga. Bragg's men, who had been hidden by the heavy woods along the banks, fell on the Union left flank. There was a sharp clash, with each side trying to win control of the fords and bridges over the creek.

During the night, both Rosecrans and Bragg prepared for the next day's battle. Rosecrans placed General Thomas L. Crittenden nearer to the center than he had been that afternoon. He moved General George Thomas, who had been at the center, to the extreme left. This meant a long night march for Thomas' troops. Alexander McCook's corps was also placed closer to the center and left. The reason for all the shifts was that Rosecrans guessed Bragg would attack close to the left and center.

Rosecrans' guess was correct. Bragg intended to turn the Union left flank, then push the Yankees into a mountain gap. The attack began on the morning of September 19, but the Union troops were not where Bragg thought they would be. The Confederates groped their way through the woods, trying to make contact with the enemy. Suddenly Thomas' men came charging at the bewildered Rebels. The Confederates were outflanked and their attack was broken. But the battle was not over.

More Confederates were thrown into the line, and they flanked and routed the Yankees. All day it went on like that, each army advancing and retreating in turn. It was a confused fight. Most of the time the commanders of the two armies were not sure exactly where their units were. Union soldiers were sent to help Thomas. Even so, the Rebels gained ground— but they took a terrible beating. By nightfall, Thomas' line was battered but unbroken. He still held the road to Chattanooga.

The night was a troubled one, with lost regiments and brigades trying to find the way to their lines in the darkness. The generals sat up late with their staffs, planning the next day's fighting. The Confederates were strengthened by the arrival of Longstreet with fresh troops from Virginia. Bragg gave him the left wing, Bishop Polk the right. Polk was to attack Thomas in the morning. As Rosecrans met this threat, Longstreet would advance.

At nine o'clock in the morning of September 20, Polk attacked. Soon Thomas had to call for help. In the confusion of reinforcing him, Rosecrans left a gap in his center. It was precisely at this spot that Longstreet struck. The Rebels poured through, splitting Rosecrans' army in half. The Yankees fell back toward Chattanooga, carrying Rosecrans with them.

Longstreet did not pursue the fleeing troops. Instead, he turned to make the rout complete by attacking Thomas. He believed that with Polk he could finish off Thomas quickly.

George Thomas was a West Pointer, a Virginian who had chosen to fight for the Union. Now he prepared to make the fight of his life. Coolly he put together a defensive line to cover his exposed flank. His men stopped one Rebel charge after another. A Confederate later remembered how "the dead were piled upon each other in ricks, like cord wood, to make passage for advancing columns. The sluggish...Chickamauga ran red with blood."

General Gordon Granger was in command of the Federal reserve. Without orders, he sent a division to aid Thomas, and a fresh supply of ammunition. Thomas could not defeat the combined forces of Longstreet and Polk. But he held out long enough to protect the Union retreat to Chattanooga. Without those few hours, one whole Union army might have been wiped out. By sunset, Thomas and his men had joined the retreat.

The name Chickamauga was said to be an old Cherokee word, meaning "river of death." It was indeed a river of death that day. Each army had lost a third of its men. The Confederate casualties numbered 17,800, the Union's only 1,200 less. Bragg was stunned and could not believe he had won a real victory. Generals Polk, Longstreet, and Forrest begged him to go after the enemy and recapture Chattanooga. This was a good chance to destroy the whole Army of the Cumberland. Bragg merely shook his head and went to bed. He finally took position on Missionary Ridge and Lookout Mountain, overlooking Chattanooga. He was preparing to lay siege to Rosecrans.

Chickamauga was a terrible defeat for the Union. But it forced the government to pay more attention to the fighting in the West, and in the end this was all to the good. Rosecrans was replaced by Thomas. Grant was given new powers, and he knew what to do with them. And so Chickamauga may have been worth what it cost, although the soldiers of the Army of the Cumberland probably would have had trouble seeing it that way.

As September ended, these soldiers were in serious trouble. They held Chattanooga, but it seemed as if they would be starved into surrender. The Confederate line ran in a vast semicircle. It touched the Tennessee River upstream from Chattanooga, following Missionary Ridge to the east and south. In the west it was anchored on the steep sides of Lookout Mountain, and touching the Tennessee again just west of Lookout.

The Confederates had no troops north of the river. They did not need any there. The country was wild, mountainous, and almost uninhabited. No military supplies could be carried across it. Supplies could reach Thomas only by the river itself, by the railroad which ran along the river's southern bank, or by the roads that were also south of the river. All of these were controlled by Bragg. The Union army could not even retreat. It seemed to Bragg that the Yankees would have to give up in a month or two. As far as he could see, all he had to do was keep his army in position.

The Federal government knew that it could not afford to lose the Army of the Cumberland, and Washington went into action. Two army corps were detached from Meade, placed under the command of Joe Hooker, and sent west by rail. This was the most effective military use of railroads yet made anywhere. The soldiers were moved with surprising speed. Leaving the banks of the Rappahannock on September 24, they reached Bridgeport, Alabama, just eight days later. Sherman was ordered to move east from Memphis with part of the Army of the Tennessee. General Grant was put in charge of almost all military operations west of the Alleghenies.

After meeting with the Secretary of War in Louisville, Grant hurried to Chattanooga to see things for himself. His trip over the mountains was a miserable one. He had injured his leg and was on crutches. At Chattanooga, he found things worse than he had thought. The soldiers were not only hungry, but also without shoes and warm clothing. Their horses and mules were dying of starvation.

Plans for breaking the Confederate hold on the city had already been made. Grant saw to it that they were carried out as quickly as possible. He ordered Hooker, who was at Bridgeport, to send his 20,000 veterans of the Army of the Potomac east over Raccoon Mountain. At the same time, a brigade of Thomas' men floated down the river on pontoon rafts. The two forces seized Brown's Ferry, a Rebel outpost on the Tennessee River west of Lookout Mountain.

This opened up a supply route from Bridgeport to Chattanooga. Steamboats, scows, a pontoon bridge, and army wagons were all used on "the cracker line," as the men called it. The soldiers cheered as the first supplies came in on creaking wagons. They would not be able to get everything they needed, but the danger of starvation was over.

Union General Hooker (on white horse at left center) drove the Confederates from Lookout Mountain.

The victory, while dramatic, was not as great as it seemed; the Rebels were outnumbered six to one.

CHATTANOOGA: Thomas, after replacing Rosecrans in command of the Federal Army of the Cumberland, fortifies Chattanooga (1). Bragg holds Missionary Ridge and Lookout Mountain, dominating the city and its supply routes. Grant, the new Western theater commander, reaches Chattanooga and moves to get food and forage for the army. Troops under Thomas and Hooker open a route called "the cracker line" (2), connecting the Bridgeport supply depot to Brown's Ferry, by road and river steamer, and thence to Chattanooga. Grant now makes plans for driving Bragg from his strong lines. On November 23 Thomas takes Orchard Knob (3), high ground in the plain before Missionary Ridge. The next day Hooker storms Lookout Mountain (4) and prepares to move on Bragg's left flank. The same day Sherman, stationed across the Tennessee, crosses the river (5) and opens the assault on the Confederate right (6). On November 25 Grant makes his major attack. Sherman, from dawn until mid-afternoon, battles Cleburne on the Rebel right (7) but makes little headway. To relieve the pressure on Sherman, Grant orders Thomas' men to seize the Rebel line at the base of Missionary Ridge (8). After taking this objective, the Yankees keep on going without orders and sweep up the mountain, reaching the crest (9) and routing Bragg's army.

RAISING THE SIEGE OF
CHATTANOOGA

Orchard Knob: November 23, 1863
Lookout Mountain: November 24, 1863
Missionary Ridge: November 25, 1863

TENNESSEE RIVER

Chickamauga Creek

TO KNOXVILLE

FORT
GROSE

WESTERN & ATLANTIC R.R.

CHATTANOOGA & CLEVELAND R.R.

THE
TUNNEL

GRANT'S
HQ

ORCHARD
KNOB

BRAGG'S
HQ

MISSIONARY RIDGE

RETREAT TO GEORGIA

5

6

7

3

8

9

David Greenspan

A sketch of Generals Grant and Sherman at Missionary Ridge. This was the last battle the two men fought together.

Sherman, meanwhile, was on his way to Chattanooga from Memphis. He had about three hundred miles to march, and he was moving very slowly. For some reason, Halleck in Washington had given him orders to repair the railroad as he moved. A few blocks away from Halleck's office, President Lincoln was fretting. Now that the troops in Chattanooga could again "board at home," he said, they should try to break Bragg's siege. Grant agreed. He told Sherman to forget about the rail lines and come as fast as he could.

By November, Grant was ready for the big fight. Sherman had arrived, and Thomas' troops were no longer half-starved. And Bragg had made a blunder that gave the Yankees an even better chance to break out.

A Union force under General Burnside had come down through the Kentucky-Tennessee mountain country to occupy Knoxville. Burnside was doing no particular harm there, but Bragg sent away 12,000 men under Longstreet to try to push him out, and more troops to help. Bragg was badly outnumbered when Grant struck on November 23.

Thomas' men took Orchard Knob, high ground on the plain in front of Missionary Ridge. It was a good spot from which to attack the ridge itself. The next day, Hooker's troops seized Lookout Mountain.

As Grant planned it, Sherman would play a big part in the main attack, which was set for November 25. Sherman was to roll up the Confederate right flank. Thomas, at the center, and Hooker, at the left, were to keep Bragg so busy he would be unable to reinforce his right. Two unexpected things happened that upset the scheme. First, Pat Cleburne, the best division commander in Bragg's army, blocked Sherman's path. Second, Thomas' men made a daring attack without orders.

The fighting began at daylight, when Sherman drove his men forward. For more than eight hours they were held off by Cleburne's Confederates, who were defending the north end of Missionary Ridge. The Rebels found that they could not lower their cannon enough to hit the Yankees, so they lit the shells and threw them down the slope. They even made a surprise counterattack from a railroad tunnel. By three o'clock in the afternoon, Sherman's troops were stalled.

Hooker was delayed, because he had to bridge a stream on his front. Grant ordered Thomas' Army of the Cumberland to take the Rebel rifle pits at the base of the ridge. It was not to be a full-scale attack. The idea was to relieve Sherman by giving Bragg something else to worry about. Thomas' men were so eager that even "servants, cooks, clerks, found guns in some way." At three-thirty, they ran forward, heading for the pits.

The first Rebel line soon fell, but killing fire rained down on the Cumberlands from above. And now came the most amazing action of all. For weeks, both Hooker's and Sherman's men had made fun of them. They had been defeated at Chickamauga, cooped up at Chattanooga, and other armies had been sent to their rescue. They were fed up, and they were out to show what they could do. Leaping from the captured pits, they began charging up the steep mountain slope without orders from either Grant or Thomas.

A Northern lieutenant noted that "little regard to formation was observed. Each battalion assumed a triangular shape, the colors at the apex...[a] color-bearer dashes ahead of the line and falls. A comrade grasps the flag....He, too, falls. Then another picks it up...waves it defiantly, and, as if bearing a charmed life, he advances steadily towards the top...." Another soldier later remembered: "Amid the din of battle the cry 'Chickamauga! Chickamauga!' could be heard."

Watching from Orchard Knob, Grant and Thomas were astounded. It seemed impossible to believe. General Granger assured them that the men had charged without orders. He added, "When these fellows get started all hell can't stop them."

Bragg's men fired desperately. The cannoneers poured hatfuls of musket balls into their pieces, shooting them like giant shotguns. Bragg, "cursing like a sailor," tried to rally his force. There was nothing he could do. The Confederates fled as the Army of the Cumberland poured over the crest of Missionary Ridge.

The battle had been won; the siege of Chattanooga was lifted. The results were tremendous. Grant was appointed commander of all the Union armies. Sherman was given command in the West. Bragg was removed as general of the Army of Tennessee. In the spring, Chattanooga would become the jumping-off place for an invasion of the South's heartland.

Union troops storm Missionary Ridge. As the Rebels fled, a Yankee cried, "My God, come and see 'em run!"

Lincoln Finds a General

IN MARCH, 1864, Ulysses S. Grant was made lieutenant general, the highest rank in the Union army.

President Lincoln and the general met for the first time at a White House reception on March 8. The next day, Lincoln presented the new commission to Grant. Grant accepted with a speech which he read poorly from a half-sheet of note paper. He did not look much like a hero, or even like a soldier. He was short, slight, a little stooped, and wore a scrubby beard. He smoked huge cigars, sometimes as many as two dozen a day.

But Grant was a brilliant strategist and understood the kind of warfare that was developing during the Civil War. He was calm, thorough, direct. Above all, he had great determination. As one of his staff officers put it, Grant looked as though he had decided to butt his head through a brick wall and was about to do it.

Lincoln had tried one general after another; every one of them had failed to defeat Lee's Army of Northern Virginia. Now at last he felt he had found a man who would fight. On March 12 he appointed Grant general in chief of all the Northern armies. The President made it clear that Grant would be given a free hand. Grant replied that he would do the best he could with the means at hand.

It seemed to Grant that his problem was quite simple. He had to destroy the main Confederate armies. The capture of cities and the occupation of Southern territory meant very little. As long as the Confederate armies were in the field, the Confederacy lived. As soon as

Lieutenant General Ulysses S. Grant, photographed at City Point, Virginia, during the siege of Petersburg.

they were destroyed, the Confederacy itself would die. His aim was to put the Southern armies out of action as quickly as possible.

The two most important Southern forces were the Army of Northern Virginia, under Lee, and the Army of Tennessee, now led by Joseph E. Johnston. Each of these numbered about 60,000 men.

Johnston was strongly entrenched on the low mountain ridges northwest of Dalton, Georgia, a few miles from the bloodstained battlefield of Chickamauga. The job of defeating him went to General Sherman, whom Grant placed in charge of all Federal operations in the West. Commanding forces of more than 100,000 men, Sherman was to set out from Chattanooga toward Atlanta. His real purpose was not to capture Atlanta, but to destroy the Rebel army in front of him. As Sherman himself said later, "I was to go for Joe Johnston."

Grant, meanwhile, would go for Lee.

Grant was not the kind of general to carry on his work from an office in Washington. He set up his headquarters in the field, moving with the Army of the Potomac. That army was still under the command of General Meade. Meade offered to resign, but Grant told him to stay where he was. Grant made only one change, bringing in Phil Sheridan, a tough infantry officer, from the West. Sheridan was put in charge of the cavalry corps.

The Union force was in camp on the northern side of the upper Rapidan River. Facing it, beyond the river, was Lee's Army of Northern Virginia. For the spring campaign, it would be reinforced by Longstreet's corps, which was returning from Tennessee. Lee would have somewhat more than 60,000 men; Grant would have nearly twice that number.

147

The job of the Army of the Potomac was as simple as Sherman's. It was to head for the Confederates and fight until something broke. For the first time all the Union armies would move together, acting as one big team. Three Federal forces would advance toward Richmond. Grant, with Meade and the Army of the Potomac, would march south across the Rapidan. Ben Butler, commanding about 33,-000 men at Fort Monroe, would move north up the Virginia Peninsula. Another Union force, under the German-born Franz Sigel, was in the Shenandoah Valley. It would protect Washington and make ready for a move east toward Richmond. And, while the armies in Virginia went into action, Sherman would begin his push from Tennessee east to Atlanta.

On May 4, 1864, Grant's machine began to roll. The Army of the Potomac crossed the Rapidan and started to march down through the Wilderness. This was the same dense forest where "Fighting Joe" Hooker had lost his nerve. Grant hoped to get through the Wilderness quickly and bring Lee to battle in the open country farther south.

But once again Lee refused to play the enemy's game. He marched straight into the Wilderness and jumped the Federal columns. Grant's general plan was to fight the Confederates whenever and wherever he could. If Lee wanted a fight here, Grant was willing to give him one, and on May 5 an enormous two-day battle got under way.

The Wilderness was a bad place for a fight. The underbrush was so thick that nobody could see fifty yards in any direction. One soldier said that it was "a battle of invisibles with invisibles." Troops were ordered to charge toward the sound of the heaviest firing. They had to fire "by earsight."

Grant had more men, but that meant little in a battle like this. He also had more cannon, but he could use few of them. The first day of the fighting, the lines swayed back and forth in charges and countercharges. The woods caught fire, and many wounded men were burned to death. The smoke of burning timber mingled with gunsmoke to make a thick, choking fog. A Northern private wrote that "it was a blind and bloody hunt to the death, in bewildering thickets, rather than a battle."

The fighting in the Wilderness was probably the most confused of the war. Yet, during all the confusion, Grant remained calm. He sat on a knoll at his headquarters, whittling, smoking cigars, listening to reports and giving com-

mands. Once Rebel guns shelled the knoll where he was sitting. An anxious staff officer hinted that it might be wise to move the headquarters out of range. Grant puffed on his cigar and replied that it would be even better to wheel up some Federal guns and hold the position. The guns were brought up and Grant went back to his whittling.

Only once did Grant lose patience. One of his generals, who had fought Lee before, feared that Lee was about to make a daring maneuver.

Grant stood up, took the cigar out of his mouth, and said that he was sick and tired of hearing what Lee was about to do.

"Some of you," he said, "always seem to think he is suddenly going to turn a double somersault and land in our rear and on both of our flanks at the same time." He dismissed the general with a sharp order: "Go back to your command, and try to think what we are going to do ourselves, instead of what Lee is going to do!"

149

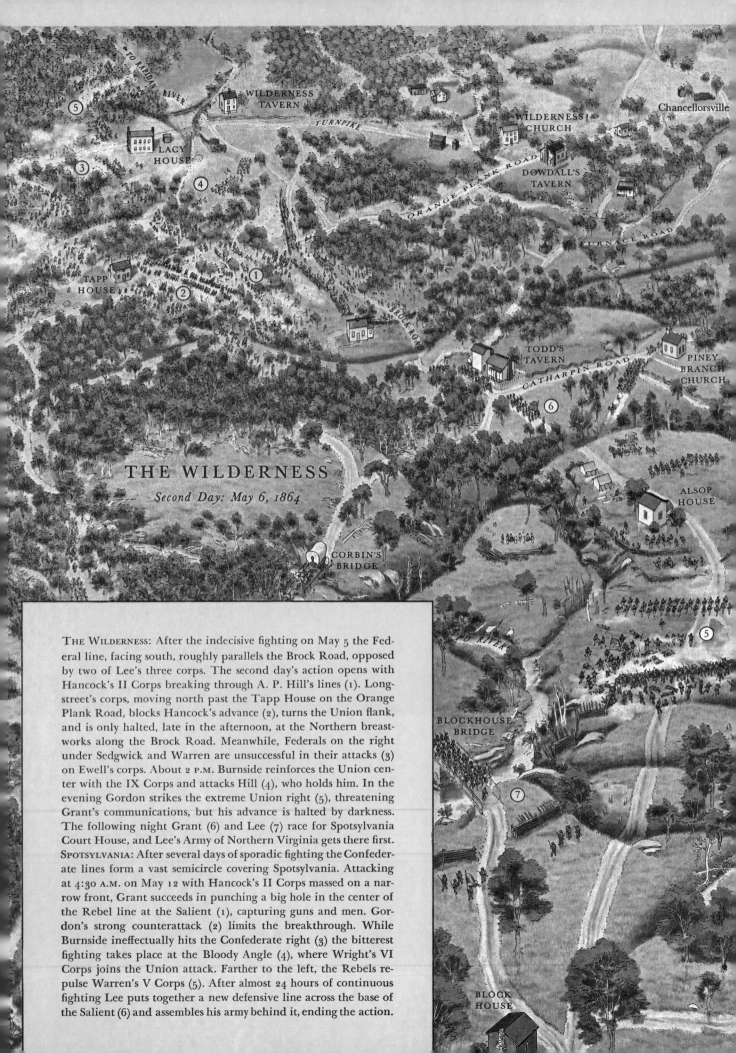

THE WILDERNESS

Second Day: May 6, 1864

THE WILDERNESS: After the indecisive fighting on May 5 the Federal line, facing south, roughly parallels the Brock Road, opposed by two of Lee's three corps. The second day's action opens with Hancock's II Corps breaking through A. P. Hill's lines (1). Longstreet's corps, moving north past the Tapp House on the Orange Plank Road, blocks Hancock's advance (2), turns the Union flank, and is only halted, late in the afternoon, at the Northern breastworks along the Brock Road. Meanwhile, Federals on the right under Sedgwick and Warren are unsuccessful in their attacks (3) on Ewell's corps. About 2 P.M. Burnside reinforces the Union center with the IX Corps and attacks Hill (4), who holds him. In the evening Gordon strikes the extreme Union right (5), threatening Grant's communications, but his advance is halted by darkness. The following night Grant (6) and Lee (7) race for Spotsylvania Court House, and Lee's Army of Northern Virginia gets there first.

SPOTSYLVANIA: After several days of sporadic fighting the Confederate lines form a vast semicircle covering Spotsylvania. Attacking at 4:30 A.M. on May 12 with Hancock's II Corps massed on a narrow front, Grant succeeds in punching a big hole in the center of the Rebel line at the Salient (1), capturing guns and men. Gordon's strong counterattack (2) limits the breakthrough. While Burnside ineffectually hits the Confederate right (3) the bitterest fighting takes place at the Bloody Angle (4), where Wright's VI Corps joins the Union attack. Farther to the left, the Rebels repulse Warren's V Corps (5). After almost 24 hours of continuous fighting Lee puts together a new defensive line across the base of the Salient (6) and assembles his army behind it, ending the action.

SPOTSYLVANIA

Fourth Day: May 12, 1864

TO RAPPAHANNOCK RIVER

TO FREDERICKSBURG →

SALEM CHURCH

TURNPIKE

UNFINISHED RAILROAD

ORANGE PLANK ROAD

N

LANDRUM HOUSE

NI RIVER

SALIENT

BLOODY ANGLE

McCOOL HOUSE

HARRISON HOUSE

TO SPOTSYLVANIA C.H.

ROAD

Library of Congress

At dawn on May 6, Grant took the offensive. His troops attacked two Rebel corps—Ewell's and A. P. Hill's—that held positions on parallel roads. Ewell drove back the attackers with heavy losses. Hill's battered troops were unable to hold off the mile-wide Yankee charge, and the Confederates were close to defeat.

Then up from the rear came Longstreet's corps, screaming the Rebel yell. In their midst was General Lee, urging them forward. "I would charge hell itself for that old man," a Rebel officer said. The Southerners crashed head-on into the Yankees, breaking the force of the charge. But Longstreet himself was accidentally wounded by his own men. He was carried away, coughing blood, to be out of action for months. The Confederate counterattack slowed down, and Lee called a halt to reorganize his lines. The fighting went on again, until darkness put a stop to it.

The next day, both armies rested. The Union forces had not gained a foot and had lost 17,500 men. Lee's losses were less than 8,000. The weary Yankees expected to do what they had done under McClellan and Hooker. They would retreat, spend dreary months in camp, and later begin a new campaign somewhere else. But Grant was a different kind of general. On the night of May 7, he rode past his troops on his big bay horse to take his place at their head. The soldiers understood. There was to be no retreat. In spite of its terrible losses, the Army of the Potomac was going to advance. The men shouted, cheered, and waved their caps. As they fell into the line of march, they began to sing.

Grant was keeping to his plan. He would force the fighting. Sooner or later, the outnumbered Confederates would be pushed into the open, where they could not win. He led his troops to Spotsylvania Court House, a crossroads settlement eleven miles southwest of Fredericksburg. It lay on Lee's road to Richmond, and if the Federals got there first, they would be between the Rebels and their capital. Lee would be forced to attack.

Lee saw what the Yankees were up to. He pulled his army out of the Wilderness and marched for Spotsylvania. His nephew, Fitzhugh Lee, delayed the Federal advance with his cavalry. Rebel infantrymen reached Spotsylvania first and were digging in when the Federal troops arrived. Now it was Grant who was forced to attack.

The fighting began on May 8, growing into a battle that went on for twelve days. No bitterer fighting was ever seen on the American continent. On May 10, a Union bayonet charge split open the center of Lee's lines. Southern artillery wrecked the supporting troops and the Federals were driven back.

The bloodiest single day of the long battle came on May 12. At least 12,000 men fell in the struggle for one square mile of ground. At a bend in the lines called the "Bloody Angle," there was savage hand-to-hand fighting. Cannon fired at point-blank range. Soldiers were "stabbed to death with . . . bayonets thrust between the logs in the parapet" which separated the men by a few feet. The fighting went on in rain and smoke until well past midnight, when Lee succeeded in strengthening the center of his line.

In the days that followed, the Rebels kept beating back the Yankee attacks. The Union army kept shifting to the left, trying to crumple Lee's flank. On May 19 the battle ended. The Federal soldiers who had been facing east when the battle began were now facing west.

Grant had lost an average of 2,000 men a day. Lee's losses in killed and wounded were far less, but he had lost thousands in prisoners. One casualty was a heavy blow for the South. Phil Sheridan had taken the Union cavalry off on a driving raid toward Richmond. "Jeb" Stuart met him on May 11 at Yellow Tavern, in Richmond's suburbs. The Yankee horsemen were driven off in a hard fight, but it was Stuart's last battle. He caught a bullet in the stomach and died the next day. Lee had lost another of his daring generals. "I can scarcely think of him without weeping," he said sadly.

Elsewhere in Virginia things went badly for the Federals. Sigel moved up the Shenandoah Valley and was routed in a battle at New Market. Ben Butler was beaten at Bermuda Hundred. He made camp on the Bermuda Hundred peninsula, and the Confederates threw a fortified line across the peninsula. As Grant said, Butler was as much out of action as if he had been put in a tightly corked bottle.

All through May Grant kept moving slowly toward the southeast, searching for a weak spot in the enemy lines. There were skirmishes almost every day, and small battles along the North Anna and Totopotomy Creek. By June 1, after a bitter struggle in which over 2,000 Federals were lost, Grant reached the crossroads of Cold Harbor, only nine miles from Richmond. Grant ordered an attack for dawn on June 2, but blunders by some of his generals

Part of Grant's army crossed the North Anna at Jericho Mills on this pontoon bridge.

With bayonets fixed, the 22nd Colored Infantry makes a desperate charge on June 16, 1864.

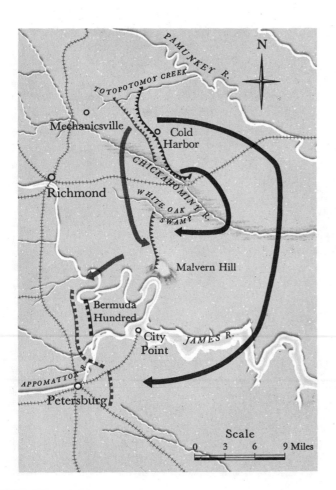

forced a delay until the next day. Lee had had time to get ready. His troops were dug in and well fortified.

Hoping to break the Confederate line once and for all, Grant put on a tremendous frontal attack. The soldiers knew it was a hopeless charge. Many of them pinned slips of paper to their coats, bearing their name and address. About 7,000 Union men fell in just half an hour. A Rebel colonel noted that "the dead covered more than five acres of ground about as thickly as they could be laid."

Grant always regretted the attack at Cold Harbor. For ten days the enemy armies faced each other from trenches, then Grant decided not to risk any more head-on attacks. On June 12, behind a screen of cavalry, his troops slipped away to the southeast. Crossing the James River, they turned west toward Petersburg, twenty miles south of Richmond.

It was a brilliant move. Most of the railroads

General Grant's flanking march from Cold Harbor to the city of Petersburg is shown on the map in black. Defensive moves of General Lee are shown in gray.

154

that linked Richmond to the South came through Petersburg. If the Federals could take Petersburg before Lee got there, the Confederates would lose Richmond. But General William F. Smith, who was leading the Union advance, bungled the job. By the time the rest of the army had come up, Lee was strongly entrenched. Grant had to settle down to a long siege of Petersburg.

For the Yankees, the siege was a time of misery. One soldier called it "hell itself . . . one-half of the line would fire while the other worked on the pits or tried to sleep." For six weeks there was blazing heat and no rain, and then there was too much rain. Artillery duels would begin at any time, day or night. Sharpshooting never stopped. Men in both armies were killed and wounded. Many others became sick, or simply deserted.

Grant sent out James H. Wilson's cavalry to strike at the rail lines west of Petersburg and Richmond. Wilson destroyed sixty miles of track before he was driven off by Rebel cavalry. Lee's railroad connections were cut off for weeks. He had a serious supply problem until the break was mended.

To relieve the pressure, Lee sent Jubal Early and 14,000 men on a dash through the Shenandoah Valley into Maryland. He hoped to throw a scare into Washington and force the Federal government to withdraw troops from Petersburg. There was even a chance that Grant might lift the siege. By July 11, Early was in Silver Spring, Maryland, on the outskirts of Washington.

A makeshift force was thrown together to defend the capital. Numbering a few thousand, it included clerks from the Quartermaster Corps headquarters and convalescent soldiers from the military hospitals. They marched to Fort Stevens, a fortified camp within sight of the capitol dome. At the last moment, as the Confederates prepared to attack, the VI Corps of the Army of the Potomac arrived from Grant's forces at Petersburg. After a skirmish, witnessed by Abraham Lincoln himself, the Rebels were driven back to Virginia.

This Confederate failure near Washington was matched by a Union failure at Petersburg. A Pennsylvania regiment that contained many coal miners dug a tunnel under the Rebel lines. At dawn on July 30, several tons of powder were set off there. The explosion opened a huge gap in the center of Lee's lines. The way was open for a march into Petersburg.

The march never took place. While two division commanders lay drunk in a dugout, the leaderless men trickled into the crater made by the explosion. Lee's artillery dropped shells on them, turning the crater into "a cauldron of hell." Confederate infantry counterattacked, and by early afternoon the break was mended. Another chance for the Union to end the war was gone. The soldiers of both sides went back to their trenches and the siege continued.

Grant was not the only Union commander who was stalled in front of a Confederate city. Farther south, at Atlanta, Sherman was having the same kind of trouble. Early in May, at the same time that Grant moved against Lee, Sherman had led 100,000 veterans of the Western campaigns against Joe Johnston and his Army of Tennessee. Both generals were men who knew their business. Johnston was an expert at defense; Sherman had more men and seldom made mistakes. Soon northern Georgia became a huge chessboard for their maneuvers.

Sherman flanked Johnston out of defense lines, one after another, at Dalton, Resaca, Cassville, and Allatoona Pass. Sherman's rugged Westerners did not see the point of direct attacks on enemy entrenchments. But they were great marchers, and ideal for this campaign of maneuver.

For four days the armies clashed at New Hope Church, with neither side able to gain an advantage. The sharpest fighting took place on May 25. On that day Hooker's attack on a Rebel division was stalled at the "Hell Hole" during a terrific thunderstorm. By the end of the month, Sherman forced Johnston into a new line a few miles north of Marietta. A Rebel

(Next page) Part of the Confederate entrenchments around Petersburg. The sharpened stakes at the left in the background were used as infantry obstacles.

prisoner complained to the Yankees that "you-uns swings around your ends like a gate."

It was near Marietta that Johnston lost one of his best corps commanders. Bishop Polk was killed by Union artillery fire. Johnston then withdrew to Kennesaw Mountain, where Sherman decided to attack on June 27.

Until now, the armies had zigzagged through northern Georgia. There were many skirmishes and several pitched battles, but nothing like the slaughter in Virginia. At Kennesaw Mountain, Sherman made the only frontal attack of the campaign. He learned the same lesson that Grant had learned three weeks earlier at Cold Harbor—head-on attacks against well-dug-in Confederates were bound to fail.

Under a broiling Georgia sun, the Union men charged bravely up the mountain. A Southern soldier later wrote, "They seemed to walk up and take death as coolly as if they were automatic or wooden men." But bravery was not enough. The entrenched Rebels could not be beaten, and the attack was a failure. Among those who were mortally wounded was Colonel Daniel McCook, who had been with Grant at Chattanooga. He was one of the fifteen "Fighting McCooks" who fought for the North, and the fourth member of the family to be killed in action.

Charging Confederates drive Yankees from a huge crater. It was formed by exploding powder in a tunnel that was dug under the Rebel line around Petersburg.

Sherman tried no more frontal attacks, and went back to his war of maneuver. He forced Johnston to the banks of the Chattahoochee River, less than ten miles from Atlanta. There Johnston made his first serious mistake. Sherman sent one of his three armies, under General McPherson, far to the east to cross the Chattahoochee and come around the Rebel flank. Johnston was caught completely by surprise, and allowed the Union force to cross the river unopposed. As a result, the Confederates had to fall back to the very edge of Atlanta.

With its rolling mill, munitions factories, and railroad connections, Atlanta was an important city to the South. Its fall would be a hard blow. As Sherman's armies massed before the city, Joe Johnston was removed from his command. Jefferson Davis, who had never trusted him, replaced him with John Bell Hood. General Hood was a fighter who was not afraid to take chances. One of Sherman's officers recalled how, in a poker game before the war, Hood "bet $2,500 with nary a pair in his hand." Now there was sure to be action.

And action was what the people of the North wanted, for they were becoming weary of the war. Grant's campaign looked like a failure. He did not seem to be any nearer the capture of Richmond than he had been when the campaign began. Sherman was deep in Georgia, but he had neither whipped the Confederate army which faced him nor taken Atlanta.

The fact was that Grant had forced Lee to go on the defensive. The North was applying strong pressure, which the Confederacy could not stand for long. But to the folks back home, it looked as though nothing had been accomplished. They only knew that the war was costing more than it ever cost before, that the casualty lists were endless, and that there seemed to be nothing much to show for all the terrible bloodshed.

General Ben Butler had his troops dig a canal so that he could send gunboats up the James River. But the canal was not completed until the war was nearly over and was of no use to the Union forces.

Behind the Lines

A LL THROUGH THE WAR, there was one man on each side who had more power and responsibility than any other. This man was the President—Abraham Lincoln, in Washington, and Jefferson Davis, in Richmond. During the spring and summer of 1864, what was happening behind the lines began to worry them almost as much as what was happening on the battlefields. After three years of fighting, many people in both the North and the South were losing their enthusiasm for the war.

Lincoln was especially worried. His first term as President was coming to an end. He would have to seek renomination, and then stand for election. For a while he doubted whether he would even get the nomination.

Some of Lincoln's troubles came from members of his own political party—a group of Republicans who were called Radicals. In their opinion, everything connected with slavery was evil. Winning the war and freeing the slaves was not enough. The South and its way of life had to be crushed. The Radicals' aim, as they put it, was "to lay low in the dust under our feet, so that iron heels will rest upon it, this great rebel, this giant criminal, this guilty murderer, that is warring upon the existence of our country."

The Radicals were dissatisfied with Lincoln from the very beginning of his administration. They felt that he was too timid, too willing to make compromises. They said he had no intention of freeing the slaves. Even after Lincoln issued the Emancipation Proclamation, they mistrusted him. They were suspicious of his plans for the South after the war. They called for "the desolation of the South as well as emancipation." Lincoln, as he later said in

his second inaugural address, wanted "malice toward none, and charity for all."

The Radicals controlled the Joint Committee on the Conduct of the War, which was made up of members of both houses of Congress. The Committee investigated every part of the war effort and often went out of its way to embarrass Lincoln. In time it became powerful enough to seriously challenge the President's role as Commander-in-Chief of the armed forces.

Lincoln also had trouble with his cabinet. At first, William H. Seward, the Secretary of State, believed that he rather than Lincoln would actually run the show. Lincoln soon put him in his place and then made a loyal supporter of him. Edwin M. Stanton, the Secretary of War, also wanted to run things his own way. Like Seward, he finally came to see that the President was boss. Salmon P. Chase, the Secretary of the Treasury, had little loyalty to Lincoln. He tried to win the Republican nomination for himself, and Lincoln had to replace him. And yet all of these men did their jobs well, and Lincoln later made Chase Chief Justice of the United States.

Lincoln's foes might have kept him from being renominated if they had been able to agree on one candidate. Instead, they began to quarrel among themselves, and Lincoln quietly went about the business of getting the nomination. On June 8, 1864, the Republicans and those Democrats who supported the war held a joint convention in Baltimore. They nominated Lincoln for President, and Andrew Johnson, Tennessee's loyal Democratic governor, for Vice President. A few days before, a group of Republicans bitterly opposed to Lincoln had

In spite of his doubts during the election campaign, Lincoln was re-elected. He is shown standing, center, making his second inaugural address. John Wilkes Booth watches from the railed balcony at right center.

met in Chicago. They nominated General Frémont, who later withdrew from the race.

In August, the Democrats put up their own candidate. He was General George B. McClellan, who was still popular. Anti-war Democrats, who were called Copperheads, said that the war had been a failure. They called for the re-establishment of the Union as it had been, "half slave and half free." They wanted to end the war, mostly on the South's terms.

161

This cartoon pictures Northern Copperheads as snakes that would strike at the Union without warning.

McClellan did not endorse this part of his party's platform, but Lincoln feared that he had little chance of being re-elected. In fact, right after the Democratic convention, he gloomily predicted his own defeat.

Even so, Lincoln never lost his sense of humor. Once he was asked how he liked being President. He answered, "You have heard about the man tarred and feathered and ridden out of town on a rail? A man in the crowd asked him how he liked it, and his reply was that if it wasn't for the honor of the thing, he would rather walk."

Jefferson Davis, the President of the Confederacy, had been elected for a six-year term and did not have to run for re-election. Nevertheless, he, too, had political troubles. He was entirely different from Lincoln, who was a master politician and could get along with all kinds of people. A proud man, Davis could not stand criticism. He could not see that other men might disagree with him and still have good intentions.

Davis' biggest problem was that the kind of

government Southerners wanted was not the kind that could win a long war. The Confederacy believed in states' rights—the right of each state to decide things for itself. Davis saw that only a strong central government could carry on the war. And when he tried to get and use the power he needed, he was bitterly criticized.

The Confederate Congress gave Davis more trouble than the Congress in Washington gave Lincoln. Often it seemed more interested in making war on Davis than in making war on the North. Almost all of its members carried horsewhips and heavy canes, and many were armed with guns and bowie knives. During stormy meetings they would wave these in the air, shouting angrily at one another. But they saved their bitterest words for President Davis.

Davis' cabinet, although it contained some good men, gave him little help. Perhaps the ablest man was Judah P. Benjamin, a lawyer and former Senator from Louisiana. He was first Attorney General, then Secretary of War, then Secretary of State. Davis trusted him as much as he could trust anybody, but, as the war went on, the Confederate government became more and more a one-man show.

Much of the criticism of Davis, like that of Lincoln, came from people who wanted a quick, easy victory. Davis knew that the South would have to fight a long war and could only win by wearing the enemy down. In the summer of 1864, he decided to take advantage of the fact that many Northerners were sick of the war. To do this, he used a device that would some day be called a fifth column.

The Confederate fifth column was operated from Canada. There Confederate agents kept in touch with other agents in the Northern states. They were also in touch with a good many Copperhead leaders, such as Fernando Wood, the mayor of New York City, and Clement Vallandigham, a former member of Congress from Ohio.

Vallandigham was eager to help the South. In and out of Congress, he spoke against the war. In January of 1863, for example, he called the war "a most bloody and costly failure" for the Union. That year he was deported to the South for supporting the enemy. He was back in a short time, becoming the Vice-Presidential candidate on the Democratic ticket.

The Confederate fifth column worked closely with a strange secret society called the Order of American Knights. It claimed hundreds of thousands of members, and was supposed to be preparing to take up arms against the Federal government. None of its plots came to anything, but it helped spread talk that the North was close to defeat. The fifth column tried other things—to burn New York City, to capture a warship on the Great Lakes, to destroy railroad bridges, to take money for the Confederacy from Yankee banks. The actual results were small, but again the talk made Northerners uneasy. Lincoln once said, "The enemy behind us is more dangerous to the country than the enemy before us."

It was not Davis' fault that the fifth-column movement of 1864 accomplished so little. If the Northern Copperhead leaders had been able to keep a fifth of their promises, the Con-federacy might have given the Northern home front a good deal more than it could conveniently handle.

Although the South failed to do much sabotage, it was highly successful with its spy system. Women played a large part in the Rebel spy network. The most famous of them was Mrs. Rose O'Neal Greenhow, a widow who had lived in Washington for many years. She knew almost everyone of importance in the capital. Even after the war broke out, she kept her friendship with Union officers and government leaders. She admitted later that she did it to learn about the Union's military plans. "To this end," she wrote, "I employed every capacity with which God has endowed me, and the result was far more successful than my hopes could have flattered me to expect."

Ten days before First Bull Run, for example, General Beauregard received a message from Mrs. Greenhow. It was delivered to one of his officers by Betty Duvall, a courier for Mrs. Greenhow.

Dressed as a farm girl, Betty Duvall had crossed a bridge from Washington to Virginia in a market cart. Once she was in Confederate territory, she changed into a riding costume. Borrowing a horse, she rode off to meet Beauregard's aide. She gave him a letter sewn up in black silk, which she had hidden in her hairdress. It contained the date McDowell would finally advance from Washington.

Mrs. Greenhow was finally arrested by Allan Pinkerton, head of the Union's Secret Service. She was put into prison, but she was never brought to trial. A trial would have let the public know that she had friends who held important offices in the government. They included Seward, the Secretary of State, and Senator Henry Wilson, chairman of the Senate Committee on Military Affairs. She was set free on condition that she go to the South. When she reached Richmond, President Davis told her, "But for you, there would have been no battle of Bull Run."

The arrest of Mrs. Greenhow did not put an end to Rebel spying. It went on throughout the war. Washington was filled with people

New-York Historical Society

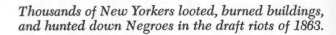

who favored the South, and it was easy to cross into enemy territory. Among the spies was Louisa Buckner, the niece of Montgomery Blair, the Postmaster General.

Miss Buckner, her mother, and a minister friend went shopping one day. Mr. Blair had lent his relatives five hundred dollars and had provided them with military passes, including a note from President Lincoln. An intelligence agent in the War Department became suspicious. He knew Miss Buckner had been born in Virginia, and he had reason to believe she was in sympathy with the South. He had the shopping party followed.

Miss Buckner visited three drugstores. She bought 600 ounces of quinine, a drug used to treat malaria and other fevers. The agent also learned that Miss Buckner was making a skirt. It was an unusual kind of skirt, with deep pockets in the folds lined with waterproof silk.

A few days later, Miss Buckner and her party were arrested for trying to deliver drugs to the Rebels. Part of the quinine was found

hidden in a wagon; the rest was in Miss Buckner's skirt. Trading with the enemy, especially supplying them with rare drugs, was forbidden. Miss Buckner and her companions went to jail, and Washington buzzed with talk about the "Quinine Lady."

Another big problem on the home front, for both Lincoln and Davis, was the draft. At the beginning of the war, the young men of the North and the South were eager to enlist. As the war went on and the casualty lists came in, enlistments dropped off. In 1862 the Confederacy passed a conscription law, the first in American history.

All able-bodied white males between the ages of eighteen and thirty-five were subject to draft in the South. The term of service was for the duration of the war, and owners of twenty or more slaves were exempt. Some men hired substitutes when they were called up in the draft, until this was stopped by law in December of 1863.

The North tried to attract men by using the bounty system. States, cities, and towns, as well as the Federal government, offered cash for enlisting. By 1864 there were many places where a man could receive more than $1,000 simply by joining the army. Some men, called "bounty jumpers," made a career of it. With no intention of serving, they would enlist, collect the bounty, and desert as soon as they could. They would repeat the process a number of times, re-enlisting under different names.

In 1863 the Union followed the Confederacy's example. Congress passed a law making all men aged twenty to forty-five liable to military service. A drafted man could be exempted by paying the government $300, or he could hire a substitute to take his place. Many Northerners complained. As one of them put it, "The blood of a poor man is as precious as that of the wealthy."

In the South the draft caused a great deal of grumbling; in the North it even caused riots.

The worst trouble came in New York City, where anti-war feeling had always been strong. The mayor and many important politicians were so-called "peace Democrats."

On Sunday, July 12, 1863, a few days after the battle of Gettysburg, the newspapers published the names drawn in the city's first draft. That afternoon angry crowds began gathering in the parks and on street corners. The next morning the drawing of names went on at a number of draft board offices throughout the city. An eyewitness described what happened at one of them: "A crowd, gradually increasing, gathered around the office, but the drawing went on until about 60 additional names had been drawn, when a sudden attack was made by the mob. The wheel [which was used to select the names] was destroyed, the papers scattered, and the building set on fire."

The news spread through the city, and 50,000 persons poured into the streets. "In a short time," according to the eyewitness account, "the aim of the leaders in the riot movement appeared to be an indiscriminate attack on the colored people, and upon those who are supposed to be in any way connected with the draft or with the Republican party."

The rioters hunted down and beat up Negroes, destroying a Negro orphan asylum. They broke into the offices of a Republican newspaper, the *Tribune*, and burned or sacked the houses of well-known Republicans. They looted, and tore up railroad tracks. For four days violence ruled the city, and about a thousand civilians were wounded or killed. The rioting was put down only after troops who had fought at Gettysburg were rushed into the city.

In the four Union draft calls, 776,829 names were drawn. Only an amazingly few draftees —46,347—actually saw military service. It was still a volunteer's war. Negroes were not allowed to serve in the Union army until 1863, after the Emancipation Proclamation was issued. The Negro troops were first given guard duty; later they were put into combat.

Yankee soldiers objected to serving with Negroes, but slowly they became used to the idea.

They finally decided that "a Negro could stop a bullet as well as a white man." Besides, most Negro regiments had white officers. This gave the soldiers a chance to get higher rank with higher pay. "The prospect of . . . $120 or $130 a month is no small temptation," one Yankee wrote.

Most of the Negro troops had escaped from slavery, and they were eager to fight. General Ben Butler said that they fought "more desperately than any white troops, in order to prevent capture, because they knew . . . if captured they would be returned to slavery."

In March, 1865, the Confederate Congress passed a law allowing the enlistment of Negro slaves. It was a desperate move, made too late, and it emphasized another of Jefferson Davis' troubles on the home front. The South was running out of manpower, as it had already run out of almost everything else.

The truth was that the South was simply not strong enough to carry on a modern war. It lacked factories, transportation, money, and skilled labor. After the North's blockade began to cut off supplies from abroad, it made an effort to support itself. The effort was a great one, and the wonder is not that it failed but that it accomplished so much. The farmers shifted from growing cotton to growing foodstuffs. Textile mills, factories, arsenals, and shipyards were built. Sash weights were melted down to make bullets. Moonshiners' stills were collected for the copper they contained. Together with the things that came in through the blockade and the material captured from the Yankees, the South managed to keep going.

As the war lengthened, the job grew harder. When the South lost territory to the Union army, it also lost mills and factories. And wherever the Yankees went, they destroyed railroad lines. Rails that were bent out of shape could be straightened and used again, but in time the Federals learned to give the rails a spiral twist. Such rails were of no use unless they could be sent to a rolling mill— and the South had very few rolling mills.

Food shortages became the South's biggest problem. The fault was not that of the farmers,

who were growing enough. But, with so much of the railroad system ruined, farm products could not be moved to where they were needed. Food prices rose higher and higher. By March of 1865, loaves of bread were made in three sizes. They sold for one, two, and three dollars. "The first is only visible by microscopick aid," a Richmond newspaper reported. "The second can be discerned with the naked eye, and the third can be seen with outline and shape distinct." Flour was selling for $275 a barrel in 1864. Bacon was nine dollars a pound; potatoes were twenty-five dollars a bushel. A Richmond newspaper reporter was forced to pay five dollars for a cup of coffee.

In April, 1864, a woman in South Carolina wrote in her diary that "you take your money to the market in the market basket, and bring home what you buy in your pocketbook." The reason was that the Confederate dollar was becoming worthless. By 1864, it was worth just five cents in gold. A Georgian predicted that "an oak leaf will be worth just as much as the promise of the Confederate treasury to pay one dollar." By the end of the war, he was proved

Brady-Handy Collection, Library of Congress

right; the Confederate dollar was worth nothing at all.

Abraham Lincoln also had financial and industrial problems, but they were different from those faced by Davis. The difference between the North and the South was pointed out by General Sherman as early as 1860. Talking to a Southern friend, Sherman said, "The North can make a steam engine, locomotive or railway car; hardly a yard of cloth or a pair of shoes can you make. You are rushing into war with one of the most powerful, ingeniously mechanical and determined people on earth — right at your doors. You are bound to fail."

The North began the war with most of the country's industrial power. Besides, it had many acres of farmland and a network of railroads that spanned more than half the continent. During the war, the North grew enormously. It was pushed into the industrial age with amazing speed. By 1865 the northeastern part of America would be an industrialized nation. What might have taken fifty years to accomplish was done with a rush in four years.

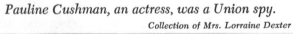

Pauline Cushman, an actress, was a Union spy.
Collection of Mrs. Lorraine Dexter

At the same time, farm production increased. The Union's farms even helped to feed foreign nations, especially Great Britain. Exports of wheat tripled during the war. There was no shortage of manpower or skilled labor. Immigration fell in 1860 and 1861, but rose after that. During the five years of 1861-65, more than 800,000 Europeans came to America, most of them from England, Ireland, and Germany. In spite of heavy casualty lists, the North's population increased.

Not that everybody in the North was prosperous. Prices rose faster than wages, and the average man had a hard time making ends meet. In some places, like the Pennsylvania coal fields, the workers were dissatisfied. People could not help being disturbed by war profiteers. The Union army needed a tremendous amount of goods to feed, clothe, and supply its men. It needed them fast—and the profiteers took advantage of this. They sold the government poor goods at the highest possible prices.

"The mania for stealing seems to have run through all the relations of Government," a New York Congressman complained. "Nearly every man who deals with the Government seems to feel or desire that it would not long survive, and each had a common right to plunder while it lived." In Louisville, for example, the government paid $58,000 for 485 horses. They were later found to be "blind, spavined . . . and with every disease that horseflesh is heir to." Outdated carbines—small, light guns—were sold by the government at two dollars apiece. They were bought by a contractor, who sold them back to the army at twenty-two dollars each. Young Jim Fisk, who was starting a career that would make him a leading financier, said, "You can sell anything to the government at almost any price you've got the guts to ask."

Another thing that disturbed Northerners was the treatment of prisoners of war. In 1862, the Union and the Confederacy worked

out a system of exchanging prisoners—general for general, private for private, or sixty privates for one general. The prisoners were to be on parole, which meant they promised not to fight again until officially exchanged.

The system broke down over the problem of exchanging former slaves captured while serving with the Union army. The South demanded that they be returned to their masters as runaways. The North demanded that they be treated like any other prisoners of war. The North also feared that paroled prisoners would be returned to the front. In 1864, Grant said, "Every man we hold, when released on parole or otherwise, becomes an active soldier against us either directly or indirectly. If we commence a system of exchanges which liberates all prisoners taken, we will have to fight on until the whole South is terminated." The South had a manpower shortage; the North did not. Grant let the exchange of prisoners stop, and thousands died in the prison camps.

As the election campaign of 1864 began, many Northerners felt that the war effort was a failure. If they still thought so by election day, the Democrats would win. Then the North would almost certainly fall out of the war, and the South would have its independence. It was no wonder that President Lincoln was worried.

Detective Allan Pinkerton (seated, right) was often wrong in his reports of enemy strength to the Union.

Total War and An Election

I N THE PRESIDENTIAL campaign of 1864, what men said made very little difference. It was what the men in uniform did that mattered. Everything depended on them. If they should start to win, Lincoln would win. If they could not win, Lincoln could not win.

No one understood this better than General Joe Johnston. Lincoln needed a smashing victory, such as the capture of Atlanta. Otherwise, McClellan would be elected President-- and his party was ready to make peace.

Johnston believed that the South's only hope was to hold out until the election. As long as he was in command of the Confederate forces at Atlanta, he would give the Union no chance for a victory. He refused to allow Sherman to lure him into a battle. He played a waiting game, delaying, stalling for time. But Jeffer-

son Davis did not see things this way, and Davis had the final say. He believed the war had to be won on the battlefield, and to do that the Confederates must fight. And so he had removed Johnston, putting General John Bell Hood in his place.

A brave and dashing fighter, Hood had been wounded in the arm at Gettysburg. He had recovered in time to fight at Chickamauga, where he lost a leg. Patched up, and riding strapped to his saddle, he was then given corps command under Johnston. Now he was in full charge of Johnston's army. The trouble was that he was not suited for the top job.

Hood realized that he was expected to fight, and he lost no time in getting to it. Rather less than half of the Union army was moving on Atlanta from the east, tearing up the Georgia

Rebels overrun a battery by the brick house and meet a counterattack in the battle of Atlanta.

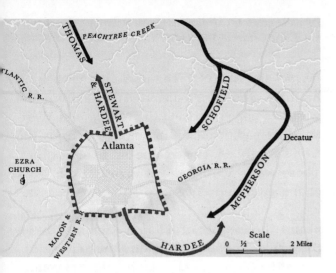

Hood's July 20 thrust at Peachtree Creek was led by Stewart and Hardee. His flank attack on July 22, led by Hardee, was known as the Battle of Atlanta.

Railroad as it advanced. The rest of the army, under General Thomas, was crossing Peachtree Creek, north of the city. Hood spotted a gap of several miles between the two Union forces and set out to destroy Thomas.

The Rebel attack, on July 20, was not quite fast enough to catch the Yankees crossing the creek. Even so, it was a hard and sudden blow, and the Union line sagged. But there never was a better defensive fighter than Thomas, who was known as the "Rock of Chickamauga." He brought up his artillery, and the Rebels were driven off with heavy losses.

Hood withdrew into Atlanta, and two days later he struck again. This time he swung east, against General James B. McPherson's Army of the Tennessee. McPherson had left one of his flanks exposed, and Hood hoped to hit it the way Jackson had hit Hooker at Chancellorsville. He almost succeeded, in a desperate fight that became known as the Battle of Atlanta.

Hood's troops went into action yelling "like demons," and slowly the Union line began to retreat. A Confederate corps punched a hole in the Union center, forcing the Yankees to fight on two fronts. At one point in the battle, McPherson's horse was seen, bleeding and riderless. McPherson was found dead, riddled by rifle bullets, and Sherman wept when the body was brought to him.

In spite of McPherson's death, the Yankees held on. Sometimes they rolled from one side of their earthworks to the other, fighting off consecutive charges from front to rear. At dark, Hood broke off the action, his flank attack a failure. He pulled his battered troops

Union battery horses (center) are killed so that the Rebels cannot remove the captured guns.

Courtesy The City of Atlanta

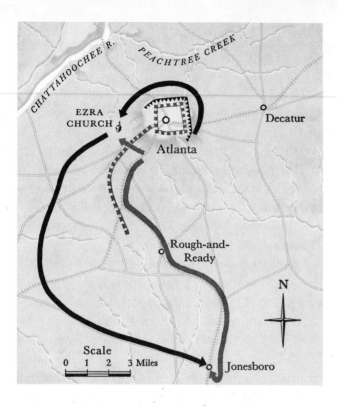

Black line shows Union moves at Atlanta. Also shown are Ezra Church and Hood's evacuation of the city.

he had the Army of Tennessee march behind his lines and sweep in on Atlanta from the west. He hoped to reach the Macon and Western Railroad, which ran southwest from the city. On July 28, Hood came out to attack him. There was a hard fight at Ezra Church, west of the city, and once again the Confederates were forced back. Sherman was a long step nearer the capture of Atlanta. Hemmed in on three sides, it was bound to fall in time.

As the siege of Atlanta began, Sherman's chief worry was his own railroad connections. The line went back to Chattanooga, down the Tennessee Valley to Bridgeport, and up through Nashville to Kentucky. His supplies came in on this line; if they were cut off he would have to retreat. And roaming the area was the rough slave trader who had become a genius of cavalry—General Nathan Bedford Forrest.

"Forrest is the very devil," Sherman had written. It was necessary to hound Forrest "to the death, if it cost 10,000 lives and break the Treasury. There never will be peace in Ten-

back inside the fortified lines of Atlanta. The two battles had cost him more than 13,000 men, and now he was pinned in his earthworks.

Sherman had already cut the railroads that came to Atlanta from the north and east. Now

Frame houses were stripped to provide lumber for Confederate fortifications at Atlanta.

Kean Archives

Sherman's men destroyed an Atlanta bank but did not touch the billiard parlor next to it.

nessee till Forrest is dead." Early in June, Sherman had sent a cavalry column under General Samuel D. Sturgis into Mississippi to stop Forrest. The two met at Brice's Crossroads, where Forrest's 3,300 troopers threw back Sturgis' 8,000 men. A soldier who took part in the day-long fight said it was "so close that guns once fired were not reloaded, but used as clubs . . . while the two lines struggled with the ferocity of wild beasts." Sturgis was badly beaten, and Forrest was free to go almost where he pleased.

Sherman tried to stop him again in July, ordering a strong expedition under General A. J. Smith to move down from Memphis into Mississippi. Near Tupelo, Smith ran into a force made up of Forrest's troopers and Rebel infantry. Forrest was wounded and the Confederates were driven off. It was clearly a Union victory, but Smith failed to follow it up. Instead, he retreated to Memphis.

In August, Smith made another try. Forrest slipped past him and entered Memphis itself. He was riding a buggy, his wounded foot

propped up on a special rack. Although his stay was brief and did no harm, it got Smith's troops recalled to Memphis. Forrest was still free to go where he pleased. At the same time, the Federal moves accomplished one thing. They kept Forrest so busy he could not strike at Sherman's supply line, and the Yankees stepped up the pressure on Atlanta. Hood pulled his troops out, retreating to the south, and on September 2 the Union army occupied the city. Sherman wired Lincoln, "Atlanta is ours, and fairly won."

Here was the victory Lincoln needed. It followed another, on August 5, when tough old Admiral Farragut had closed the port at Mobile. He had steamed in through a mine field, and mines were called "torpedoes" in those days. His battle cry of "Damn the torpedoes—full speed ahead!" stirred the entire North.

Still a third Union victory was in the making, farther north, in the Shenandoah Valley. The valley was of great importance to the Confederacy. Immensely fertile, it supplied

171

The Federals fight a delaying action in the West.

Lee's army with meat and grain. Besides, any Rebel army moving through the valley could threaten Washington and such cities as Philadelphia and Baltimore. Grant's master plan called for laying waste the rich farmlands of the valley so that it could no longer support a Confederate army.

Franz Sigel, the first general assigned to the job, failed completely. David Hunter, who replaced him, did not do much better. After defeating a small Confederate force, he turned east to Staunton, burning and destroying as he went. Near Lynchburg he found Jubal Early, ready as usual to make a stand. Although the Union force outnumbered Early's 15,000 men, Hunter cautiously fled to the mountains of West Virginia.

Early was chased back into Virginia after threatening Washington, but his pursuers could not catch him. Using tactics much like "Stonewall" Jackson's, he dodged and outmaneuvered 45,000 Federals. Grant realized he had to stop Early, and he picked Phil Sheridan to do it.

The thirty-three-year-old Sheridan was young for such an important command. Bowlegged, short, and slight, he did not look impressive, but he turned out to be a brilliant leader and a tough fighting man. His orders from Grant were to destroy both Early and the valley. He was to lay waste the farmlands, so that even a crow flying over them would have to carry its own rations.

On August 7, 1864, Sheridan took command of the newly named Army of the Shenandoah. He began cautiously, for Early was a hard hitter and his men were rugged veterans. On September 19, Sheridan attacked near Winchester. The attack was bungled, and the Federals were soon in trouble. Riding his big black horse Rienzi, Sheridan galloped to the front. He waved his hat and shouted to his officers, "Give 'em hell. . . . Press them, General, they'll run!" The Union army surged forward, breaking the Confederate lines. Early retreated, after losing 4,000 men. Three days later he tried to make a stand at Fisher's Hill, and again he was badly beaten.

As the Rebels retreated south, Sheridan followed them, burning and destroying. Crops ready for harvest went up in smoke and flame. Two thousand barns were burned, mills and storehouses were destroyed, cattle were either slaughtered or driven off. Never again would the Confederate army feed off this once-fertile garden. Nothing would be planted in the burned-over land until after the war. As the Federals finally withdrew, a Rebel saw "great columns of smoke which almost shut out the sun by day, and . . . the red glare of bonfires which . . . crackled mockingly in the night air."

By early October Sheridan was able to report to Grant that "the Valley, from Winchester to Staunton, ninety-two miles, will have but little in it for man or beast." The middle of the same month found Sheridan's men encamped at Cedar Creek, twenty miles south of Winchester. Sheridan left them there while he traveled to Washington to attend a conference.

A Union cavalryman's drawing of Quantrill's raid on Lawrence, Kansas

Colonel Mosby, on white horse at right, watches his rangers return from a raid on a Yankee supply train.

Early was not far from the Union force. His supplies were dangerously low, and it was impossible for him to live off the valley. He had to either get out or fight. He decided to fight, and at dawn on October 19 he attacked.

That morning Sheridan was at Winchester, where he had stopped overnight on his way back from Washington. He was awakened by the sound of gunfire, and at first he thought it was his own artillery feeling out the enemy. Still, he was uneasy. After a quick breakfast, he started riding his horse Rienzi toward Cedar Creek.

Sheridan later wrote that at the crest of a hill "there burst upon our view the appalling spectacle of a panic-stricken army . . . all pressing to the rear in hopeless confusion." He soon learned from the soldiers what had happened. Early had smashed the Union's left flank, and with it an entire army corps. Taken by sur-

prise, the Yankees had been shoved back four miles, and many of them had fled.

Sheridan rose in the saddle and said, "We will go back and recover our camp." Spurring his horse, he waved his hat and rallied his troops. "Turn back! Turn back! Face the other way!" he shouted. Groups of stragglers turned to follow him. Soldiers who had been making coffee by the roadside kicked over their coffee cans and swung into line. Sheridan rode furiously, pushing on to the battlefront.

Late that afternoon, the re-formed Union army charged the Rebels. The Confederate line crumbled, and by sundown Early had been driven off. The Confederacy's hold on the Shenandoah Valley was broken for good.

Sheridan's ride became a legend; a song about it went all across the North. His victory in the valley, together with those of Sherman at Atlanta and Farragut at Mobile Bay, made

174

General Jubal Early demands $200,000 for the Rebels from leading citizens of Frederick, in Maryland.

the people forget their war weariness. No longer could the Democrats say that the war was a failure. Not that they gave up their campaign against Lincoln. They still called him an ape, a gorilla, a buffoon, and whispered all sorts of stories about him.

The Republicans also played rough. In control of the government, they used every political trick they could to win the election. They forced government employees to contribute money to the party treasury. They passed laws allowing soldiers to vote in camp, and whole regiments were furloughed so that the men could go home and vote.

Election day, November 8, 1864, was cold and wet in Washington. Few people visited Lincoln in the White House that day. At seven o'clock in the evening he splashed through the rain to the War Department telegraph office to get the election returns. As the Republican votes began to pile up, Lincoln relaxed and began telling funny stories. At two in the morning, when he left the telegraph office, his re-election seemed certain.

Complete election returns gave Lincoln 2,203,831 votes to McClellan's 1,797,019, with an electoral vote of 212 to 21. In some states, such as New York, Lincoln barely managed to win. McClellan got forty-five per cent of the national vote, which showed that a surprisingly large number of Northerners were dissatisfied. However, they were still a minority. A substantial majority of the people had told Lincoln that they wanted him to carry on the war to a victorious end.

What had happened on the battlefield was only part of the reason Lincoln was re-elected. He had made many mistakes, especially in the way he handled military matters during the first two years of the war. He had been criticized both for going too far on the slavery question and not going far enough. At times he had seemed more of a politician than a

leader. But, in spite of everything, he had kept on waging war. The people re-elected him because they believed in him and in what he was doing.

While Sherman and Sheridan and Farragut had been winning their victories, Grant was still dug in at Petersburg. His Army of the Potomac had had a fearful campaign. For more than five months it had been in almost daily contact with the enemy. It had fought the hardest, longest, costliest battles ever seen on the American continent.

The Army of the Potomac had won no glory. Its casualties had been extremely heavy, and yet it had no really clear-cut victory to its credit. It had done just one thing—the one thing that was needed for the final Union victory. It had forced Lee to stay near Richmond and fight a defensive war he could not win.

Destruction by Rebels at Chambersburg

*Phil Sheridan's famous ride from Winchester stirred
the North and helped win the election for Lincoln.*

Lee's Army of Northern Virginia and
Grant's Army of the Potomac had worn each
other out. The campaigns that would decide
the war would therefore be made far to the
south and west, where the Confederates were
at a disadvantage. Lee's army no longer had
the room and strength to maneuver as it did
in the past. Grant had seen to that. Lee could
do no more than protect the capital, while
Federal armies crushed all the life out of the
Confederacy.

Lincoln's re-election was the clincher. It
meant that Lincoln would support Grant, who
would never let up in his pressure on the
South. After the election in November, victory
for the Union could only be a question of time.

Even so, the fighting went on, and there
was hate in the land. During all of his campaign in the Shenandoah Valley, Sheridan was
troubled by Confederate guerrillas. They were
bands of irregular fighters who raided out-
posts, burned Yankee wagon trains, and shot
sentries and couriers. Because of them, Sheridan had to use a sizable number of men for
guard duty. The Union soldiers considered
the guerrillas to be criminals, and usually

Western Reserve Historical Society

*In this drawing of the battle of Winchester, Yankee
cavalry is capturing a fortified Confederate battery.*

176

hanged any they captured. The guerrillas hanged Yankees in return, and the hate grew more bitter.

Many of the guerrillas were no better than organized outlaws. They often raided civilians, and they did the Confederacy more harm than good. A Rebel cavalryman complained that "they roam broadcast over the country, a band of thieves, pillaging, plundering . . . an injury to the cause." The Confederate commanders discouraged guerrilla warfare, and Lee said, "I regard the whole system as an unmixed evil."

The most successful of the guerrillas was Colonel John S. Mosby. He controlled the area north of the Rappahannock in Virginia, and it was called Mosby's Confederacy. Sheridan gradually cleared the Shenandoah Valley of guerrillas, but there seemed to be no way of stopping Mosby's bands. Late in November, Union cavalry rode across the Blue Ridge Mountains, into Mosby's Confederacy. Their search failed to turn up Mosby and his men. Hoping to starve the guerrillas out, the troopers set the area aflame, and the once-lovely valley was left a blackened ruin.

West of the Mississippi, in Kansas, Missouri, and Arkansas, guerrilla warfare was especially violent. Fighting between Union and pro-slavery men had begun in the 1850's, and dur-

Century Club, New York

This painting, Guerrilla Warfare, Civil War, *shows Yankees firing from ambush at Southern irregulars.*

ing most of the Civil War the area lived under a rule of terror. In the Ozark Mountains, Southern sympathizers hanged men "with no charge against them except that they had been feeding Union men." James H. Lane, a Senator from Kansas, led Unionist troops in sacking and burning pro-Confederate settlements. Sometimes neighborhood feuds got all mixed in with the business of fighting the enemy, and old grudges were settled in blood.

The most murderous of all the guerrillas was William C. Quantrill, who led a pro-Southern band in Kansas. Among his followers was Bill Anderson, who tied the scalps of his victims to his horse's bridle. Jesse James and Cole Younger learned their trade as outlaws under Quantrill.

Quantrill made his worst raid on August 21, 1863, when with 450 men he attacked the town of Lawrence in Kansas. About 150 unarmed citizens were butchered. An eyewitness wrote, "The whole business part of the town, except two stores, was in ashes. The bodies of dead men . . . were laying in all directions." Another eyewitness said, "It is doubtful whether the world has ever witnessed such a scene of horror. . . ." In October Quantrill staged another massacre at Baxter Springs. Union troops hunted him for months, but he was not caught until after the war. In May, 1865, he was shot while trying to escape capture in Kentucky.

Guerrilla warfare went on even after the fighting between the regular troops had stopped. In the fall of 1864, the Confederates made their last offensive west of the Mississippi. Sterling Price and 12,000 troopers rode into Missouri, threatening St. Louis, Jefferson City, and Kansas City. On October 23, a Union force under Samuel Curtis met Price near the town of Westport. Curtis had won the battle at Pea Ridge in 1862, and once again he was successful. Aided by cavalry, he whipped the Rebels, driving them into Arkansas. The war in that part of the West was practically over.

The March to the Sea

Two DAYS after Sherman occupied Atlanta, he ordered the civilians to leave. His answer to protests was, "You might as well appeal against the thunderstorm as against these terrible hardships of war." He was determined to make Atlanta safe from a Confederate counterattack, and the civilians would only get in the way. More than half the population fled to the Confederate lines. Sherman fortified all the approaches to the city, refitted his army, and began to make plans for the future. His problem was where to go next.

General Hood, too, had a problem—how to get Sherman out of the South. Hood did not have enough men to risk a direct attack. He decided to go west of Atlanta, swing north, and attack Sherman's communications. Sherman would be forced to follow him. In the tangled countryside of northern Georgia, the Confederates might possibly win a battle.

While Hood started his march, Forrest went up into Tennessee. Forrest's troops broke an important section of the railroad between Nashville and the Tennessee River. If this move had been made before the capture of Atlanta, it would have given Sherman serious trouble. As it was, a force of 30,000 Federals was assigned to get Forrest, and Sherman sent General Thomas to take charge at Nashville. Forrest withdrew, reaching northern Mississippi just as Hood began operations against Sherman's railroad line in Georgia.

Sherman left an army corps to hold Atlanta and set out after Hood. For more than two weeks the two armies maneuvered for position. On October 5, Hood tried to capture a large Union supply depot at Allatoona Pass. It was guarded by a small detachment under

Brigadier General John M. Corse. The Yankees held on stubbornly, and the Rebels were forced to retire.

Hood was unable to make a real break in Sherman's supply line. Sherman, on the other hand, was unable to pin down the Confederates for a finish fight. Hood decided on a bold and desperate gamble. He would march his entire army into Tennessee. He hoped that this would force Sherman to give up Atlanta and come after him. Even if it did not, Hood might take Nashville, drive into Kentucky, and threaten Cincinnati. He might even cross the Cumberland Mountains, fall on Grant's rear, and relieve the pressure on Lee before Rich-

The gray line indicates Hood's long route from Atlanta toward Nashville. Black lines show moves of Union forces under Generals Schofield and Sherman.

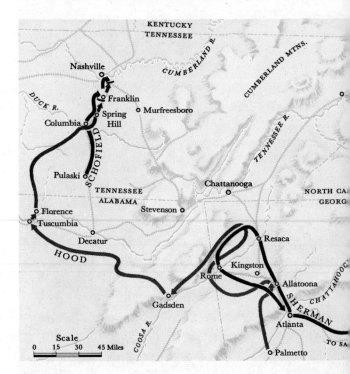

A battery of Negro troops, part of the force Sherman sent to oppose Hood at Nashville

mond. As it turned out, Hood's plan was a great mistake. But nothing he could have done would have been much better; he simply had no good choice to make.

Meanwhile, Sherman was deciding on a bold gamble of his own. He was tired of chasing Hood. "Damn him," he said, "if he will go to the Ohio River, I'll give him rations . . . my business is down South." Sherman's plan was different from the one Grant had made six months earlier. Grant had wanted to destroy the Confederate armies. Sherman said he would pay no attention to Hood's army. Instead, he would march toward Savannah and the sea, through the heartland of the South. His men would live off the land and destroy anything of use to the enemy.

Sherman's action would do more than destroy things the Confederates badly needed. It would destroy their spirit as well. It would prove, once and for all, that the Confederacy could not protect its own people and property

and was too weak to live. Grant was at first against the plan, but he finally agreed, and Sherman put it into operation.

Sherman's destruction began with Atlanta itself. He ordered the burning of warehouses, factories, railroad depots and yards, and similar buildings. His enthusiastic soldiers went even further than that, and most of the city went up in smoke.

On November 15, 1864, Sherman set out for the sea. "I can make . . . Georgia howl!" he promised. His 62,000 troops moved slowly, covering a front sixty miles wide. Georgia was a rich land, and to the soldiers the march seemed more like a long picnic than like regular war. An Illinois soldier wrote, "This is probably the most gigantic pleasure excursion ever planned. It already beats anything I ever saw soldiering and promises to prove much richer yet."

Each morning foraging parties were sent out to bring in supplies. Instead of salt pork

181

and hardtack, the soldiers ate chicken, beef, ham, and fresh vegetables. A Georgia woman told what happened when a foraging party arrived at her plantation. "To my smoke-house, my dairy, my pantry, kitchen and cellar," she wrote, "like famished wolves they came, breaking locks and whatever is in the way. The thousand pounds of meat in my

smokehouse is gone in a twinkling, my flour, my meat, my lard, butter, eggs, pickles . . . wine, jars and jugs are all gone. My eighteen fat turkeys, my hens, chickens, and fowl, my

In this painting, symbolizing Sherman's march to the sea, Sherman is shown at left center, riding the dark horse. The march began November 15, 1864, after Sherman promised, "I can make . . . Georgia howl!"

Still marked by bullet holes is the Carter House at Franklin, where the Union battle line was formed.

young pigs, are shot down in my yard and hunted as if they were Rebels. . . ."

The foraging parties returned at night with wagons piled high with booty. If the army wagons were not enough, they would use "anything that had wheels, drawn by anything that could pull." When the army moved on, it destroyed more food than it had eaten, or gave it to the runaway slaves.

These runaway slaves followed the marching columns by the thousands. The army was also trailed by swarms of lawless stragglers called "bummers." Among them were deserters from the Union army who had no intention of returning to their regiments, and men temporarily absent without leave, who would later return to duty. Oddly enough, there were also a certain number of deserters from the Confederate army. The bummers not only took food, they carried away things like silverware and watches. They robbed and looted and burned all the way from Atlanta to the sea.

Sherman could probably have controlled the bummers if he had tried hard enough. He did not try. He said that his job was to get his army safely to the sea, and that he could not spare the manpower or energy to protect the people of Georgia. But the plain fact was that the bummers were helping to make Georgia howl. They were more brutal than Sherman would have liked them to be, but they were laying waste the Confederate homeland—and this was all that mattered.

For Sherman was waging total war. He was tearing down and burning bridges, railroads, machine shops, warehouses. Barns and their contents were also burned. Food to feed the army and its animals was taken, and three or four times as much as the army needed was simply spoiled. And partly because of all of this Lee's soldiers would be on starvation rations and the Confederate war effort would grow weaker and weaker. The destruction was not pleasant to watch, but it was helping to bring the war to an end.

As Sherman went on toward the sea, Hood was making his way northward into Tennessee. On November 18, Hood joined forces with Forrest's cavalry, so that his army now numbered 30,000 men. But Union General Thomas was getting together a force of 40,000 men at Nashville. Twenty-three thousand more, under General John Schofield, were moving up from Atlanta. To have any chance at all to take Nashville, Hood had to stop Schofield from reaching the city.

Hood led his men in an elaborate flanking movement, trying to cut off Schofield at Spring Hill, less than thirty miles from Nashville. Hood almost succeeded. He was in position to put Schofield's whole force out of action. Then, for some unexplained reason, he ordered his army to encamp for the night.

While the Rebels slept, the Yankees remained awake. With the Confederates less than 600 yards away, Schofield's men slipped quietly away in the darkness. All night they

FRANKLIN: Having escaped the Rebels at Spring Hill, Schofield's army reaches Franklin by noon of November 30. The supply wagons are moved across the Harpeth River (1), as the troops form behind breastworks south of town. Hood approaches two hours later and at 3 P.M. orders the attack (2). This onslaught sweeps the Federal advance back along the Columbia Pike, and the Rebels pour through the Union line near the Gin House (3). At the Carter House (4) General Emerson Opdycke rallies enough Northerners to plug the gap. Further attacks along the Federal line (5) prove fruitless, and the battle sputters out at 9 P.M. That night Schofield pulled his army out of Franklin and joined Thomas' force at Nashville on December 1.

FRANKLIN

November 30, 1864

FORT GRANGER

TO NASHVILLE

Franklin

CARTER HOUSE

GIN HOUSE

COLUMBIA PIKE

LEWISBURG PIKE

HARPETH RIVER

NASHVILLE & DECATUR R.R.

pushed on toward Nashville on the double. They did not even fall out to eat, but munched hardtack and salt pork as they marched.

The following morning, November 30, Hood exploded when he learned what had happened. "The best move in my career as a soldier," he complained, "I was thus destined to behold come to naught." He drove his men after the enemy, determined to attack.

Forrest's cavalry stabbed at Schofield's columns, and were answered by the Union artillery, firing at close range. A Yankee later said, "You could see a Rebel's head falling off his horse at one side and his body on the other. . . . Others you could see fall off with their feet caught in the stirrup, and the horse dragging and trampling them. . . . Others, the horse would get shot and the rider tumble head over heels, or maybe get caught by his horse falling on him."

Forrest was beaten off, but the Federals had to stop before they got to Nashville. At Franklin they found that the bridge over the river had been burned. While the engineers built a new one, the infantry took positions just south of the town.

By noon of that hazy Indian-summer day, all of Schofield's weary troops had reached Franklin. Entrenched in a vast semicircle, they waited to see what the Rebels would do. About two o'clock in the afternoon the Confederates appeared on the rim of the hills south of the town. Within an hour they had formed a line of battle. "It was a grand sight such as would make a life-long impression . . ." a Federal officer later recalled. "For the moment we were spell-bound with admiration, although they were our hated foes, and we knew that in a few brief moments . . . all that orderly grandeur would be changed to bleeding, writhing confusion. . . ."

Behind the magnificent Confederate line, General O. F. Strahl was saying to his men, "Boys, this will be short but desperate." A signal volley was fired, the Rebel yell filled the air, and the Southerners swept forward "as steady and resistless as a tidal wave." The center of the Union line was cracked, and the Rebels poured through. For a while the Federals to the rear were unable to fire. They were afraid of hitting their own men, who were fighting hand-to-hand with the attackers. Then the Union line stiffened. Most of the Confederates who had broken through were killed, captured, or driven off.

Hood refused to give up. The Confederates charged again and again. Some Union soldiers counted as many as thirteen separate assaults. "It is impossible to exaggerate the fierce energy with which the Confederate soldiers, that short November afternoon, threw themselves against the works, fighting with what seemed the very madness of despair," a Federal colonel wrote long afterwards. At some of the earthworks the men crowded in so thickly that the dead could not fall and remained upright.

At about nine o'clock in the evening, Hood halted the slaughter. He had lost 6,252 men; the North had lost 2,326. Five Confederate generals had been killed in the battle. Six had been wounded, one mortally, and a twelfth had been captured. The Southerners had fought heroically, but they had gained nothing. Hood had only weakened his army. Worse yet, his men had lost confidence in him.

Two hours after the fighting was over, under cover of darkness, Schofield pulled his men out. After another all-night march, they reached Nashville the next day. Hood followed them. He put his men in camp on high ground a few miles south of Nashville and waited. Just what he was waiting for, nobody knew. The Federals had occupied the city for three years, and it was one of the best fortified places in the country. Union General Thomas had a force at least twice the size of Hood's. It was impossible for Hood to storm the city. He did not have enough soldiers to lay siege to it. He could not side-step and march north without leaving himself open to an attack on his flank and rear. He was afraid that if he retreated his army would fall apart. Once again, he had no real choice, and so he dug in on a five-mile line. His one small hope was that he would lure Thomas out, stop the Union attack, and counterattack.

NASHVILLE: Thomas advances from his solid entrenchments (1) on December 15 to drive the Rebels back to a position astride the Franklin and Granny White pikes. On December 16 the initial Federal attacks launched against the Rebel right at Overton Hill (2), are unsuccessful, but later that afternoon the storm tactics of McArthur and Couch overwhelm the Confederate left (3). To Hood's rear, dismounted Union cavalry (4) force him to fight a three-sided battle. With his left and center (5) in complete rout, Hood orders a retreat (6) down the Franklin Pike to the south. Several delaying actions were fought later by Forrest's cavalry before the decimated Army of Tennessee reached safety in Mississippi.

NASHVILLE

Second Day: December 16, 1864

David Greenspan

Wrecking railroads was part of General Sherman's plan of "smashing things to the sea" during his march from Atlanta, and his men became especially skillful at it.

But Thomas was still holding back. He preferred not to strike until everything was ready. He had just completed his preparations when a hard sleet storm came down. The roads and hills were coated with ice, and he decided to wait a few days for a thaw. Far off in Virginia, Grant was worried. Usually very calm, he had a bad case of jitters. The war was almost won, but Hood might still get away from Thomas. If Hood marched north to Ohio, the Union would be in for trouble.

Grant did not know that Thomas was completely in control of the situation. He sent one message after another demanding an immediate attack. At last, losing patience, he sent General John Logan to Nashville. In Logan's pocket was an order relieving Thomas from command. That order would remain in Logan's pocket. Early on the morning of December 15, Thomas checked out of his Nashville hotel room, paid his bill, and gave his packed valise to an orderly. A thaw had melted the ice and he was ready for battle.

At six o'clock, in a dense fog, Negro troops under James B. Steedman attacked the Rebel right. Then the main Union drive against Hood's weak left got under way. One Union corps was to strike at the Rebel center, as a pivot on which cavalry and infantry would swing left along the Hillsboro Pike. Unexpectedly, a detached Rebel artillery unit of 148 men held off a 4,000-man infantry division. After two hours, the Federals again advanced, and the Confederate left began to crumble.

Hood recalled some of the soldiers from his right to reinforce his hard-pressed left. But Schofield's men, who had been held in reserve, were brought up, and the Rebels fell back along the muddy road.

Mary Bradford, a plucky Southern girl, rushed out among Hood's fleeing soldiers. Tears streaming down her face, she begged them to halt. It was no use. At nightfall Thomas called off the battle, convinced that he had won. Schofield did not agree. "You don't know Hood," he said. "He'll be right there, ready to fight, in the morning."

Schofield was right. By the morning of December 16, Hood had re-formed his lines. Thomas decided to repeat the tactics he had used the day before. He would try to bend back Hood's flanks and keep him from retreating south. This time, however, it seemed to take the Union soldiers longer to get into line. The reason was that many of them had to find their units, from which they had become separated the night before.

Two Union commanders, Darius Couch and John McArthur, became impatient at the delay. They volunteered to storm the two steep slopes that made up the Confederate left. At about four o'clock in the afternoon they began their attacks. In the Federal rear, spectators held their breath as they watched the tiny blue figures climbing the slopes. In a matter of minutes, the Stars and Stripes waved from the summit. A cheer echoed across the valley—"the voice of the American people," Thomas called it. Another Northerner wrote, "It was more like a scene from a spectacular drama than a real incident of war . . . so exciting was it all that the lookers-on instinctively clapped their hands. . . ."

Hood's left collapsed, and then his center. Still his troops fought on. "I doubt if any soldiers in the world ever needed so much cumulative evidence to convince them that they were beaten," Schofield said later.

A heavy rain began to fall, and Hood ordered a retreat toward Franklin. "I beheld for

The waterfront at Savannah, Georgia, after it fell to Sherman three days before Christmas in 1864. Bales of captured cotton are being put aboard vessels for shipment to New York.

the first and only time," he said, "a Confederate Army abandon the field in confusion."

That night, a Rebel private stumbled into General Hood's tent by mistake. There sat the beaten commander with tears of bitter disappointment running down his cheeks. Within a month he would resign his commission. His army had fallen apart, his career had ended in a crushing defeat, and the war in the West was practically at an end.

While Hood sat weeping, Thomas was riding down stragglers with the Union cavalry. To anyone who listened, he shouted, "Didn't

I tell you we could lick 'em? Didn't I tell you. . . ."

Farther south, Sherman's men were still marching through Georgia, bummers and all. At Milledgeville, the state's capital, they easily routed a small force of militiamen. They made their campfires of Confederate money, and repealed secession in a mock legislative session. Here, too, they found several Yankees who had escaped from the prison camp at Andersonville. An officer wrote that the sight of these living skeletons "sickened and infuriated the men who thought of them starving in

When Fredericksburg was sacked in 1862, a Union officer was horrified by the way his men "seemed to delight in destroying everything." A few years later destruction helped to defeat the Confederacy.

the midst of plenty." The angry Northerners made Georgia howl even louder.

From Milledgeville they marched for Savannah, 175 miles away. The North waited impatiently for news. Sherman had cut off his lines of communication when he left Atlanta, and was completely out of touch with the home folks. His brother, Senator John Sherman, asked Lincoln what the general's goal was. Lincoln replied, "I know the hole he went in at, but I can't tell you what hole he will come out of."

After a month of silence, the North learned that Sherman had reached Savannah. The city was defended by 10,000 troops, but they retreated and moved up into South Carolina. On December 22, 1864, Sherman proudly marched into Savannah. It meant more feasting for his men. As one soldier wrote, they were a little tired of "beefsteak, porksteak, broiled chicken, sweet potatoes." Now they could enjoy "oyster soup, oysters on the half shell, roast goose, fried oysters, rice, raisins, coffee, and roast oysters."

Two days later, Sherman sent Lincoln a telegram, offering him the city of Savannah as a Christmas present. Included in the gift were 250 cannon and 40,000 bales of cotton.

Sherman left Savannah untouched, but behind him was a wide path of destruction that cut through Georgia. He estimated the damage at one hundred million dollars. Eighty million was "simply waste and destruction."

As 1864 came to an end, the position of the Confederacy was hopeless. It still had an army west of the Mississippi, but this could have no real effect on the war. It had no forces to throw against Thomas' victorious troops in Tennessee. There was no chance of bringing together enough men to keep Sherman from coming north from Savannah whenever he decided to try it. Lee was still pinned in the lines at Petersburg, unable to do more than hold on.

The South had had only one recent success. In December, a combined army-navy expedition under Union General Benjamin Butler had tried to capture Wilmington, North Carolina. This was the South's last remaining sea-

This sketch of a bummer, loaded with loot after a foraging expedition, was drawn by a Yankee soldier.

port through which it could communicate with the rest of the world. A Union fleet bombarded Fort Fisher, which guarded the entrance to the Cape Fear River. Butler managed to get troops ashore, then grew panicky. He pulled his men out and sailed north.

The North did not allow the South much time in which to enjoy the victory. In January, Grant sent down another expedition. Admiral Porter commanded for the navy and General A. H. Terry commanded for the army. The fleet pounded the fort hard, and Terry got his troops on the beach. They swarmed over the defenses, and Fort Fisher surrendered. The Confederacy's last door to the outside world was closed.

Sherman was now preparing to march north. In Tennessee, a powerful mounted force of 12,000 Federals, armed with repeating carbines, was getting ready to cut down into Alabama. Another Federal army was besieging Mobile. Grant was ordering 21,000 Western troops brought east, to move inland from captured Wilmington and join Sherman as he came north.

The war was all but finished.

Northern soldiers denied setting the fire that destroyed most of Columbia, South Carolina.

Victory

ON THE FIRST day of February, 1865, Sherman and his army started north from Savannah. The 60,000 tough veterans—all of them now called bummers, even by Sherman—had made a remarkable march across Georgia. They were ready to make another, through the Carolinas.

They faced little opposition from the Confederates. Only 30,000 threadbare and hungry Rebels stood between them and Grant's army at Petersburg. In North Carolina the Yankees would be reinforced by 21,000 more troops,

while the Rebels had no way of increasing their forces. About all the Southerners could hope to do was slow down Sherman's march. They could not possibly stop it.

Realizing this, the Confederate leaders tried to find out if the Federal government was willing to discuss peace terms. A meeting between Southern and Northern delegations was arranged for February 3. It would be held on a Federal steamer in Hampton Roads, Virginia. The Southern delegation included Vice President Alexander Stephens; speaking for the

Union would be President Lincoln and Secretary of State Seward.

To reach Hampton Roads, the Confederate officials had to cross the lines of the armies at Petersburg. There was a deep silence as the soldiers of both sides watched them from the parapets of the trenches. Suddenly the troops began to cheer. They had had enough of war; they wanted peace. When the Southern officials had gone on their way, the Rebel troops gave three cheers for the Yankees. The Yankees answered with three cheers for the Rebels. Then the men settled back in their trenches to talk about the chances of getting home.

Nothing came of the meeting. Lincoln said there would be no peace until the South disbanded its armies and accepted the authority of the Federal government. This meant the abolition of slavery. The thirteenth amendment to the Constitution, ending slavery forever, had already gone to the states for ratification.

The Southerners saw that Lincoln was simply offering them unconditional surrender. What would happen to the South once the war was over would depend on the Federal government. There was no doubt that Lincoln himself would be generous. He planned no punishment for the Rebels. He was even willing to try to get the Federal government to pay slaveowners for the loss of their slaves. But there were many Northerners, including a number in Congress, whose ideas were very different from Lincoln's. By surrendering, the South would be at their mercy. The delegation went back to Richmond, and Confederate President Davis told his people that they must fight to the last ditch.

The Confederacy tried a number of things to put off defeat. It offered to abolish slavery if France and Great Britain would recognize it as a legal government. The Confederacy had been trying to get such recognition since the beginning of the war. Two or three years earlier, an offer to abolish slavery might have brought the South what it wanted. Now it was clear to everyone that the Rebels were losing, and the offer fell flat.

Even so, the Confederate Congress voted to make soldiers out of Negro slaves. A slave who became a soldier had to be given his freedom. If some slaves were freed, all would have to be freed in time. But the Confederacy needed manpower, and the bill was passed in spite of bitter opposition. As spring came, some steps were taken to arm and train Negro troops.

Robert E. Lee was named commander in chief of the Confederate armies. Lee brought Joe Johnston back from retirement to try to halt Sherman. Johnston knew it was impossible. "I can do no more than annoy him," he confessed sadly.

As it turned out, Sherman found Johnston less annoying than the weather and the geography. The Union's line of march went through swampy lowlands cut by many rivers. In rainy weather the streams flooded and roads turned into mud. Surprisingly, Sherman's army moved through South Carolina as quickly as it had moved through Georgia. The men forded icy rivers and built their own bridges over the floodwaters. To make the roads passable, they felled trees, cut logs, and laid the logs crosswise in the mud. Roads like these were called "corduroyed roads." A Confederate prisoner complained, "If your army goes to hell, it will corduroy the road." General Johnston himself later said that there had been no such army since the days of Julius Caesar.

Sherman's men were rough on South Carolina. They had been on their good behavior in Savannah, but they fell back into their old habits once they left Georgia. They burned and looted and destroyed with a kind of fury they had not shown before. They felt that South Carolina, the first state to leave the Union, had started the war. It was the "mother of secession" and the "hell-hole of secession," and its people deserved the roughest kind of treatment. Sherman said that "the devil himself could not restrain his men in that state."

On February 17, Columbia, the capital of South Carolina, fell into Union hands. The city was two-thirds destroyed by fire, but Sherman claimed that his troops were not responsible. He put the blame on General Wade

The artist who painted this picture exaggerated the welcome given to Lincoln when he visited Richmond.

Hampton, a Confederate cavalry commander, whose men were among the last Rebels to leave the city. Sherman said that Hampton had "ordered that all cotton . . . should be moved into the streets and fired, to prevent our making use of it." Tufts of burning cotton, blown by the wind, carried the flames to houses and other buildings. "Without hesitation," Sherman wrote, "I charge General Hampton with having burned his own city of Columbia. . . ." He added that his Federals had worked hard to put out the fires. Whoever was responsible, the Northern soldiers "smiled and felt glad" as they watched the burning city, and Columbia was left a "howling waste."

A week after the capture of the city, Sherman and Hampton quarreled over another matter. Sherman accused Hampton's troops of murdering Union soldiers. He charged that a lieutenant and seven privates on a foraging mission had been captured by the Rebels and then killed. He said that he had "ordered a similar number of prisoners in our hands to be disposed of in like manner."

Hampton sent back a hot reply. "I beg to assure you," he wrote, "that for every soldier of mine murdered by you, I shall have executed at once *two* of yours. . . ." He went on to accuse Sherman of ignoring the plight of the people of the city, "leaving amidst its ruins thousands of old men and helpless women and children, who are likely to perish of starvation and exposure."

There was little Sherman could say. Thousands of people had been made homeless in Columbia. As Sherman had written to a friend while marching through Georgia, "War is cruelty, and you cannot refine it."

No matter what the Southerners thought, they could not stop Sherman's march. After Sherman's advance had cut off all rail communication to Charleston, General Beauregard ordered that city evacuated on February 17. He had no choice. Federal troops threatened Charleston from the land, while ships of the Union navy were at the entrance to the harbor. Fort Sumter was abandoned, and the Union fleet steamed into the harbor—the first Yankee vessels to do so since April 14, 1861.

Sherman's army swept northward, into North Carolina. On February 22, units under General Schofield took Wilmington, another key Southern port. On March 16, Sherman defeated a Confederate force under General Hardee at Averasboro. Three days later, at Bentonville, a surprise attack by Johnston forced him to fall back. After reinforcements were brought up, the Union troops counterattacked. Johnston's force was too small to hold the line, and the Confederates retreated toward Raleigh. Sherman did not even bother to pursue him. There was just no point to it. Instead he moved to Goldsboro, where 30,000 additional troops were waiting to join him. He arrived there on March 23.

Sherman's bummers were again on their good behavior. They did not feel the hatred for North Carolina that they felt for its sister state, and destruction was kept to a minimum. As a matter of fact, there was now no military reason for destruction. The war could not possibly last much longer.

On March 2, Sheridan had destroyed Early's remaining troops in the Shenandoah Valley at Waynesboro, Virginia. He then started his two veteran cavalry divisions for Petersburg. Lee had to act quickly to prevent Sheridan's troopers from cutting off his communications and supplies. At the same time, Grant was extending the Union lines to the west of Petersburg. Lee's own lines were dangerously extended, and he had half the number of troops facing him. The only other Rebel troops left were in Johnston's small force, in South Carolina. The North, on the other hand, had 280,000 men to throw into battle.

There was just one last chance for Lee and the Confederacy—and a very slim chance it was. He must somehow give Grant the slip, get his army into North Carolina, join forces with Johnston, and defeat Sherman. Then Lee and Johnston might turn back toward Virginia and attack Grant. It was unlikely that all of this could be done, but it had to be tried.

Grant's army, in Lee's front, occupied a huge semicircle more than forty miles long. The northern tip of it was opposite Richmond, the southern tip curled around southwest of Petersburg. Once again Lee decided on a bold move. He would strike at Grant's center and try to break the military railroad that supplied the Union army. If he was successful, the Union left would have to be pulled back to avoid being cut off. That would allow Lee to march his troops south and carry out the rest of his plan.

At dawn on March 25 Lee launched his last great attack. General John B. Gordon led the charge against Fort Stedman, a fortified point not more than 150 yards from the Rebel line. The Federals, taken by surprise, were driven from the fort. Gordon sent patrols back toward the railroad and seized some of the Federal trenches. But the Union troops rallied quickly. Gordon was hit hard by artillery fire and counterattacks, and in less than four hours he pulled his troops back to their own lines. The Confederate attack had failed.

The battle for the fort was witnessed by President Lincoln. A few days earlier he had journeyed from Washington to spend some time at Grant's headquarters at City Point, on the James River. At night he slept aboard a steamer. During the day he wandered about the camp, talking with the soldiers and visiting the wounded in the hospitals. Once he delighted the troops by picking up an axe and helping to build a cabin. After four years of war, Lincoln knew that victory was near, and he wanted to be in on it.

During the final days of March, Grant tried to drive in past Lee's extreme right. Phil Sher-

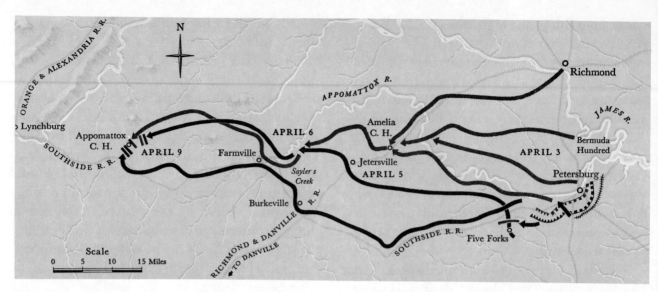

The final campaign of the Civil War lasted a week. Lee's flight from Petersburg and Richmond to Appomattox is shown in gray, Grant's pursuit in black. Some units marched over forty miles in a day.

idan with 12,000 horsemen moved out to Dinwiddie Court House, which was south and west of the place where the Union and Confederate infantry were fighting for control of the flank. On March 31, Sheridan moved north to Five Forks, a road center west of the Petersburg defenses. If Lee lost this, he would also lose the Southside Railroad, his last rail connection with the South. He would be forced to give up Petersburg, and then Richmond itself would fall.

The job of holding Five Forks was assigned to General George Pickett, the hero of the famous charge at Gettysburg. His orders were to "hold Five Forks at all hazards." But Sheridan beat off all his attacks on the first day of the battle. On April 1, reinforced by a corps of infantry, Sheridan smashed Pickett's line. Five thousand Confederates were taken prisoner, and Pickett barely managed to escape capture himself. He wrote his wife: "We were completely entrapped . . . overpowered, defeated, cut to pieces, starving, captured. . . ."

The way was now clear for Grant to get in behind Lee's army. He ordered a general attack on the main Petersburg lines for dawn on April 2. The Federal infantry broke through, and in a short time the entire Rebel right wing collapsed. A. P. Hill, another of Lee's trusted generals, was killed. A Confederate officer,

who was at headquarters when word came of Hill's death, wrote, "I will never forget the expression on General Lee's face."

April second was a Sunday, and in Richmond Jefferson Davis was at church. In the midst of the services a courier arrived with a message from the War Department: "General Lee telegraphs he can hold his position no longer." Davis quietly left the church and set about removing his government from Richmond. That same day, shortly after dark, Lee's troops gave up Petersburg.

As the Confederate government and the army garrison left Richmond, its factories, arsenals, and mills were ordered destroyed. Some were blown up, others were burned, and the fires were soon out of control. Crowds rushed to the commissary depots, which had been thrown open. Whiskey stocks were broken into, and "the streets ran with liquor."

Through the night, drunken mobs of civilians and army deserters roamed the city, looting and burning. A Rebel gunner described the wild, terrible scene: ". . . an ocean of flame is dashing, as a tidal wave of destruction . . . from street to street. . . . Miles on miles of fire; mountain piled on mountain of black smoke . . . one ceaseless babel of human voices, crying, shouting, cursing; one mighty pandemonium of woe."

On the morning of April 3, Grant's troops took over the city. A Richmond woman saw "a body of men in blue uniforms. . . . The Confederate flag that fluttered above the Capitol came down and the Stars and Stripes were run up. . . . We covered our faces and cried aloud."

The Federal troops got the fire under control and restored order. The next day Lincoln himself arrived. He came into the ruined city quietly and rode through the streets. Visiting the Confederate White House, he sat for a moment at Jefferson Davis' desk, "a serious, dreamy expression" on his face.

Lee's Army of Northern Virginia, meanwhile, was making its last march. The hungry, worn-out troops stumbled on toward Amelia Court House, on the Richmond and Danville Railroad. Here Lee hoped to pull together his troops from Petersburg and Richmond and move south to join Johnston. But

(Next page) Between ranks of Federal troops, Lee's army stacked its arms at Appomattox Court House.

Sheridan blocked the railroad south of the Rebels. Lee had to head for Lynchburg, about sixty miles to the west. During the past year, the two armies had raced each other to such important places as Spotsylvania Court House, Cold Harbor, and Petersburg; now the soldiers realized that they were on their final race. "We grew tired," a Yankee wrote, "but we wanted to be there when the rebels found the last ditch of which they had talked so much."

Sheridan kept stabbing at the Southern columns. On April 6 he cut out a Rebel wagon train and called up an infantry corps to attack Lee's rear guard at Sayler's Creek. More than 6,000 Confederates were captured. Watching the fighting from high ground, Lee said to one of his officers, "General, that half of our army is destroyed."

Rebel veterans furl the Stars and Bars for the last time before starting for home.

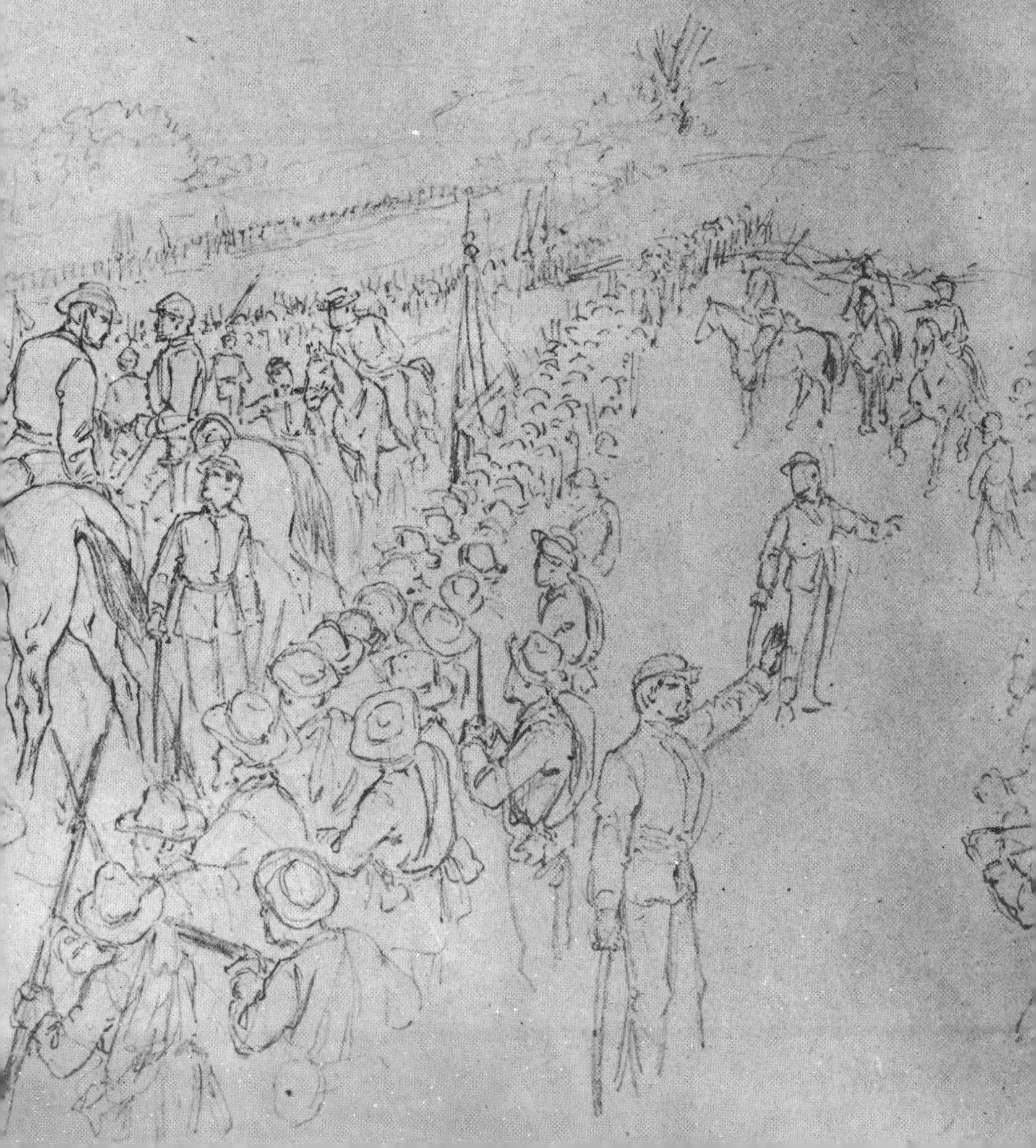

Lee pushed on toward the west, but he was outpaced by the Union cavalry. On April 8, Yankee troopers under General George Custer—who would later become famous as an Indian fighter—reached Appomattox Station, west of Lee. They seized four trains of supplies meant for the Confederates. Sheridan wrote Grant that if "the 5th Corps can get up tonight we will perhaps finish the job in the morning."

The next day Lee found Sheridan's cavalry across his line of march, near the little town of Appomattox Court House. He pushed the horsemen aside, only to face solid lines of infantry. The road to Lynchburg was blocked. Other powerful forces were on his flank, and a huge mass of infantry was at his rear. Lee could not get in touch with Johnston. He could neither continue his march to the west nor put up a fight. He had fewer than 30,000 soldiers by now, and less than half of them were armed. The rest were worn-out men who could not be used in battle.

The Union forces prepared to launch a massive attack, and the Confederates waited under their red battle flags. Then out between the lines rode a Confederate horseman with a white flag fluttering at the end of a staff. A sudden quiet fell on the broad field. The soldiers in both armies stared at one another, unable to believe that the fighting at last was over. Lee had made his decision. "There is nothing left for me to do but go and see General Grant," he told a staff officer. He added, "And I would rather die a thousand deaths."

Early in the afternoon of April 9, 1865—Palm Sunday—the two generals met in Wilmer McLean's farmhouse. McLean had lived near Manassas Junction, where the first important battle of the war had been fought in 1861. When his farm was overrun during the Second Battle of Bull Run, he moved his family to the quiet little village of Appomattox Court House. Now after four years, the war was coming to an end in his parlor.

Lee was the first to arrive. He wore a new uniform and carried a sword at his side. Grant was in a fatigue uniform and carried no side arms. Lee's aide thought Grant looked "as though he had had a pretty hard time . . . dusty and a little soiled."

Both men wanted a good peace. Instead of surrendering, Lee might have told his troops to carry on guerrilla warfare as long as there was a Yankee south of the Mason-Dixon Line. Lee realized that this would mean years of brutality, bitterness, and hatred, and he was against it. His men had lost their fight, and they must now try to make the best of what remained to them.

Grant believed that the whole point of the war was to prove that Northerners and Southerners were and always would be fellow citizens. Now that the fighting had stopped, they ought to begin behaving that way. In the North were many men who wanted the leading Confederates hanged, but Grant was opposed to any punishment of the Rebels. His terms of surrender were generous. They stated that "each officer and man will be allowed to return to his home, not to be disturbed by the United States authorities. . . ." Officers could keep their side arms and baggage. Men who owned horses and mules would be allowed to take them home.

By four o'clock, the surrender of the Army of Northern Virginia was completed. Lee shook hands with Grant. "Sad-faced and weary," he mounted his horse Traveller and rode slowly back to his army. The Union artillery began to fire salutes in celebration, but Grant stopped it. "We did not want to exult over their downfall," he explained later.

The next day Lee addressed his troops for the last time, praising their "unsurpassed courage and fortitude." Then the men stacked their guns, furled the Stars and Bars, and prepared to go home.

With the surrender of Lee, the Confederate armies collapsed. General Forrest gave up in Alabama. Mobile, the last Confederate stronghold on the Gulf coast, fell on April 12. Two weeks later Johnston surrendered to Sherman in North Carolina. The only hold-outs were some small Rebel forces in Mississippi, Alabama, and Texas. By late May, these, too, had laid down their arms. A New York newspaper ran the headline: "The Old Flag Waves From Maine to the Rio Grande!"

Jefferson Davis and his cabinet had moved across the Carolinas and into Georgia, hoping to keep the Confederacy going somehow. It could not be done, and the cabinet at last scattered. Davis himself was captured by Federal cavalry, and the government of the Confederate States of America went out of existence. The war was over. Some Northerners wanted Davis tried and hanged for treason. He was sent to prison in Fort Monroe, but was released after two years.

On April 15, 1865, Robert E. Lee rode through the rain into Richmond. An eyewitness wrote, "His steed was bespattered with mud, and his head hung down as if worn by long travelling. The horseman himself sat his horse like a master; his face was ridged with self-respecting grief; his garments were worn in the service and stained with travel. . . ." A great crowd gathered and greeted Lee with cheers. Union officers respectfully raised their caps as he passed.

As one of the Confederate leaders, Lee was indicted for treason, but he was never brought to trial. However, he was not granted the Federal pardon he asked for. In September, he wrote, "The war being at an end . . . I believe it to be the duty of every one to unite in restoration of the country, and the establishment of peace and harmony. . . ."

That month he became president of Washington College in Lexington, Virginia. He held this position for the five remaining years of his life. On October 12, 1870, when he lay dying, his old opponent, Ulysses S. Grant, was President of the United States. "Strike the tent," Lee murmured, and died.

News of the Confederate surrender set off celebrations everywhere in the North.

End and Beginning

THE WAR had lasted for four years, and it had cost hundreds of thousands of lives and billions of dollars. It had destroyed one of the two American ways of life forever, and it had brought great changes to the other. It ended as it had begun, in a kind of mystery. No one could say exactly why it had come about in the first place; no one could quite say what it meant now that it was finished.

Of all men, Abraham Lincoln came the closest to understanding the meaning of the war. And yet even he had to confess that something had happened in the land which could not be put into words. In his second inaugural address, on March 4, 1865, he could do no more than remind his countrymen that they had somehow done more than they intended to do.

"Neither party," he said, "expected for the war the magnitude or the duration which it has already attained. Neither anticipated that the cause of the conflict might cease with, or even before, the conflict itself should cease."

He was referring to the fact that the Congress of the United States had already passed the thirteenth amendment, ending slavery. In Richmond, the Congress of the Confederacy was preparing to vote regiments of slaves into the Confederate service. Slavery was dead no matter how the war came out.

He went on, speaking of the two sides in the war: "Both read the same Bible and pray to the same God, and each invokes His aid against the other. . . . The prayers of both could not be answered; that of neither has been an-

swered fully. The Almighty has His own purposes."

Lincoln believed that both sides shared in the blame for the war, just as they had shared in the cost of it. Both sides must, therefore, also share in the victory. The peace that would come out of the war must be broad enough to mean some sort of gain for everyone—for the Northerner and for the Southerner, for the Negro and for the white. In such a peace, there could be no question of punishing the South.

"Let 'em up easy," was the way Lincoln put it. He said these words to Grant and Sherman, just before the beginning of the last campaign of the war. "Let 'em up easy." He wanted to see the Confederate armies disbanded and the men back at work on their farms and in the shops. He wanted civil governments set up again in the Southern states as soon as possible.

So, when Johnston surrendered, Sherman was guided by what he thought Lincoln wanted. Two things, however, were wrong. Sherman seems to have gone much further than Lincoln would have gone—and, by this time, Lincoln was dead. Sherman and Johnston met near a place called Durham's Station, a few days after Lee had given up. On April 18, they agreed on surrender terms. Sherman, the man who struck without mercy, laid waste whole states, and was considered the South's most pitiless enemy, came up with an amazing document.

To begin with, it covered not only Johnston's army, but all the remaining armed forces of the Confederacy. Johnston had no authority over any troops but his own. But with him was John C. Breckenridge, the Con-

Union armies paraded up Washington's Pennsylvania Avenue in a final Grand Review, May 23-24, 1865.

Abraham Lincoln, as he appeared in Springfield on June 3, 1860.

federate Secretary of War, who did have such authority.

Confederate regiments were to march to their state capitals, deposit their arms, and disband. Every soldier would sign a pledge not to take up arms again. The government of each Rebel state would be recognized as lawful once its officers had taken an oath to support the Constitution of the United States. No one was to be punished. All property rights guaranteed in the Constitution were to be respected. This might have allowed the South to keep its slaves, for the thirteenth amendment had not yet been ratified.

When the surrender terms were sent on to Washington, the cabinet refused to approve

Five years later, on April 10, 1865, his face showed the mark of war.

them. Sherman was ordered to withdraw the agreement. On April 26, Johnston and Sherman signed another agreement, much like the one signed by Grant and Lee. It said nothing about the Rebel state governments or the property rights of Southerners.

Sherman then issued ten days' food rations to the hungry Southern soldiers. Johnston later wrote him that this "reconciles me to what I have previously regarded as the misfortune of my life, that of having you to encounter in the field." He never forgot Sherman's generosity. Twenty-six years later Joe Johnston died of pneumonia, after standing hatless in the rain at Sherman's funeral.

But there was no generosity in Washington toward Sherman. The surrender terms he had at first offered Johnston were considered too easy. Lincoln himself would almost certainly have changed them. From the moment that a Confederate surrender seemed likely, he insisted that his generals were not to decide political matters. Anything that had to do with slavery, the rights of Southerners, or the Rebel states coming back into the Union was to be left to him. In spite of the opposition of the Radicals, he thought he could put through a moderate reconstruction program for the defeated South.

An actor named John Wilkes Booth upset everything. On Good Friday evening, April 14, he entered the President's box at Ford's Theater and fired a bullet into Lincoln's brain. The peace that Lincoln wanted—"with malice toward none, and charity for all"—died with him. The South would be held responsible for the President's murder, and the peace would be a harsh one.

Secretary of War Stanton charged that Booth had acted on the orders of the Confederate leaders. The United States government issued a proclamation stating that Jefferson Davis and two other Confederate officials had actually plotted the murder. Rewards were offered for their arrest. Many Northerners agreed with a Washington newspaper, which said that Davis had "guided the assassin's trigger and dagger. . . . The tragedy-cracked player who did the deed . . . was no such criminal as the cold-blooded politician who laid out

Collection of Frederick Hill Meserve

John Wilkes Booth led the conspirators shown below.

the work." Later it became clear that Booth had acted on his own.

The story of the plot that took Lincoln's life is one of the strangest in all American history. Booth's father, Junius Brutus, and his brother, Edwin, were both famous actors. At the age of 26, John Wilkes Booth was himself a popular actor. He spent the winter of 1864 in Washington, hatching out a wild scheme to kidnap Lincoln alive and take him

Lewis Paine

George Atzerodt

down to Richmond. After Lee surrendered and Richmond was captured, he changed his plans. He would kill Lincoln, Grant, Vice President Johnson, and Secretary of State Seward. To help him, he got together a weird band that could hardly have carried out a plan to rob a corner newsstand. The plot to kill Grant and Johnson went astray.

Booth knew that Lincoln was to be at Ford's Theater on the evening of April 14. That afternoon the tired President said to a friend, "It has been advertised that we will be there, and I cannot disappoint the people. Otherwise I would not go. I do not want to go."

The President and Mrs. Lincoln reached the theater about nine o'clock. They were accompanied by a young officer and his fiancée. The Presidential party was shown to a flag-draped box, where Lincoln eased himself into an upholstered rocking chair to enjoy the play.

A half hour later, Booth arrived at the theater. Lincoln's unreliable guard had left his post, and the entrance to the Presidential box was unguarded. Booth slipped along a back corridor and hurried to the door of the box. He sighted Lincoln through a hole he had drilled in the door that morning. He silently entered, aimed a six-inch brass derringer at the back of Lincoln's head, and fired. After grappling with the young officer for a moment or two, Booth jumped from the box. He landed on the stage, breaking his leg as he fell. Quickly he rushed out through the wings and escaped on a horse waiting in the alley.

Across town, at the same time, Lewis Paine was making an unsuccessful attempt on the life of Secretary of State Seward. He forced his way into Seward's sickroom, slashed him with a knife, and then fled.

Lincoln was carried into a private house across the street from the theater. Through the night doctors did what they could to save Lincoln's life, but at twenty-two minutes past seven the next morning, Abraham Lincoln died. At seven-thirty, church bells began to toll and flags were lowered to half-mast. Shortly after, a coffin was carried down the steps of the house in which Lincoln died. A group of army officers, bareheaded, followed the coffin the less than a dozen blocks to the White House. People stood silently along the streets, many of them weeping.

At sunrise on April 19, the city was awakened by a twenty-one-gun salute. Early that morning, people hurried to places from which they could see the funeral procession. From the White House to the Capitol, the streets were a solid mass of humanity. When the procession reached the Capitol, a funeral sermon was preached and the closing prayer spoken. For two days the body lay in state in the rotunda of the Capitol. Then it was placed on the seven-car funeral train for a 1,700-mile journey to Springfield, Illinois.

As the train passed Lancaster, Pennsylvania, a tired old man in a carriage watched from the edge of the crowd. It was James Buchanan. who had been President before Lincoln. In Phil-

Mary Surratt
Collection of Frederick Hill Meserve

David Herold
Collection of Frederick Hill Meserve

Union veterans on Decoration Day in Boston in 1890. General Sherman is in the front rank at right.

adelphia, the coffin was taken to Independence Hall. In New York, a hundred thousand hushed mourners marched with the procession through the streets. In Cleveland, no building was large enough to hold the crowds that were expected, and a special platform was put up in a city park. Bonfires lit up the route to Chicago, and thousands stood in the rain all night to catch a glimpse of the passing train.

On February 11, 1861, setting out from his home town, Lincoln had said: "I now leave, not knowing when or whether ever I may return. . . ." On May 4, 1865, he was laid to rest in Springfield.

Meanwhile, on April 26, Booth was trapped in a burning barn in Virginia and shot. A military court sentenced four of his band to be hanged; the others were given prison sentences. The bullet that Booth had fired harmed both the North and the South, for it made reuniting the country a long and difficult job.

The millions who stood in silence to watch the funeral train were the people who had supported Lincoln through thick and thin. They had fought in his armies and voted for him in the elections. Lincoln had spoken to their hearts, in a way no one else had ever done, in his speeches at Gettysburg and at his second inaugural. He expressed the best that was in them, and he had gone with them through four years of death and destruction. As the war ended, they had come to understand his greatness. Now that he had been killed, they felt a terrible anger.

It was this anger that prevented the kind of peace that Lincoln wanted. President Johnson did try to bring it about, but the job was too much for him. The Union was reconstructed at last, but at the price of bitterness and injustice. Much work was left for later generations to do. Perhaps the wonder is not that the job was done so imperfectly, but that it was done at all.

For it was done, finally. If not finished, it was at least put on the road to completion. As the years passed, the war became a legend and a memory. In the cities and small towns of the North, Union veterans marched in parades every Decoration Day. They tramped down dusty streets, with bands playing and flags flying. Year after year they grew older, and their ranks grew thinner, until finally nobody remained to march at all. In the South, too, the old soldiers marched, although the date on the calendar was different.

The South had the bitterer memories. Ruined plantation buildings, with empty verandas slowly falling apart, somehow spoke for the dream that had died. There were cemeteries in both sections—quiet, peaceful fields where soldiers lay in the last sleep. There were statues, too, with great men frozen in cold marble, staring out over drowsy battlefields which would never again know violence or bloodshed.

And, finally, there was the simple memory of personal bravery. The most ordinary people had shown that they could value something more than they valued their own lives. When the last of the veterans had gone, and the sorrow and bitterness had worn away, this memory remained. The men who fought in the war, speaking for all Americans, had said something the country could not forget.

Robert E. Lee, shortly after the end of the war

CHRONOLOGY OF THE CIVIL WAR

MAY 1860

18 Republicans nominate Abraham Lincoln and Hannibal Hamlin.

JUNE 1860

23 Regular Democrats nominate Stephen A. Douglas and Herschel V. Johnson. Anti-Douglas Democrats choose John C. Breckinridge and Joseph Lane.

NOVEMBER 1860

6 Lincoln is elected President.

15 Maj. Robert Anderson is given command of Charleston defenses.

23 Anderson asks for reinforcements.

DECEMBER 1860

4 In his annual message to Congress, President James Buchanan declares that secession is unconstitutional but denies that the Federal government has power to force states to remain in the Union.

20 South Carolina secedes.

22 Lincoln's opposition to the key Crittenden proposal protecting slavery in the territories is made public.

24 The Senate Committee of Thirteen rejects the Crittenden Compromise.

JANUARY 1861

5 The *Star of the West* sails from New York with men and supplies for Fort Sumter.

9 South Carolina gunfire prevents the *Star of the West* from entering Charleston Harbor.

9 Mississippi secedes from the Union.

10 Florida secedes from the Union.

11 Alabama secedes from the Union.

19 Georgia secedes from the Union.

26 Louisiana secedes from the Union.

29 Kansas is admitted to the Union.

FEBRUARY 1861

1 Texas secedes from the Union.

4 The seceded states open a convention in Montgomery, Ala.

8 The Constitution for a provisional Confederate government is adopted.

15 The Montgomery convention, acting as the provisional Confederate Congress, passes a resolution to take Fort Sumter and Fort Pickens, Fla., by force if necessary.

18 Jefferson Davis is inaugurated at Montgomery as provisional President of the Confederacy.

MARCH 1861

4 Abraham Lincoln is inaugurated.

6 The Confederacy calls for 100,000 volunteers.

11 The Confederacy adopts a permanent Constitution.

APRIL 1861

4 Lincoln orders a relief expedition to Fort Sumter.

8 The relief expediton sails from New York.

12 Confederates fire on Fort Sumter.

13 Fort Sumter surrenders.

15 Lincoln calls for 75,000 volunteers.

18 Robert E. Lee is offered command of the Federal armies.

18 The Union garrison abandons Harpers Ferry.

19 The 6th Massachusetts Regiment clashes with a Baltimore mob.

19 Lincoln proclaims a blockade of Confederate ports from South Carolina to Texas.

20 Lee resigns from the U.S. Army.

27 Ports of North Carolina and Virginia are included in the blockade.

MAY 1861

3 Lincoln calls for 42,034 three-year volunteers and enlarges the regular army and navy.

6 Arkansas secedes from the Union.

7 Tennessee, in effect, secedes from the Union by forming an alliance with the Confederacy.

10 Capt. Nathaniel Lyon secures Federal control of St. Louis.

12 Troops restore full Federal control in Baltimore.

16 The Confederate Congress authorizes the recruiting of 400,000 men.

20 North Carolina secedes.

20 Kentucky proclaims its neutrality.

21 The Confederate Congress votes to move the capital to Richmond.

23 Virginia votes overwhelmingly to join the Confederacy.

24 10,000 Federal troops enter Virginia and occupy Alexandria.

28 Brig. Gen. Irvin McDowell is appointed Union commander of the Dept. of Northeastern Virginia.

29 Federal troops occupy Newport News, Va.

JUNE 1861

3 Maj. Gen. George B. McClellan's army, invading western Virginia, routs Confederates at Philippi.

10 Federal troops are forced to withdraw after Battle of Big Bethel, Va.

11 Western Virginia counties refuse to secede and set up a state government, recognized by Washington as the loyal Virginia government.

JULY 1861

11 McClellan wins the Battle of Rich Mountain in western Virginia.

16 McDowell's Union army advances upon Manassas Junction, Va.

20 Maj. Gen. Joseph E. Johnston's Rebel troops from the Shenandoah Valley join Brig. Gen. P. G. T. Beauregard at Manassas Junction.

21 The First Battle of Bull Run (First Manassas) ends in a rout of McDowell's Union forces.

21 Maj. Gen. John C. Frémont assumes command of Union forces in the West, at St. Louis.

27 McClellan replaces McDowell as commander of Federal troops in the Washington area.

AUGUST 1861

10 Brig. Gen. Nathaniel Lyon is killed and his army is defeated by Confederates at Wilson's Creek, Mo.

28 Brig. Gen. Ulysses S. Grant is given command of Federals in southeastern Missouri and southern Illinois.

SEPTEMBER 1861

4 Confederate Maj. Gen. Leonidas Polk seizes Columbus, Ky., ending the state's neutrality.

6 Union troops take Paducah, Ky.

10 General Albert Sidney Johnston is given command of the Confederate armies in the West.

20 Rebels capture the Union garrison at Lexington, Mo.

OCTOBER 1861

8 Brig. Gen. William T. Sherman assumes command of the Federal army in central and eastern Kentucky, replacing Robert Anderson.

21 Federal troops are defeated at Ball's Bluff, Va.

NOVEMBER 1861

1 Winfield Scott resigns as Federal general in chief, to be replaced by McClellan.

2 Frémont is relieved of the Western command.

6 Davis and Stephens are elected to full six-year terms as Confederate President and Vice-President.

7 Grant suffers a tactical defeat at Belmont, Mo.

7 Flag Officer Samuel F. Du Pont's Federal forces take Port Royal, S.C.

9 Brig. Gen. Don Carlos Buell replaces Sherman.

19 Maj. Gen. Henry W. Halleck replaces Frémont in Missouri.

JANUARY 1862

19 Brig. Gen. George Thomas defeats the Confederates at Mill Springs, securing Union control of eastern Kentucky.

FEBRUARY 1862

6 Grant and Flag Officer Andrew Foote lead a successful joint army-navy attack upon Fort Henry on the Tennessee River.

7 A. S. Johnston orders a Rebel retreat from southwestern Kentucky.

8 A Federal expedition takes Roanoke Island, N. C.

16 Fort Donelson unconditionally surrenders to Grant.

22 Jefferson Davis is inaugurated as permanent President of the Confederate government.

25 Rebels abandon Nashville, Tenn.

MARCH 1862

2 Polk abandons Columbus, Ky.

8 Confederates lose the two-day Battle of Pea Ridge, Ark.

8 The *Merrimac* enters Hampton Roads, destroying or damaging three U.S. warships.

9 The *Merrimac* and the *Monitor* meet in an indecisive battle at Hampton Roads.

11 Halleck is given command of all Federal forces in the West.

11 McClellan is removed as Federal general in chief but retains command of the Army of the Potomac.

14 Southern forces abandon New Madrid, Mo., opening the way for a Union attack on Island No. 10.

14 Brig. Gen. Ambrose E. Burnside takes New Bern, N.C.

17 Grant takes command of the Federals at Pittsburg Landing, Tenn.

23 Maj. Gen. Thomas J. (Stonewall) Jackson is defeated at Kernstown, Va., in the first battle of the Shenandoah Valley Campaign.

29 A. S. Johnston reassembles Rebel Western forces at Corinth, Miss.

APRIL 1862

4 McClellan's Union army on the Peninsula starts its advance.

5 McClellan besieges the Confederate defenses at Yorktown, Va.

6 Confederates maul Grant's army in a surprise attack at Shiloh, Tenn. (Pittsburg Landing); A. S. Johnston is killed, and Beauregard takes command of the Rebel army.

7 Buell's reinforcement of Grant at Shiloh turns the battle in the Federals' favor, forcing Beauregard to retreat to Corinth, Miss.

8 Rebels on Island No. 10 surrender.

11 Fort Pulaski is taken by Federals, insuring blockade of Savannah, Ga.

16 The Confederate Congress votes conscription of able-bodied men between 18 and 35.

25 Flag Officer David G. Farragut captures New Orleans.

29 Halleck, taking over Grant's army, begins to advance on Corinth.

MAY 1862

1 Maj. Gen. Benjamin Butler occupies New Orleans.

4 The siege of Yorktown, Va., ends as Confederates retreat.

5 Maj. Gen. James Longstreet fights a successful rear-guard action against McClellan at Williamsburg.

8 Stonewall Jackson defeats Brig. Gen. Milroy at McDowell, Va.

9 McClellan's advance on Richmond forces Rebels to abandon Norfolk.

11 The *Merrimac* is burned to prevent its capture.

12 Federals occupy Baton Rouge, La.

23 Jackson drives the Federals from Front Royal, Va.

25 Jackson routs Maj. Gen. Nathaniel P. Banks at Winchester, Va.

25 Halleck arrives at Corinth, Miss., after a 26-day, 20-mile advance.

30 Beauregard evacuates Corinth.

31 Joseph E. Johnston is severely wounded at the inconclusive Battle of Fair Oaks (Seven Pines).

JUNE 1862

1 Robert E. Lee succeeds to command of the Confederate forces defending Richmond as the fighting ends at Fair Oaks.

6 Memphis, Tenn., is occupied after a Federal naval victory.

8 Jackson defeats Frémont at the Battle of Cross Keys, Va.

9 Jackson defeats Shields at Port Republic, Va.

15 Brig. Gen. J. E. B. Stuart completes a four-day reconnaissance ride around McClellan's army.

17 Jackson's army leaves the Shenandoah Valley to join Lee's Army of Northern Virginia at Richmond.

25 McClellan attacks at Oak Grove, Va., starting the Seven Days' Battles.

26 Lee attacks McClellan's right wing at Mechanicsville, Va., but fails to destroy Brig. Gen. F. Porter's corps.

26 Pope is given command of the Federal Army of Virginia, newly formed from the commands of Frémont, McDowell, and Banks.

26 Farragut's ships start bombarding Vicksburg, Miss.

27 General Braxton Bragg replaces Beauregard in command of the Confederate Army of Mississippi.

27 Lee continues his attack on Porter, achieving a breakthrough at Gaines' Mill and forcing McClellan to retreat toward the James River.

29 Lee continues his attack on the Army of the Potomac in the Battle of Savage's Station, Va.

30 Lee fails to cut off McClellan's retreat at Frayser's Farm, Va.

JULY 1862

1 Lee is repulsed at Malvern Hill, Va, ending the Seven Days' Battles.

2 Lincoln calls for 300,000 three-year enlistments, but response is disappointing.

3 McClellan entrenches at Harrison's Landing, Va., on the James River.

11 Halleck becomes general in chief of the Union armies.

14 Pope leads a Union advance upon Gordonsville, Va.

AUGUST 1862

4 Lincoln issues a new call for 300,-000 nine-months militia.

9 Jackson defeats Banks at the Battle of Cedar Mountain, Va., as Lee seeks to destroy Pope before McClellan's army joins him.

14 Maj. Gen. Edmund Kirby Smith opens the Confederate invasion of central Kentucky.

14 McClellan begins to withdraw the Army of the Potomac from the Peninsula as ordered by Halleck.

26 Jackson destroys Pope's supply depot at Manassas Junction, Va.; Pope turns to pursue Jackson.

28 Jackson fights Brig. Gen. Rufus King at Groveton, Va., revealing his position to Pope.

28 Bragg's army leaves Chattanooga to join Kirby Smith in Kentucky.

29 Pope attacks Jackson, beginning the Second Battle of Bull Run (Second Manassas), but fails to dislodge him; Jackson is reinforced by Longstreet.

30 Longstreet envelops Pope's left flank, and the Second Battle of Bull Run ends in a Federal rout.

30 Buell orders the pursuit of Bragg and Kirby Smith.

SEPTEMBER 1862

1 Jackson attacks Pope's forces at Chantilly, Va.

2 Pope is replaced by McClellan, who takes over the defense of Washington.

2 Kirby Smith takes Lexington, Ky.

5 Lee crosses the Potomac into Maryland, opening invasion of the North.

7 Lee reaches Frederick, Md.

9 Lee splits his army and sends Jackson to capture Harpers Ferry, Va.

13 McClellan finds a lost copy of Lee's orders revealing troop plans.

14 McClellan breaks through the South Mountain passes at the Battles of Crampton's Gap and South Mountain, forcing Lee to concentrate at Sharpsburg, Md.

15 Jackson captures 12,000 Union troops at Harpers Ferry.

16 McClellan is in position at Antietam Creek near Sharpsburg; Jackson rejoins Lee.

17 McClellan repeatedly attacks Lee in the Battle of Antietam (Sharpsburg), but neither side can claim a victory in the bloodiest single day of the war.

18 Lee retreats to Virginia, ending his invasion threat.

19 Grant sends Maj. Gen. William S. Rosecrans to defeat Maj. Gen. Sterling Price at Iuka, Miss.

22 Lincoln issues the preliminary Emancipation Proclamation.

22 Bragg reaches Bardstown, Ky., abandoning his drive on Louisville.

29 Buell reaches Louisville, Ky.

OCTOBER 1862

4 Rosecrans defeats Maj. Gen. Earl Van Dorn at Corinth, Miss., isolating Bragg.

8 After Bragg's inconclusive battle with Buell at Perryville, Bragg and Smith retreat toward Tennessee.

12 Stuart completes his second ride around McClellan's army.

30 Rosecrans replaces Buell in command of the Union Army of the Cumberland.

NOVEMBER 1862

2 Grant launches a campaign to capture Vicksburg, Miss.

7 Burnside replaces McClellan as commander of the Army of the Potomac.

17 Burnside reaches the north bank of the Rappahannock River, opposite Fredericksburg, Va.

21 Lee's army entrenches in a defensive position at Fredericksburg.

30 Jackson arrives at Fredericksburg from the Shenandoah Valley.

DECEMBER 1862

11 Burnside's troops start to cross the Rappahannock at Fredericksburg.

11 Brig. Gen. Nathan Bedford Forrest launches a cavalry attack upon Grant's communication lines in Tennessee.

13 Burnside's assaults on Lee's lines are repulsed with heavy loss in the Battle of Fredericksburg.

15 The Army of the Potomac withdraws across the Rappahanock.

20 Van Dorn destroys Grant's supply depot at Holly Springs, Miss., halting his advance on Vicksburg.

20 Sherman leaves Memphis and heads down the Mississippi River for Vicksburg.

21 Brig. Gen. John Hunt Morgan starts a cavalry raid on the Federal supply lines in central Tennessee.

29 Sherman's attack on Chickasaw Bluffs above Vicksburg is repulsed.

31 The *Monitor* sinks in a storm off Cape Hatteras, N.C.

31 Bragg holds the edge over Rosecrans after a day of heavy fighting at Murfreesboro, Tenn.

JANUARY 1863

1 Lincoln issues the Emancipation Proclamation.

2 Bragg renews his attacks on Rosecrans at the Battle of Murfreesboro (Stones River) but is beaten off.

3 Bragg withdraws from Murfreesboro despite a tactical victory.

26 Maj. Gen. Joseph Hooker succeeds Burnside as commander of the Army of the Potomac.

FEBRUARY 1863

2 Grant cuts the levee at Yazoo Pass, Miss., to open a passage for gunboats to reach the rear of Vicksburg.

MARCH 1863

3 The U.S. Congress passes a conscription act applicable to all men between 20 and 45.

8 Grant abandons his attempts to bypass Vicksburg's river defenses via the Canal and Lake Providence.

17 Grant's Yazoo Pass expedition is blocked at Rebel Fort Pemberton.

21 Sherman rescues Rear Adm. David Dixon Porter's ironclads, trapped in Steele's Bayou, ending another attempt to reach Vicksburg's rear.

25 Burnside is appointed commander of the Dept. of the Ohio with orders to operate in eastern Tennessee.

APRIL 1863

2 Bread riots take place in Richmond.

16 Porter's flotilla runs past the Vicksburg guns, preparing the way for Grant's new campaign.

17 Col. Benjamin H. Grierson leads a Federal cavalry raid to disrupt Rebel communications with Vicksburg.

29 Maj. Gen. George Stoneman leads a Federal cavalry raid behind Lee's lines in Virginia.

30 After crossing the Rappahannock and Rapidan rivers, Hooker concentrates his Union forces at Chancellorsville, Va.

MAY 1863

1 Grant defeats the Confederates at Port Gibson, Miss.

2 Jackson routs Hooker's exposed right flank at Chancellorsville; Jackson is accidentally shot by his own men.

2 Grierson reaches Union lines at Baton Rouge, La.

3 Stuart replaces Jackson; he and Lee push Hooker back toward the Rappahannock River.

3 Maj. Gen. John Sedgwick moves to Hooker's aid after breaking through the Rebel line at Fredericksburg.

4 Lee attacks Sedgwick at Salem Church and drives him back toward Fredericksburg.

4 Longstreet lifts siege of Suffolk, Va.

6 Hooker retreats across the Rappahannock after his defeat at Chancellorsville.

10 Stonewall Jackson dies.

12 Grant defeats the Confederates at Raymond, Miss.

13 Joseph E. Johnston assumes command of the Confederate troops in Mississippi at Jackson.

14 Grant turns toward Vicksburg after driving Johnston from Jackson.

16 Grant defeats Lt. Gen. John C. Pemberton at the Battle of Champion's Hill.

17 Grant routs Pemberton's rear guard at the Battle of the Big Black River.

18 Pemberton withdraws into Vicksburg defenses.

19 Grant's assault on Vicksburg fails.

22 Grant opens the siege of Vicksburg after a second frontal assault fails.

27 Banks besieges Confederate-held Port Hudson, La.

JUNE 1863

3 Lee launches a second invasion of the North from Fredericksburg.

15 Lt. Gen. Richard S. Ewell, leading Lee's invasion, destroys the Union garrison at Winchester, Va.

20 West Virginia is admitted to the Union as the thirty-fifth state.

23 Rosecrans advances on Tullahoma to dislodge Bragg from Tennessee.

25 Stuart departs on a cavalry raid, intending to ride around Hooker's army and then screen Lee's advance into Pennsylvania.

25 Hooker begins crossing the Potomac River to check Lee's advance.

28 Maj. Gen. Jubal Early's division of Lee's army seizes York, Pa.

28 Maj. Gen. George Gordon Meade replaces Hooker as commander of the Army of the Potomac.

29 Lee, learning that the Federals are north of the Potomac, orders his forces to concentrate near Gettysburg, Pa.; Stuart is still absent.

JULY 1863

1 Confederates A. P. Hill and Ewell rout Meade's advance forces at Gettysburg; Lee concentrates on Seminary Ridge, Meade on Cemetery Ridge.

2 Lee's heavy attacks on both ends of Meade's Gettysburg lines are repulsed.

2 Stuart rejoins Lee.

3 Lee orders an attack on Meade's center; "Pickett's Charge" is broken, ending the three-day Battle of Gettysburg.

3 Bragg, outmaneuvered by Rosecrans, retreats to Chattanooga.

4 Vicksburg with 30,000 troops surrenders to Grant.

5 Lee retreats from Gettysburg.

7 Finding the Potomac flooded, Lee entrenches at Williamsport, Md.

9 The surrender of Port Hudson, La., gives the Federals control of the Mississippi and splits the South.

13 In New York City a mob of 50,000 begins four-day draft riots.

14 Lee completes his withdrawal across the Potomac River; Rebel Gen. Harry Heth fights a rearguard action at Falling Waters, Md.

24 The Army of Northern Virginia begins to concentrate at Culpeper, Va.

26 Morgan surrenders at New Lisbon, Ohio.

AUGUST 1863

15 Burnside opens his drive on Knoxville, Tenn.

16 Rosecrans begins to move on Chattanooga.

21 Col. William C. Quantrill's Rebel raiders burn Lawrence, Kan.

SEPTEMBER 1863

2 Burnside occupies Knoxville.

4 Bragg retreats as Rosecrans crosses the Tennessee River in his advance upon Chattanooga.

7 Fort Wagner, guarding Charleston, is occupied by Union troops.

8 Union Rear Adm. John Dahlgren's attack on Fort Sumter is repulsed.

9 Federals enter Chattanooga after Bragg retreats into Georgia.

10 Union Maj. Gen. Frederick Steele seizes Little Rock, Ark.

17 Rosecrans concentrates his dispersed troops near Chickamauga Creek in northern Georgia.

18 Longstreet's corps begins to arrive from Virginia to reinforce Bragg.

19 The Battle of Chickamauga opens as the Federal left under Thomas absorbs Confederate assaults.

20 Longstreet breaks the Federal line at Chickamauga; Thomas holds long enough for Rosecrans' beaten army to escape to Chattanooga.

23 Bragg occupies Missionary Ridge and Lookout Mountain to begin the Rebel siege of Chattanooga.

24 Hooker with 15,000 men leaves the Army of the Potomac in Virginia for Chattanooga.

OCTOBER 1863

9 Lee moves toward Bristoe Station, Va., in an effort to damage the reduced Army of the Potomac.

17 Grant is made supreme commander of the Federal forces in the West.

19 Thomas replaces Rosecrans as commander of the Union Army of the Cumberland at Chattanooga.

23 Grant arrives at Chattanooga to command the Union forces.

27 The "cracker line" supply route into Chattanooga is opened.

NOVEMBER 1863

4 Longstreet's troops are detached from Bragg to attack Burnside at Knoxville.

10 Lee withdraws to a line on the Rapidan River after the indecisive Bristoe Campaign.

19 Lincoln delivers his Gettysburg Address.

20 Sherman arrives at Chattanooga with reinforcements from the Army of the Tennessee.

23 Thomas opens the Battle of Chattanooga by taking Orchard Knob in front of Missionary Ridge.

24 Hooker pushes Bragg's men off Lookout Mountain; Sherman crosses the Tennessee River to attack the opposite end of Bragg's Missionary Ridge line.

25 Sherman's attack on Bragg's right is halted; Thomas' Army of the Cumberland charges up Missionary Ridge to rout the Confederates; Bragg retreats into Georgia.

26 Meade crosses the Rapidan River

to probe the Army of Northern Virginia's defenses along Mine Run, west of Chancellorsville, Va.

29 Longstreet unsuccessfully attacks Union Fort Sanders.

DECEMBER 1863

1 Meade withdraws the Army of the Potomac into winter quarters at Culpeper, Va.

1 Bragg is removed from the Army of Tennessee to become military adviser to President Davis.

4 Longstreet retreats toward southwestern Virginia after ending the siege of Knoxville.

27 Joseph E. Johnston assumes command of the Confederate Army of Tennessee.

FEBRUARY 1864

22 Forrest defeats Brig. Gen. W. S. Smith's cavalry at Okolona, Miss.

MARCH 1864

3 A Union cavalry raid on Richmond led by Brig. Gen. Judson Kilpatrick and Col. Ulric Dahlgren fails.

4 Sherman's troops return to Vicksburg after a damaging, month-long raid on Meridian, Miss.

12 Grant, promoted to the rank of lieutenant general, becomes general in chief of the U. S. armies.

15 Porter's Union flotilla reaches Alexandria, La., to spearhead the Red River Campaign.

18 Sherman assumes command of the principal Union armies in the West.

23 Frederick Steele advances from Little Rock, Ark., to join the Union Red River Campaign.

25 Nathaniel P. Banks assumes command of the Red River Campaign.

APRIL 1864

8 At Sabine Crossroads, La., Rebel Maj. Gen. Richard Taylor blocks Banks' advance on Shreveport, halting the Red River Campaign.

12 Forrest captures Fort Pillow, Tenn.

17 Grant halts prisoner exchange, increasing the Confederate manpower shortage.

25 Banks retires to Alexandria, La.; low water in the Red River temporarily traps Porter's gunboats.

30 Steele, defeated by the Confederates at Jenkins Ferry, Ark., is forced to withdraw to Little Rock.

MAY 1864

4 Grant crosses the Rapidan River to attack Lee.

5 The armies of Lee and Grant collide in the Wilderness; fighting is indecisive.

5 Butler's Union Army of the James leaves Fort Monroe to attack Petersburg and Richmond.

6 Longstreet's arrival halts Grant's offensive in the Wilderness; Rebel counterattacks push in both Union flanks; in the fighting Longstreet is wounded by his own men.

6 Sherman opens the Atlanta Campaign against Johnston's Army of Tennessee.

8 Lee wins the race to Spotsylvania and repels Grant's advance units.

9 The Army of Northern Virginia entrenches at Spotsylvania.

9 Col. P. H. Sheridan launches a heavy Union cavalry raid on Richmond.

9 Sherman's first attempt to flank Johnston at Dalton, Ga., fails.

10 Grant's attacks on Lee's Spotsylvania lines are repulsed.

10 Butler withdraws to Bermuda Hundred after a sortie toward Petersburg, Va., fails.

11 Rebel cavalry halts Sheridan's Richmond raid at Yellow Tavern; Jeb Stuart is mortally wounded.

12 After a day-long fight at the "Bloody Angle," Lee mends the break in his Spotsylvania lines.

13 Johnston withdraws from Dalton to Resaca, Ga.

13 Porter's flotilla safely passes the rapids at Alexandria, and Banks continues his withdrawal from the Red River Campaign.

15 Sherman resumes his flanking movement, forcing Johnston to abandon Resaca.

15 Maj. Gen. John C. Breckinridge defeats Maj. Gen. Franz Sigel at New Market, Va.

16 Beauregard drives Butler from Drewry's Bluff back into the Bermuda Hundred defenses.

17 Grant continues his effort to flank Lee at Spotsylvania.

19 The Rebel attack under Ewell at Spotsylvania fails.

19 Johnston is flanked out of his Cassville, Ga., defense line.

20 Grant leaves his Spotsylvania lines in an attempt to flank Lee.

24 Grant finds Lee's new position at the North Anna River too strong.

24 Sherman advances toward Dallas, Ga., after flanking Johnston from his Allatoona Pass defenses.

24 Sheridan rejoins Grant.

25 A four-day fight between Johnston and Sherman opens at New Hope Church, Ga.

28 Grant and Lee begin a skirmish along Totopotomoy Creek, Va.

JUNE 1864

1 Lee begins to entrench at Cold Harbor, Va.; Grant takes up a position facing him.

3 Grant is severely repulsed in the Cold Harbor assault; the Federals entrench after the battle.

4 Johnston shifts his lines to Lost, Pine, and Brush mountains, to check Sherman's advance.

8 The Republicans nominate Abraham Lincoln and Andrew Johnson.

10 Forrest crushes a Federal force at Brice's Crossroads, Miss.

12 Sheridan abandons his cavalry raid on the Shenandoah Valley after being repulsed by Maj. Gen. Wade Hampton at Trevilian Station, Va.

14 Grant, having moved his army across the Peninsula, begins to cross the James River in order to attack Petersburg, Va.

15 Grant's advance guard under William F. Smith fails to take the thinly held Petersburg line.

16 Beauregard abandons the Bermuda Hundred lines to repulse the Union attacks at Petersburg.

17 Lee's army reoccupies the Bermuda Hundred lines before Butler can advance.

18 Lee's troops begin to arrive in the Petersburg lines, and Grant opens the siege of Petersburg after further assaults fail.

18 Union Maj. Gen. David Hunter, replacing Sigel in the Shenandoah Valley, is defeated by Early at Lynchburg, Va.

19 Johnston withdraws to Kennesaw Mountain, Ga.

19 The Confederate raider *Alabama* is sunk by the U.S.S. *Kearsarge* off Cherbourg, France.

23 A. P. Hill blocks Union troops advancing on Weldon Railroad which leads south from Petersburg.

23 Early opens a Confederate offensive in the Shenandoah Valley.

27 Sherman's frontal assault on Kennesaw Mountain is driven back.

JULY 1864

3 Johnston withdraws from Kennesaw Mountain to his Chattahoochee River defenses to escape Sherman's flanking movement.

6 Early crosses the Potomac River into Maryland.

9 Johnston withdraws from the Chattahoochee River line as Sherman pushes toward Atlanta.

9 Early reaches Frederick, Md., and wins a victory at Monocacy.

11 Reinforcements from the Army of the Potomac arrive in Washington to protect the capital.

12 Early is forced to withdraw to the Shenandoah Valley after reaching the outskirts of Washington.

17 General John Bell Hood replaces Johnston in command of the Confederate Army of Tennessee as Sherman nears Atlanta.

20 Hood's attack on the Federals at Peachtree Creek, Ga., is repulsed; Sherman moves to cut Atlanta's rail connections.

22 Hood fails to turn Sherman's flank at the Battle of Atlanta; Union Maj. Gen. James B. McPherson is killed.

24 Early defeats Union troops at Kernstown.

28 At Ezra Church, Ga., Hood's third attack on Sherman is broken.

30 A Federal mine breaches Lee's Petersburg lines, but the Rebels halt the Union breakthrough.

30 Brig. Gen. John McCausland's Rebel cavalry burns Chambersburg, Pa.

AUGUST 1864

5 Farragut is victorious in the Battle of Mobile Bay.

7 Sheridan assumes command of Union forces in the Shenandoah Valley.

10 Wheeler begins a month-long Confederate cavalry raid on Sherman's communication lines between Atlanta and Nashville.

21 After the Battle of Globe Tavern, Grant seizes the Weldon Railroad.

21 Forrest reaches Memphis, Tenn., on a cavalry raid.

22 Judson Kilpatrick's five-day Union cavalry raid fails to destroy Hood's supply line into Atlanta.

23 The fall of Fort Morgan ensures Union control of Mobile Bay.

29 The Democrats nominate McClellan for President and George H. Pendleton for Vice-President.

31 Federals cut the Macon and Western Railroad, Hood's last rail connection into Atlanta.

SEPTEMBER 1864

1 Hood evacuates Atlanta after Sherman reaches Jonesboro.

2 Hood establishes a Confederate defense line at Lovejoy's Station.

2 Sherman occupies Atlanta.

4 Sherman orders civilians out of Atlanta.

4 Confederate raider John Hunt Morgan is killed at Greeneville, Tenn.

8 McClellan accepts the Democratic Presidential nomination without endorsing the peace platform.

19 Sheridan defeats Early at Winchester, Va., in the Shenandoah Valley.

19 Sterling Price opens a Confederate raid on Missouri.

22 Sheridan routs Early at Fisher's Hill, Va.

22 Frémont withdraws from the Presidential race.

28 Hood crosses the Chattahoochee to strike at Sherman's supply lines.

28 Sherman sends Thomas to Nashville to contain Forrest in western Tennessee.

29 In an attempted advance on Richmond, Grant captures Fort Harrison but is repulsed at Fort Gilmer in the Battle of New Market Heights, Va.

OCTOBER 1864

4 Hood strikes at Sherman's rail communications at Big Shanty, Ga.

5 Hood's effort to capture the Federal position at Allatoona, Ga., fails.

6 After pursuing Early to Harrisonburg, Va., Sheridan devastates the Shenandoah Valley as he withdraws toward Winchester.

13 Hood damages Sherman's rail communications to Chattanooga; Sherman moves his army from Atlanta to Resaca.

18 Hood retreats into Alabama.

19 Sheridan defeats Early at Cedar Creek, Va., driving the Confederates from the Shenandoah Valley.

23 Price's Rebel raiders are defeated at Westport, Mo., and driven from the state.

27 A. P. Hill repulses Grant's attack on the railroad at Hatcher's Run, Va.

30 Sherman sends Maj. Gen. John Schofield to reinforce Thomas at Nashville and repel Hood's invasion of Tennessee.

31 Nevada is admitted to the Union.

NOVEMBER 1864

8 Lincoln and Johnson are elected President and Vice-President.

15 After burning Atlanta, Sherman starts his March to the Sea.

19 Hood, joined by Forrest's cavalry, opens a drive on Nashville, Tenn.

23 Sherman, pursuing a scorched-earth policy, reaches Milledgeville.

29 Hood attempts to trap Schofield at Spring Hill, Tenn., but Schofield escapes to Franklin.

30 Hood makes a frontal attack on Schofield at Franklin, Tenn., but fails to cut off his retreat to Nashville; five Rebel generals are killed.

DECEMBER 1864

2 Hood takes up a defensive line south of Nashville.

13 Sherman captures Fort McAllister, guarding Savannah, and establishes contact with Dahlgren's Union blockading fleet.

15 Thomas assaults Hood's army in front of Nashville.

16 Hood suffers a defeat at Nashville and retreats into Mississippi.

21 Lt. Gen. Hardee evacuates Savannah; Sherman occupies it.

25 Butler's joint army-navy expedition fails to take Fort Fisher, N. C.

JANUARY 1865

15 Fort Fisher falls to Union Maj. Gen. A. H. Terry, closing Wilmington, N. C., the last major Rebel port.

15 Hood is relieved of command of the Army of Tennessee at his own request.

31 The U.S. Congress submits to the states the Thirteenth Amendment, abolishing slavery.

FEBRUARY 1865

1 Sherman begins his invasion of the Carolinas.

3 Lincoln and Seward meet the Confederate leaders Alexander H. Stephens, R. M. T. Hunter, and J. A. Campbell in an unsuccessful peace conference at Hampton Roads, Va.

6 Robert E. Lee is named commander in chief of the Rebel armies.

17 Sherman occupies the South Carolina capital, Columbia, which is destroyed by fire that night.

18 After Fort Sumter is abandoned, the Federals seize Charleston.

22 Wilmington, N. C., surrenders to Schofield.

22 Johnston is recalled to command of the Army of Tennessee to oppose Sherman's advance.

MARCH 1865

2 Sheridan destroys Early's remaining troops in the Shenandoah Valley at Waynesboro, Va.

4 Lincoln is inaugurated for a second term.

11 Sherman reaches Fayetteville, N.C., and re-establishes contact with Federal forces on the coast.

13 The Confederate Congress authorizes the use of slaves as troops.

16 Sherman defeats Hardee at Averasboro, N. C.

17 Maj. Gen. E. R. S. Canby opens a Federal attack on Mobile, Ala.

19 Sherman repulses Johnston's attack at Bentonville, N. C., and the Rebels retreat toward Raleigh.

23 Sherman occupies Goldsboro, N. C.

25 Maj. Gen. John B. Gordon captures Fort Stedman at Petersburg but is forced to retreat.

27 Sheridan rejoins the Army of the Potomac.

28 Lincoln discusses peace terms with Grant and Sherman.

APRIL 1865

1 Sheridan turns Lee's flank at Petersburg by defeating Maj. Gen. George Pickett at Five Forks, Va.

2 Grant breaks through Lee's lines at Petersburg; Confederate Lt. Gen. A. P. Hill is killed.

2 Abandoning Petersburg, Lee begins to retreat westward toward Amelia Court House.

2 The Confederate government flees from Richmond.

3 Federal troops enter Richmond.

4 Lincoln visits Richmond.

5 Sheridan blocks Lee's escape route south from Amelia Court House; Lee moves toward Lynchburg, Va.

6 Grant cuts off and captures Lee's rear guard at Sayler's Creek, Va.

7 Lee's troops fight off a Union attack at Farmville.

7 Grant and Lee enter into correspondence leading to surrender.

8 Sheridan reaches Appomattox Station to cut off Lee's retreat.

9 Lee surrenders the Army of Northern Virginia to Grant at Appomattox Court House, Va.

12 Wilson's Union cavalry captures Montgomery, Ala.

12 Federal troops enter Mobile, Ala.

12 At Greensboro, N. C., Johnston tells Jefferson Davis that further resistance is impossible.

13 Sherman enters Raleigh, N. C.

14 Maj. Gen. Robert Anderson raises over Fort Sumter the same flag he had lowered four years earlier.

14 John Wilkes Booth shoots Lincoln at Ford's Theatre in Washington, and Lewis Paine wounds Secretary of State Seward.

15 Abraham Lincoln dies, and Andrew Johnson succeeds to the Presidency.

18 Johnston and Sherman meet near Raleigh, N. C., where they sign a broad armistice agreement.

21 President Johnson and the cabinet disapprove Sherman's armistice with Johnston and send Grant to North Carolina.

26 Johnston accepts from Sherman the same terms Grant offered Lee.

26 John Wilkes Booth is trapped and killed by Federal cavalry near Bowling Green, Va.

26 The Confederate cabinet meets for the last time at Charlotte, N. C.

MAY 1865

10 Jefferson Davis is taken prisoner by Union cavalry at Irwinsville, Ga.

13 The last fighting of the war takes place at Palmito Ranch, near Brownsville, Texas.

23 A two-day Grand Review of the Federal armies up Washington's Pennsylvania Avenue begins.

26 Kirby Smith surrenders Confederate troops west of the Mississippi to Canby, ending the Civil War.

Index

Numbers in *italics* refer to illustrations.